THE CHISHOLM TRAIL

BY WAYNE GARD

with drawings by Nick Eggenhofer

THE
CHISHOLM
TRAIL

NORMAN
University of Oklahoma Press

BY WAYNE GARD
Book Reviewing (New York, 1927)
Sam Bass (Boston, 1936)
Frontier Justice (Norman, 1949)
The Chisholm Trail (Norman, 1954)
Fabulous Quarter Horse: Steel Dust (New York, 1958)
The Great Buffalo Hunt (New York, 1959)
Rawhide Texas (Norman, 1965)

This book is printed on paper designed for an effective life
of at least three hundred years.

Library of Congress Catalog Card Number: 54–6204

FOREWORD

For more than a dozen tempestuous years, beginning in 1867, the Chisholm Trail was the Texas cowhand's road to high adventure. It held the excitement of sudden stampedes, hazardous river crossings, and brushes with Indian marauders. It promised, at the end of the drive, hilarious celebration in the saloons, gambling parlors, and dance halls of frontier Kansas towns.

> *I woke up one morning on the old Chisholm Trail,*
> *Rope in my hand and a cow by the tail.*
>
> *Feet in the stirrups and seat in the saddle,*
> *I hung and rattled with them Longhorn cattle.*

For others the Chisholm Trail meant more than rousing experiences. It carried what probably was the greatest migration of domestic animals in world history. In a period when Texas still lacked railroads for shipping its surplus cattle to northern markets, the trail to Kansas served an urgent need. This pathway, which took the imprints of several million Longhorns, helped Texas dig herself out of the poverty that followed the Civil War. It also spurred railroad construction in the West and the Southwest.

Some of its effects were felt even farther away. Cattle trailed over this route helped to relieve the beef shortage in other parts of the country. Some of them provided an item of export needed to serve European wants and to help balance this country's foreign trade. Others were used to stock new ranches and thus spread cattle raising into the northern part of the Great Plains and the Rocky Mountain region. The trail gave quick expansion to meat-packing industries in Chicago, Kansas City, and elsewhere. It also sped the development of refrigeration for the transportation of meat.

Those who have exploited the frontier cowboy in fiction, on the screen, and in the comic strip have made much of the Chisholm Trail. They have depicted it as a heroic highway, but sometimes they have distorted the true story of this famous cattle route. From serious historians, the trail has not had the attention it deserves. Few have bothered to look into surviving records of the period of the trail.

Even in Texas, as a result of this neglect, there still is much popular confusion on the location of the Chisholm Trail. Many a Texan, on hearing the trail mentioned, recalls that it went right through his grandfather's ranch. These hazy recollections, added together, would put the trail in almost all of the 254 counties of Texas. Some have loosely applied the Chisholm name to all of the several cattle trails that led northward from Texas. One such person, from Oklahoma, tried to attach a Chisholm Trail marker to a landmark of the Western, or Dodge Trail, which succeeded the Chisholm Trail. Another, a woman who went up the Western Trail two years after the Chisholm Trail had been abandoned, mistitled her book of reminiscences, *A Bride on the Old Chisholm Trail in 1886*.

On the other hand, some have held that the name Chisholm Trail should not be applied to the Texas part of the route. Their reason is that Jesse Chisholm, whose name the trail took, blazed only the part in the Indian Territory and Kansas, from the North Canadian to the mouth of the Little Arkansas. The Old Trail Drivers Association of Texas took this narrow view in a resolution adopted in 1931. Both history and folklore, though, have applied the Chisholm name to the entire route, including feeder branches in Texas and terminal branches in Kansas. That definition is used here.

The main stem of the Chisholm Trail, which had many feeder lines coming in from both sides, began near the southern tip of Texas. It led through or past San Antonio, Austin, and Fort Worth and entered the Indian Territory—now Oklahoma—at Red River Station. Its route through the Indian country, which then had few white inhabitants, is now marked roughly by a line of cities and towns. They include Duncan, Chickasha, El Reno, Kingfisher, Enid, Pond

Creek, and Medford. The first terminus of the trail was Abilene, Kansas. Beginning in 1872, Ellsworth and Wichita were the principal cattle markets for several years. Then they gave way to Dodge City and Caldwell. The later Western Trail led to Dodge City.

When the present work was begun, nearly all the cowmen who had ridden the Chisholm Trail had died. Fortunately, the reminiscences of many of them were published by J. Marvin Hunter in *The Trail Drivers of Texas*. Other firsthand accounts were available in other sources. Joseph G. McCoy, who set up the Abilene market that gave rise to the trail, wrote an informative book on his project. To a later edition of McCoy's *Historic Sketches of the Cattle Trade*, Ralph P. Bieber added a scholarly introduction and many useful notes. J. Frank Dobie told superbly the story of *The Longhorns*.

The present author learned what he could from talking with surviving trail drivers. In addition, he made a diligent search through public records, manuscripts, railroad archives, and newspaper files. He traveled over the route of the Chisholm Trail and visited the towns that were its chief terminals. He has tried to piece together, for the first time, a comprehensive account of this historic trail.

In doing this, it has seemed needful to glance at the origin of the Longhorn breed and the trailing of cattle from Texas before the Chisholm route was opened. A broad view of the trail has called, too, for a look at the life the cowmen led in their short stays in the Kansas towns at which they sold their stock.

Many librarians, archivists, historians, and others gave generous help and advice. J. Frank Dobie of Austin and Ramon F. Adams and Dan Ferguson of Dallas lent valuable source material. Counsel came also from other historians, among them T. C. Richardson of Dallas, Professor Edward Everett Dale of the University of Oklahoma, Professor Carl Coke Rister of Texas Technological College, Professor Ralph P. Bieber of Washington University, and Floyd Benjamin Streeter of Fort Hays Kansas State College. The author is grateful also to his wife, Hazel D. Gard, for making many helpful suggestions. All opinions and errors are the author's own.

WAYNE GARD

Dallas, Texas

Photograph by Elwood Payne

Lord of the range

CONTENTS

ix

ILLUSTRATIONS AND MAPS

THE CHISHOLM TRAIL

Jesse Chisholm, whose name the trail bears

MAVERICKS IN THE BRUSH

Like mighty armies the herds moved slowly northward, each with its cloud of dust. The cattle grazed as they plodded along, every step taking them farther from their Texas range. The herd's only banner was the flapping canvas of the chuck wagon, its only trumpets the bawling of the cows. Yet on and on the Longhorns marched.

Even those Kansans who had seen their plains darkened with buffalo herds were bewildered. Never, it seemed, had there been such an invasion as that of the half-wild cattle pouring in by the Chisholm Trail. The ferocious-looking brutes with sharp, spreading horns overflowed the prairies and crowded the banks of rivers and creeks. From a hilltop, one could look for miles without seeing any end to the herds.

The Longhorns that tramped up this and other dusty trails from Texas belonged to a tough breed. They were even hardier than the wind-beaten men on horseback who kept them pointed in the right direction. For nearly four centuries they had been adapting themselves to a new world and a new way of life. They had learned to fend for themselves and to survive without human aid.

Most of their ancestors had grazed in the highlands of Andalucía or Castile. Some had crossed the buffeting Atlantic in fragile caravels of Christopher Columbus and those who followed him. They had stocked the ranches of the Spanish conquerors in the West Indies and in Mexico. They had marched northward with Coronado and other explorers. They had grazed in the pastures of frontier missions. They had run wild in the brush, where they fought off snarling beasts and wily Indians.

At the close of the Civil War, five million Longhorns were roaming the Texas grasslands. There some stockmen considered them hardly worth capturing. The cities where beef was in demand were far away, and there was no cheap and convenient means for shipping the cattle. Thousands of them were slaughtered for their hides and tallow. It looked as if King Ferdinand and Queen Isabella of Spain, who had sent the first cattle to the Americas, had succeeded too well.

The Longhorns were entirely of European ancestry, with the Spanish strain dominant. In 1493, the year after he had discovered the New World, Columbus had brought cattle and other livestock on his second westward voyage across the Atlantic. The Spanish monarchs had instructed him to have his cavalrymen take fifteen stallions and ten mares. They took also a royal bull from Andalucía, cows, calves, a band of sheep, and a few goats and hogs.

The mariners loaded the cattle, horses, and other animals on four wooden sailing ships at Cádiz in May. When the voyage ended, they were taken off at Hispaniola—Santo Domingo—on November 3. They then were put on ranches that the Spaniards had established. By mid-December the colonists had taken some of the breeding stock to new settlements in Cuba. Later ships brought more stock.

The cattle multiplied rapidly. Gregorio de Villalobos took some calves from Santo Domingo to New Spain—Mexico—to start beef herds on the mainland. That was in 1521, two years after Hernando Cortés had begun his conquest of Mexico. Cortés had a ranch in Cuba, from which he stocked his estate in Mexico. The latter he called Cuernavaca, or Cow Horn.

Probably the first cattle to reach Texas were those brought in 1541 by Francisco Vásquez de Coronado. In the preceding year Coronado had left western Mexico with 336 European adventurers and several hundred Indians, who served as scouts and herdsmen. His aim was to find legendary cities of gold, about which earlier travelers had brought exciting rumors. Coronado took along large

4

herds of cattle, sheep, goats, and swine. These animals were intended not for propagation but as food for the travelers. There were at least five hundred cattle at the start.

Although some of the cattle had fallen exhausted or escaped to become wild, Coronado still had a large number when he reached what later became the United States. In Texas, he and his men went as far east as Palo Duro Canyon, then turned north. But if the disappointed explorers left any of their remaining cattle on the high plains of western Texas, those animals apparently did not propagate there. The first cattle to become permanent residents did not arrive until more than a century later.

A French explorer may have brought the next Spanish cattle to Texas. He was René Robert Cavelier, Sieur de la Salle. At Santo Domingo he had taken on chickens, hogs, and cattle before he sailed for the mouth of the Mississippi and, overshooting his mark, landed on the shore of Lavaca Bay in February, 1685.

Other cattle came overland from Mexico. General Alonso de León, governor of Coahuila, took horses and cattle along on his four expeditions across the Rio Grande between 1687 and 1690. On the last of these excursions, De León was said to have left a bull, a cow, a stallion, and a mare at each river he crossed. In 1690, De León and Father Damián Massanet established the San Francisco and Santa Maria missions, the first in Texas. They were situated among the Asinai Indians on and near the Neches River, near the Louisiana border. They had two hundred cattle brought from below the Rio Grande.

Soon more Spanish cattle were headed northward. Domingo Terán los Ríos, who in 1691 was made governor of the newly formed province of Texas, brought a supply of domestic animals with him. Some of this stock he left when the province was abandoned two years later. Ownerless horses and cattle wandered across the prairies and plains. On June 22, 1715, a French trader, Louis Juchereau de St. Denis, remarked on the abundance of these animals, which he believed the Indians feared to kill. Livestock left by the Spaniards, he said, had "increased to thousands of cows, bulls, horses, and mares, with which the whole country is covered."[1]

[1] Jose Antonio Pichardo, *Pichardo's Treatise on the Limits of Louisiana and Texas*, IV, 526.

In the following year, Captain Domingo Ramón headed an expedition that took more than a thousand cattle, sheep, and goats into Texas. On this journey, in which he established missions and roads, Captain Ramón noted in his diary the survival of cattle brought earlier. Two of his men had seen, in the brush of the Trinity River bottoms, "wild cattle lost by the Spaniards on their first expedition into Texas. They killed a fat cow."[2]

Later visitors made similar reports. On May 12, 1718, Fray Francisco Celiz, chaplain of Martín de Alarcón's expedition to Texas, wrote that the party saw a black Castilian bull in the woods near the San Marcos River. This made them believe that the animal trails they had crossed were made "by the cattle which General Alonso de León left exhausted on the return from his first trip to Texas."[3] By 1731 the mission ranches were well stocked, and the raising of cattle and sheep was the chief civilian occupation. In 1757, Spaniards trailed fourteen hundred cattle from the San Antonio River to the mission they established that year on the San Saba. Many of the Indians in Texas profited by stealing Spanish cattle and horses and selling them in Louisiana.[4]

As the mission herds proved prolific and as Spaniards brought more stock from Mexico to establish permanent settlements, Texas acquired vast numbers of cattle. By 1770 the Mission of Espíritu Santo, near Goliad, claimed forty thousand head, many of them without brands. Its cattle grazed upon the prairies between the San Antonio River and the Guadalupe. West of the San Antonio, the Mission of Rosario pastured ten thousand branded cattle and twenty thousand unbranded. The Spaniards had two names for the unbranded cattle. Those tame enough to be rounded up they called *mestenas*. Those too wild for human control were *cimarrones*.

In the 1770's, a market slump and Indian depredations sent cattle raising into a decline along the San Antonio River. The Apaches, Comanches, and Lipans, no longer afraid to kill the horned beasts, were said to have driven off twenty-two thousand head in a single

[2] "Captain Diego Ramón's Diary of His Expedition Into Texas in 1716" (ed. by Paul J. Foik), *Preliminary Studies of the Texas Catholic Historical Society*, Vol. II, No. 5 (April, 1933), 17.

[3] Fray Francisco Celiz, *Diary of the Alarcon Expedition Into Texas, 1718–1719* (trans. and ed. by Fritz Leo Hoffman), 52.

[4] Herbert Eugene Bolton, *The Spanish Borderlands*, 236.

raid. Also discouraging was the lack of buyers. Only a small part of the increase was required to supply the local need for beef and hides. The few herds trailed across the coastal prairies to Louisiana didn't always bring a price high enough to justify the long drive. Nor was the demand for dried beef in Coahuila enough incentive for the tedious trip with pack animals.

Yet many of the ranchers hung on, hoping that some day they could obtain wealth from the wild cattle that wandered over the ranges and hid in the brush. There seemed no end to these scattered brutes, no matter how many the savages drove off. While crossing the Brazos and Colorado valleys in 1778, when English colonists on the Atlantic coast were fighting for independence, Athanase de Mézières, lieutenant-governor of Natchitoches, saw what he termed "an incredible number of Castilian cattle."[5]

II

On the spreading grasslands, cattle continued to multiply faster than they were slaughtered. After Mexico won independence from Spain in 1821, more settlers from the United States began to filter into Texas. Most of them were farmers; and many brought with them a few scrub cattle and other stock, mainly of British breeds. Their cattle, although not of impressive quality, were on a par with the "Arkansas travelers and Louisiana canebrake splitters"[6] of nearby states. On the unfenced frontier, then and later, the blending of British and Spanish breeds was inevitable. While the resultant Longhorns looked and behaved more like the wilder and dominant Spanish cattle, they had an appreciable amount of British blood.

In that period the wild cattle ranged over southern and eastern Texas and northwestward to the upper Brazos River. Usually they grazed in small bunches, hiding in thickets during the day and feeding mainly at night. To get the first scent of any danger that might approach, they pointed their noses into the wind as they grazed. "We have only to go out a few miles into a swamp between the Big and Little Brazos to find as many cattle as one could wish," wrote

[5] *Athanase de Mézières and the Louisiana-Texas Frontier, 1768–1780* (trans. and ed. by Herbert Eugene Bolton), II, 187. The Colorado River mentioned here and later is not the one which flows through the Grand Canyon but is the Colorado River of Texas.

[6] *Prose and Poetry of the Live Stock Industry of the United States*, 394.

a visitor in Texas in 1822. He and other hunters had amused themselves by shooting wild cattle. It was dangerous to camp on the east side of the Little River, he said, "on account of the cattle coming in for water, the night being the only time they drink."[7]

When settlers from the United States pushed into the valley of the San Marcos River in 1833–35, they found it stocked with wild cattle. These unbranded animals apparently were the offspring of a herd that Don Felipe Partilleas had brought to his ranch there but had abandoned as a result of Comanche raids. "So wild were they," one settler recalled, "that only the most expert hunters might hope to come up with them."[8]

During the fifteen years in which Texas was under Mexican rule, cattle raising increased but without bringing much return to the ranchmen. Indian marauders still were a menace. Although most of the redskin raiders preferred buffalo meat to beef and came mainly to steal horses, they often drove off cattle as well. Some of the stock raisers, most of them Mexicans, slaughtered cattle for their hides and tallow, which they shipped on slow sailing vessels to New Orleans or to Europe. Most of the meat was wasted. Surely there must be a way to put such cattle to better use.

The Texas Revolution in 1836, although it did not last long, led many ranchmen, both Anglos and Mexicans, to abandon their homes and herds. More domestic cattle wandered off and in some instances joined the wild herds. After the war, wild cattle in vast numbers ranged on the luxuriant grass between the Nueces River and the Rio Grande. Save for their wildness, most of these cattle were of acceptable quality. In the early days of the Republic, Texas Army commanders sent detachments into the region between the Nueces and the Rio Grande to round up and bring out cattle needed to feed the troops.

Soon the unclaimed cattle began to tempt veterans of the Texas Revolution and other hardy and adventurous settlers of both races. In small bands, the men set out after the wild brutes. Their activities gave rise to the saying that to become a cowman, a fellow needed only a rope, a branding iron, and the nerve to use them. The cap-

[7] W. B. Dewees, *Letters From an Early Settler of Texas*, 22, 25–26.
[8] John J. Linn, *Reminiscences of Fifty Years in Texas*, 338.

tured cattle were used to start new herds or to replace beeves that had been marketed in Louisiana.

Before long the Mexican *vaqueros* were rivaled and even out-done by English-speaking Texans. The latter were beginning to be called cowboys, although some called them stock boys, cow herders, or cow drivers. Often the cattle hunters worked by moon-light. A group of them would drive off several hundred wild cattle and keep them moving for two or three days. By that time, the ani-mals would be so worn out that the horsemen could manage them almost as readily as domestic cattle.

Besides wearing down the wild cattle, the cowboys had other means of capturing them. One was to drive a decoy herd into the woods or brush and try to take the wild cattle out with the tame ones. Another was to rope the cattle and either tie them to trees until subdued or "hog-tie" them by fastening their feet together. Sometimes a cowboy would "tail" a cow or yearling by riding up behind and catching its tail. Giving the tail a twist around the horn of his saddle, he would spur his horse and jerk the victim to the ground. Usually he could tie the animal before it recovered from the shock. In other cases, the hunters would trap wild cattle at a water hole and drive them into a pen. Obstreperous ones, after being captured, would be "necked," or tied to work oxen that would lead them into a corral.[9]

Some of the cowboys became so enthusiastic in this new enter-prise that they did not stop with driving wild cattle. They stole gentle cattle from many a Mexican rancher on the Texas side of the Rio Grande. Occasionally they did not halt at the border river. In 1839 Dr. James H. Starr reported that he saw, about twelve miles from La Grange, a band of Texas cowboys who had stolen hundreds of cattle, as well as horses and mules, from the inhabitants of Chihuahua.[10] While most of the settlers frowned on such forays, some condoned them on the ground that Mexicans were a hostile people and should be treated as enemies. Cattle raids in the border country led to retaliation and occasional armed clashes.

9 *Western Texas, the Australia of America*, 39–40; James H. Cook, *Fifty Years on the Old Frontier*, 18–25.

10 James H. Starr, private journal, 1839–40, entry for September 21, 1839, Starr Papers (MS, University of Texas Library).

Elsewhere in Texas, wild cattle were also abundant. A traveler who crossed the central Brazos Valley in 1840 reported that, along with buffalo, deer, and mustangs, "wild cattle were forever in sight on the extensive prairies."[11] Many hunted these cattle for sport or for meat. In 1841, Buck Barry, a noted Indian fighter, roamed for a month in the Red River country near Clarksville, hunting wild cattle and other game in the canebrakes and oak thickets.[12]

Cattle raising in Texas was disrupted again by the Mexican War, which closely followed annexation. Approaching troops caused many Mexicans in southwestern Texas to flee across the Rio Grande, abandoning their homes and their livestock. When these Mexicans came back after the war to reclaim their homes and to hunt for their scattered herds, they often were treated as trespassers and thieves, despite guarantees in the peace treaty.

The attitude of many Texans toward the uprooted Mexicans was reflected in a letter that Major J. H. Lamotte, commander of the United States Army forces on the Rio Grande, wrote from his headquarters at Camp Ringgold on November 10, 1848. The letter was addressed to J. Maria G. Villareal, the alcalde of Camargo, across the river. Noting that many persons from Mexico had been crossing the Rio Grande to hunt mustangs and wild cattle, the commander said that these animals were the property either of individuals or of the state. He asked the alcalde to caution his people against such hunting. "Cattle and horses so caught in the future will be liable to confiscation," he added, "and the persons engaged in it to a process under the law of trespass."[13]

By this and other means, hundreds of Mexican families were driven from Texas land which they and their ancestors had owned and occupied for a century. Some of the newcomers used force or threats. More misapplied Texas headrights. These headrights were grants of land, usually for 640 acres, issued by the state of Texas to war veterans. They could be bought and sold, and the owner could locate his claim on any land not already occupied or in lawful possession of another. Many of the settlers pounced on land that Mexicans had improved. They used the headrights, plus litigation

[11] A. B. Lawrence, *History of Texas, or the Emigrant's Guide*, 78.
[12] James Buckner Barry, reminiscences (MS, University of Texas Library).
[13] Corpus Christi *Star*, February 10, 1849.

or intimidation, to oust the original owners. Some of the new Anglo settlers made raids across the Rio Grande to enlarge their herds.

Such injustices brought swift vengeance. From the Mexican side of the Rio Grande, raiders preyed on Texas herds for many years. Chief among the leaders of Mexican bands that terrorized the border during the 1850's was the red-bearded Juan L. Cortinas. Not only did Cortinas plague ranchmen by driving off their stock but once he held the whole city of Brownsville in subjection for a day. Although he was driven across the river by Texas Rangers, Cortinas continued to sponsor depredations, causing losses that Texas stockmen placed at more than a third of a million dollars.

Yet there still were free cattle in abundance for those who wanted to hunt and capture them. On the Blanco River, one settler recalled, "these wild cattle were wilder than the deer."[14] In 1851, Captain Richard Ware, who wintered on the San Marcos River while on his way farther west, complained of them. He lost many of his cattle from their mingling in the thickets with the wild stock, perhaps descendants of the Partilleas herd. To prevent loss of their tame cattle in this manner, stockmen sometimes joined forces to kill off all the wild cattle within reach, taking only their hides.[15]

John Washington Lockhart, who came from Alabama and settled in the lower valley of the Brazos River, found many Spanish cattle there. He recalled the wild cattle as "trimly made, with legs and feet built for speed. It would take a good horse to outrun one of them. They ran to one color, being black with brown backs and bellies. In time, they became mixed with domestic cattle, and their calves took on mixed colors. When harried or wounded, they were vicious and would fight any living thing. Their sharp horns made them a formidable foe."

Likewise, Noah Smithwick, who lived near the Colorado, found many wild cattle in the thickets along that river. Some of them, he noted, were "handsome brutes, coal black and clean limbed, their white horns glistening as if polished."[16]

14 A. J. Sowell, *Early Settlers and Indian Fighters of Southwest Texas*, 284–85.
15 C. N. Jones, *Early Days in Cooke County*, 49–53; *Western Texas, the Australia of America*, 39.
16 Jonnie Lockhart Wallis (ed.), *Sixty Years on the Brazos*, 328; Noah Smithwick, *The Evolution of a State*, 29.

III

Not all of those who went out after cattle had to choose between stealing and the hazardous capturing of wild stock. The ranges had many unbranded cattle that had strayed from domestic herds but that had not yet become wild and unmanageable. They were what the Spaniards had called *mestenas,* in contrast to the fierce *cimarrones.* Such were many that had wandered from the herd that a San Antonio lawyer and land speculator, Samuel A. Maverick, had bought.

Maverick, of South Carolina birth, had arrived in Texas in 1835 and was one of the signers of the Texas Declaration of Independence. In 1847, while living temporarily at Decrows Point, on Matagorda Bay, he accepted a herd of four hundred cattle from a neighbor in payment of a debt of $1,200. In 1854, after many of his cattle had strayed or been stolen, he decided to move the remnant of his herd. With the aid of his two sons and several others, he brought most of the cattle to his ranch at Conquista, on the San Antonio River, about forty-five miles south of the city. In charge of them he placed a Negro, with several Mexican helpers. In Maverick's absence, most of the calves were left unbranded and many of the cattle were allowed to stray. In 1856, Maverick sold his land, cattle, and brand to a nearby ranchman, A. Toutant Beauregard, a brother of the famous general. In hunting for strays from Maverick's herd, Beauregard's men ranged over several counties. Whenever they came upon unbranded cattle, they claimed them as Maverick's and applied the branding iron. Hence, any unbranded and unclaimed animal came to be called a maverick.[17]

In a day when the prairies and thickets were full of unbranded cattle of unknown ancestry, cowmen did not regard the hunting of mavericks on public land as stealing. Honest stockmen didn't take calves under a year old if they were with branded cows, but any unbranded animal that was more than a year old and had been

[17] Maverick Papers (MS, University of Texas Library); George Madison Maverick and John Henry Brown, *Re Maverick* (pamphlet); Mary A. Maverick, *Memoirs of Mary A. Maverick;* James Cox, *Historical and Biographical Record of the Cattle Industry of Texas and Adjacent Territory,* 595; Maury Maverick, *A Maverick American,* 73–79; Rena Maverick Green (ed.), *Samuel Maverick, Texan: 1803–1870,* 321, 357, 359, 411–20.

weaned was fair game. Many a cattle fortune was started by such
mavericking. Only much later, when unbranded cattle had become scarce and their ownership easy to determine or subject to
division at a roundup, did the ranchmen begin to frown upon mavericking as a form of rustling.

In the period between the Mexican War and the Civil War, a
slow rise in prices gave some encouragement to cattle raisers. In the
first years after annexation, ranchmen received only four to five dollars a head for stock cattle and eight to ten dollars for fat beeves.
As steamships began to carry cattle to New Orleans and as some
herds were taken to distant markets on the hoof, prices gradually
rose. In 1860, twenty dollars a head was regarded as an average
price for good beeves.

This period saw the rise in Texas of what then was called the
cowboy system of cattle raising. Texas set a pattern for cowboy life
that was to spread over the whole West and to persist in song and
legend long after it had been altered in practice to fit changing conditions. From Mexican *vaqueros* the Texas cowmen learned to become expert at riding, roping, trailing, and branding. "Mount equally the best *sabruer* and a Texas lassoer for a combat," wrote one who
had seen both, "and I would back the roper at any odds."[18] The
Texans trained cutting horses to separate from a herd the individual
animals they wanted out. They developed the cow hunt, the fore-
runner of the more formal roundup.

The branding of animals to show ownership had, of course, been
practiced since ancient times. And in backwoods sections of the
South Atlantic colonies, stockmen had held cattle roundups of a
sort while Texas was still a Spanish province. Yet Texas cowmen
tied these and other practices into a recognized system.

For those who had their own herds of marked cattle grazing on
public lands, it was necessary to brand the calves before they were
weaned and while they still could be identified by the brand of
the mother. For this purpose, stockmen using common ranges joined
in spring and fall cow hunts. A typical hunt would bring out ten
to fifteen men, each with one to three spare horses. Every man took

[18] "Wild Cattle Hunting in Texas," *Leisure Hour*, No. 632 (February 6, 1864),
85.

a pack horse for his blankets and provisions. Wild game and un-branded yearlings provided plenty of fresh meat; but the men took coffee, sugar, salt, hard bread, and bacon.

Such a cow hunt was described by a stockman who wrote from Lamar, Refugio County, on June 17, 1860. "Provided for a hunt of several weeks," he noted, "they sally forth, each man with a lasso at saddle bow and armed with an excellent six-shooter and bowie knife. They traverse a wide extent of country, driving into close herds large numbers of cattle at places most convenient to a pen. Then they cut out—select from the herd—such cattle as belong to the men who compose the crowd and those for whom they brand. They drive them into the pen and mark, brand, and alter the calves. Each man can tell his own calves by observing what cow the calf follows and sucks. But some few calves among so large a number of cattle escape the branding. These calves, when afterwards dis-covered, if they have ceased to suck their mothers and cannot be identified, are accounted common property and divided pro rata among the stock growers of the neighborhood."[19]

Captain R. H. Williams, at his ranch on the Frio River, was an energetic cow hunter. All through one spring, he recalled, "we were generally in the saddle soon after daybreak and by midday would drive home from ten to twenty cows, with their calves on foot. Then, after a short dinner hour, out again on fresh horses, returning home before sundown with another bunch. This hunting of cows and calves, where the cattle ranged over miles of country, was no child's play. The cows, half wild, with the instinct of their race, hid their calves in the chaparral, where it was hard to find them. But they had to be found, for success in ranching depends on the careful and thorough manner in which calf hunting is done. If you don't look sharply, half your crop will be lost, killed by lobos or coyotes or eaten by maggots. That spring and early summer we branded more than a thousand calves."

In May of that year, Captain Williams and two of his neighbor ranchers, Louis Oje and Mont Woodward, hunted stray cattle in the forks of the Nueces. "We took eight *vaqueros* and plenty of spare horses. Making our headquarters in a dilapidated mustanger's hut, with corrals nearby, handy for penning the cattle, we spent a week

[19] *Texas Almanac* for 1861, 150.

there, doing some good driving. At night we sat around the camp fire, smoking and yarning."[20]

As beef prices rose in the 1850's, most of the Texas cowmen prospered, especially those on the coastal plains of the Gulf of Mexico. Their herds increased rapidly and did not require expensive care. "Every person in this section who has given his attention to stock raising has become well off by it," wrote the Lamar ranchman quoted earlier. "All commenced on small beginnings but are now in comfortable circumstances and many comparatively rich." By 1860, Thomas O'Connor owned more than twenty thousand cattle and was branding five thousand calves a year.

IV

This period and the four years of war that followed seemed to bring a more definite fixing of the Longhorn breed. The mixture of some blood from frontier cattle of British descent didn't make this predominantly Spanish breed any less hardy. The Texas cattle had long legs and lanky bodies that lent them speed. Their elongated heads made their faces narrow and gave them a sullen and often sinister expression. Their colors ranged from yellow to black, often with strange combinations. Their horns swept out horizontally and served ably for defense or attack. Frank Reaugh, who set up his easel on the Texas prairies in a later day, found the Longhorn steers majestic subjects for his brush.

Environment had done much for the breed. A century or so of running wild had given it toughness and vitality hard to equal. The Longhorn had withstood drouths and blizzards. It had survived attacks by swarms of insects and rapacious wolves and had escaped Comanche arrows. Ranchmen said a steer or a dry cow would walk fifteen miles to water and would make one drink last two days. The Longhorn was ready for almost any ordeal that cowmen could devise.

Cattle of this breed, wrote a cavalry officer, "become so wild that to kill one you would have to stalk it as you would a deer. In fact, it is much more difficult to get a shot at a wild Texas cow than it would be at the most cautious and wary old buck. To kill a buffalo

[20] R. H. Williams, *With the Border Ruffians*, 217, 224.

is but child's play compared with it."[21] The Longhorn cow had a strong sense of smell that made it easy for her to find her own calf in the brush. Her cunning in hiding the calf often was matched by ferocity in its defense.

Occasionally a wild Longhorn bull would be found alone, apparently driven out of the herd as are rogue elephants in India. "A wounded bull fights in earnest," testified one who had hunted wild cattle in Texas in 1857. "His rush, his weight, his stubborn anger make him a formidable opponent. The hunting knife is not easily brought into play with him, should your gun be empty. If I had my choice, I should prefer a wounded bear to a wounded bull, half a dozen times over."[22]

Similar testimony came from other sources. Colonel Richard Irving Dodge called the Texas cattle "fifty times more dangerous to footmen than the fiercest buffalo." Writing of the Longhorn from encounters in his hunting days, he described it as "the domestic animal run wild, changed in some of its habits and characteristics by many generations of freedom and self-care." He added:

A footman is never safe when a herd is in his vicinity. Every sportsman who has hunted quail in Texas will have experienced the uneasiness natural to any man around whom a crowd of long-horned beasts are pawing the earth and tossing their heads in anger at his appearance.

I admit some decided frights. On more than one occasion I have felt exceedingly relieved when an aggressive young bull has gone off bellowing and shaking his head, his face and eyes full of No. 8 shot, and taking his herd with him. The wild bull is "on his muscle" at all times. Though he will generally get out of the way if unmolested, the slightest provocation will convert him into a most aggressive and dangerous enemy.

The wild cattle are not found in herds. A few cows and their calves may associate together for mutual protection, but the bulls are almost always found alone. Should two meet, a most desperate combat determines the mastery then and there, frequently with the life of one of the combatants.

He who would enjoy the favors of a cow must win his way to them by a series of victories. The result of this is that the number of bulls is greatly disproportioned to the number of cows.

[21] H. H. McConnell, *Five Years a Cavalryman*, 307, quoting W. W. W. in the *Youth's Companion*.

[22] "Wild Cattle Hunting in Texas," *Leisure Hour*, No. 632 (February 6, 1864), 85–87.

As an example of Longhorn ferocity, Colonel Dodge recounted the army story of what happened to General Zachary Taylor's command. During the march from Corpus Christi to Matamoros, a soldier came upon a wild bull and fired upon it. "The bull immediately charged; and the soldier, taking to his heels, ran into the column. The bull, undaunted by the number of his enemies, charged headlong, scattering several regiments like chaff. He finally escaped unhurt, having demoralized and put to flight an army which, a few days later, covered itself with glory by victoriously encountering five times its number of human enemies."[23]

Cowmen who went out on the prairies or into the brush for Longhorn stock had to be well mounted and well armed. No one knew when he might encounter a bull in a ferocious mood, ready for stamping and goring. The speed of the bull, his powerful muscles, and his great and sharp horns made him, when enraged, a terrifying beast. Those mighty horns usually measured three and one-half to six feet from tip to tip but in rare animals were more than eight feet.

Pioneer plainsmen called the Longhorn bull as mean a creature as ever went on four legs. "The longer he lived, the meaner he became," wrote one of them. "While in an ordinary frame of mind, he was always much of a blusterer and went swaggering around and threatening destruction to everything that came near him. His temper became ungovernable when he was aroused and made him a dangerous animal." As fighters of each other, he added,

the Texas bulls were much like the bulls among the wild cattle of the southern plains. These were sullen, morose, solitary, and pugnacious. When two of them met, there was sure to be a fight. So savage were many of the battles of these wild warriors that the number of living bulls was one to about twenty-five or thirty cows.

The old Texas bulls did not carry hostilities quite so far as that; yet their duels frequently were fatal to one or the other of the gladiators. A bull thoroughly whipped but still able to navigate usually would break off to another bunch of cattle, with which he might or might not succeed in making himself recognized as a bad bull and in becoming the ruler of the outfit.

Whipped bulls seldom allowed their fondness for trouble to lead

[23] Richard Irving Dodge, *The Hunting Grounds of the Great West*, 148–52.

them to attack their victors a second time, for they knew when they had met their masters. Several successive defeats often would bear so heavily upon their spirits that it was not uncommon for them to withdraw entirely from bovine society and lead a hermit life for awhile to recover some of their self-respect and to give their damaged confidence in their prowess a chance to reassert itself. Bulls that had been vanquished repeatedly lost standing in the herds so that even the cows would begin to shove them aside or to dig them with their horns.

The conduct of the victors was even more humiliating to their humbled foes. Nothing was too low for them to do in bringing general attention to the fact that they were in command and must be obeyed. They became tyrannical and lorded it over their herds until, in their turn, they were either killed or deposed from power and driven forth into outer darkness by vigorous and valiant younger rivals.

A fight to the finish between two infuriated Longhorn bulls was a desperate and bloody combat. After much preliminary defiant bellowing, roaring, and earth-pawing, in the fashion of the buffalo bull, they would pitch into each other with great fury. When one got advantage of the other, he made the most of it with relentless ferocity, driving his horns deep into the body of his adversary, ripping and tearing, and usually disemboweling him. However, the weaker or less determined fighter, when he realized that the battle was going against him and that he was likely to get more than enough of it, would, if he could, get out of the scrape, even if his retreat covered him with ignominy. Notwithstanding his blustering, furious temper and quarrelsome disposition, deep down in his heart he placed his life above military fame and glory.[24]

This hardy breed, whose habits J. Frank Dobie has depicted in much more detail in his excellent book *The Longhorns*, appealed to Texas stockmen returning home from the Civil War. They saw in the several million unbranded cattle an opportunity to retrieve their fortunes, even though war conditions had tumbled stock prices at home. In such local markets as existed, ordinary cattle brought only three to four dollars a head, mature beeves five dollars. Yet in the cities of the North and East, where meat was in strong demand, the same cattle would command prices up to ten times that much. The big Texas problem was to link a four-dollar steer to a forty-dollar market.

[24] *Prose and Poetry of the Live Stock Industry of the United States*, 442–43.

Finding a way to deliver surplus Longhorns to people who wanted beef was not easy. Steamships, although used to some extent, could carry only a small fraction of the load. Railroads still were beyond reach. Texas had made only a start at railroad building when the Civil War diverted men and equipment to other channels. Now, with capital as tight as it was, progress would be slow. It would be years before Texas could have a rail line to St. Louis.

There remained the possibility of rounding up large herds of Longhorns and taking them on foot to distant cities or railheads, as some had done before and even during the war. If this method of marketing could be put in operation on a much larger scale, it might rid the Texas ranges of surplus cattle and put needed money in the pockets of stockmen. Many were ready to give it a try.

REACHING FOR MARKETS

For decades before Longhorns surged up the Chisholm Trail, some Texas cowmen had been taking herds overland to markets beyond their borders. Already they had begun to prove the words of Berta Hart Nance:

> *Other states were carved or born;*
> *Texas grew from hide and horn.*

The drovers had gone in several directions to find buyers. They had faced and overcome many obstacles. Barring their way were rivers that sometimes raged with floods. Along some trails were Indian warriors who might lift the hair of the drovers and steal their horses. Often there were white desperadoes ready to stampede the herds and drive off many of the cattle. In Kansas and Missouri there were farmers determined that Texas cattle should not pass through their counties.

Those Texans who had taken their cattle to market on the hoof had met with varying degrees of success. Many had found the reward enough to warrant the risk. As a result, the northward trailing of Longhorns had grown steadily until interfered with by disease outbreaks in the 1850's and by war embargoes in 1861.

The Texas drovers were following a method that had been a common practice since the day of Abraham and that had long been used in other parts of this country. In the early years of the Atlantic colonies, some stockmen had walked their meat animals to butchers. As far back as 1655, John and William Pynchon began taking livestock over the roads from Springfield, Massachusetts, to Boston. By 1700, farmers in many sections of New England were trailing cattle and hogs to the cities for slaughter. Soon those who lived farther south began making similar drives to Philadelphia, Baltimore, and Charleston.

After 1800, as frontier Kentucky and Ohio became important livestock regions, farmers began making longer drives. Many took herds from Ohio and even Indiana to Baltimore in the 1820's. Often they used rough backwoods roads, sometimes handling cattle and hogs together. Usually the boss rode horseback, carrying a blacksnake whip. Also mounted was a flanker who helped keep the animals in line, especially at crossroads and in wooded country. The other men were afoot. One led an ox at the head of the procession, while the others kept after stragglers in the rear.

At night the drovers bedded their herds on farms where they could buy corn in the shock. The cattle forded or swam most of the rivers, though sometimes the lead ox and a few steers were ferried across. By 1830, herds from Missouri were passing through Illinois and Indiana on their way to eastern markets. Some of the trails that stockmen used became the routes of railroads that later pushed westward from the seaboard.

In the 1830's, as the center of cattle raising followed the movement of pioneers westward, Illinois began to challenge the position of Ohio as the leading beef state. Drovers gathered large herds in Indiana, Illinois, and Missouri and took them to Ohio and sometimes beyond. Benjamin F. Harris pointed herds of several hundred each eastward from Illinois. He swam them across the Wabash River at Attica and trailed them through Muncie, Springfield, and Columbus and on to markets in Pennsylvania and Maryland. In 1845 young John T. Alexander trailed 250 fat Illinois cattle all the way to Boston, by way of Albany, showing some of the enterprise that later made him the country's leading cattle shipper. Another Illinoisan, Isaac Funk, sometimes walked as many as 1,500 cattle a year from his farm to the Chicago market. Other Funk cattle were trailed to Buffalo, New York.

Soon Funk, Jacob Strawn, and other Illinois cattle kings were making buying trips into the frontier. In Missouri, in the Indian country, and even in Texas they obtained cattle which they trailed to Illinois for fattening. In 1855 Funk and James Nichols paid a reported $27,000 for 1,200 Texas cattle and trailed them home. Later Alexander bought Longhorns extensively in Texas to supply his big Illinois feeder ranches. Meanwhile, many small herds were walked into Illinois from Kentucky.

By the outbreak of the Civil War, Illinois was crisscrossed by railroads. Although Texas then had more cattle than any other state, Illinois, the second state, was at the top of the list in shipments of fat cattle to eastern markets. It continued in that position through the next decade.[1]

Rail shipments did not end for some time the trailing of beef cattle from the central and border states to eastern cities. In the fall of 1863, with the supply of Texas Longhorns cut off by war, Walt Whitman watched immense herds in the streets of Washington. Some of the drovers, he noted, led the cattle with a wild, pensive call, "between the cooing of a pigeon and the hoot of an owl."

Whitman liked to stand and look at the herds but kept a little way off to avoid the dust. "There are always men on horseback, cracking their whips and shouting," he wrote in *Specimen Days*. "The cattle low—some obstinate ox or steer attempts to escape—then a lively scene. The mounted men, always excellent riders and on good horses, dash after the recusant and wheel and turn. A dozen mounted drovers, their great slouched, broad-brimmed hats, picturesque. Another dozen on foot. Everybody covered with dust, long goads in their hands. An immense drove of perhaps a thousand cattle —the shouting, hooting, movement."

Texas enterprise in trailing cattle to distant markets got under way slowly. Even under Spanish and Mexican rule, there had been

---

[1] Quincy *Whig*, July 3, 1854; *Illinois State Journal*, January 16, 1869; Clarence P. McClelland, "Jacob Strawn and John T. Alexander, Central Illinois Stockmen," *Journal of the Illinois State Historical Society*, Vol. XXXIV, No. 2 (June, 1941), 177–208; Paul Wallace Gates, "Cattle Kings in the Prairies," *Mississippi Valley Historical Review*, Vol. XXXV, No. 3 (December, 1948), 379–412; Helen M. Cavanagh, *Funk of Funk's Grove*.

a few small drives to Louisiana. This activity increased in the early years of the Texas Republic. James Taylor White, who had started a ranch on Galveston Bay in 1819, took a herd over the Opelousas Trail through the bayou country to the Mississippi River in 1838. Although records are lacking, others are believed to have trailed herds over this route to various Louisiana points in the next few years. A census report mentions the trailing of Texas cattle to New Orleans, beginning in 1842. In 1845 the *Planter's Banner,* published at Franklin, Louisiana, noted this movement. It cited the deputy collector of customs at Vermilion as saying that large droves of Texas cattle were ready to cross the line for the New Orleans market as soon as the duty was abolished.[2]

Although a herd of fifteen hundred Texas cattle was said to have been trailed to Missouri in 1842, the first large northward drive of definite record was made in 1846. In that year Edward Piper took a thousand head overland from Texas to Ohio, where he fed and sold them. Other northward drives followed.

Two years after the Piper drive, the acquisition of the Pacific Southwest by the United States and the discovery of gold in California opened a new and attractive market for beef cattle. Despite the danger of Indian raids on the long trail, some Texas cowmen were quick to take advantage of this opportunity. T. J. Trimmier of Washington County walked five hundred beeves to California and sold them at a hundred dollars a head. As he returned to Texas the next year, he met other herds on their way west.

Several herds left Fredericksburg, on the Texas frontier, in 1849.[3] Although not all the drovers received prices like that obtained by Trimmier, most of the ventures were successful. The supplying of Texas cattle to California reached its peak in 1854 and continued until the outbreak of the Civil War. Other herds were trailed to the mining region from Illinois, Missouri, Arkansas, and the Indian Territory. This movement of cattle to California paralleled a similar one in which sheep from midwestern states were taken over long mountain trails to California in 1852–60.

The drives to California were highly speculative. Cattle bought on the Texas frontier at $5 to $15 a head might bring $25 to $150

2 *Texas National Register,* August 28, 1845.
3 Houston *Telegraph,* March 8, 1849.

in California, depending on market conditions at the moment. Even those drovers who received high prices had taken heavy risks and often had lost some of their stock on the trail. They had run the gauntlet of Apache raiders. They had contended with dust, hot winds, drouth, and parched grass. Often the rough trail had left cattle and horses with cut hoofs and sore feet. Poison came from alkaline lakes and from strange weeds. Many a carcass was left beside the barren trail.[4]

Among those who trailed Texas cattle to California was James Campbell of San Antonio. He took herds in both 1853 and 1854.[5] Others included Michael Erskine of Seguin and John James of San Antonio. The latter had in his outfit a young trail hand of Tennessee birth, James G. Bell. In a diary, Bell described this trip in some detail.[6] The main loss of stock came from the eating of poisonous weeds near the end of the long drive. There were, of course, occasional inconveniences such as the scarcity of water and the night activity of coyotes, which threatened to stampede the cattle. But the Apache raiders who had killed one of the Texas drovers on the trail ahead and had stolen twenty cattle didn't bother the James herd. At the ferry near Fort Yuma, Bell was told that more than ten thousand cattle had crossed that season. In Los Angeles, beeves were selling at twenty-five to thirty dollars a head.

The trailing of Texas cattle to California did not interrupt the selling in other markets. Beginning in 1848, steamers carried some Longhorns from various Texas Gulf ports to New Orleans. Those shipped from Galveston from 1850 to 1856 were reported to range from 2,900 to 6,000 head a year. Yet many of the cattle bound for Louisiana continued to go on their own motive power. Not every herd walked all the way to New Orleans; some were trailed to one point or another on the Red River or the Mississippi, whence they went to the Crescent City by boat. Late in 1855, two cowmen from central Texas trailed 175 head to Alexandria and shipped from there

[4] *Texas State Gazette*, July 29, 1854, April 21, 1855.

[5] *Colorado Tribune*, July 21, 1854.

[6] James G. Bell, "A Log of the Texas-California Cattle Trail, 1854" (ed. by J. Evetts Haley), *Southwestern Historical Quarterly*, Vol. XXXV, No. 3 (January, 1932), 208-37, Vol. XXXV, No. 4 (April, 1932), 290-316, Vol. XXXVI, No. 1 (July, 1932), 47-66.

to New Orleans. They found the market dull but cleared about $4.50 a head.[7]

This trailing grew in volume through the 1850's. A resident of Beaumont estimated that about forty thousand head had crossed the Neches River there that year. At Liberty, farther west, a local citizen who kept a record of cattle crossing the Trinity River by ferry there reported for 1855 twenty-five herds with a total of 5,843 head. His figures for 1856 were thirty-one droves and 6,869 head. During the first ten months of 1856, the Galveston *News* reported, 32,412 beeves from western Texas crossed the Sabine River into Louisiana. Most of them were headed for New Orleans. Some of the cattle received in New Orleans were shipped to other points in the South or to the West Indies.

Even those herds shipped from Texas by boat usually required some trail driving from pasture to port. Abel H. (Shanghai) Pierce, then a gangling youth of twenty who had been in Texas only a year, made his first drive in southern Texas in 1855. Pierce had acquired his nickname because he looked like a long-legged, long-necked Shanghai rooster. At that time he was working for W. B. Grimes, who had a large spread near Tres Palacios. Grimes raised his pay to $22.50 a month and put Shanghai in charge of buying a herd and trailing it to the coast for shipment to New Orleans.

II

The northward drives also continued, those to Missouri becoming larger in 1849 and 1850. "Several droves of cattle have passed through this place en route to Missouri," reported the Dallas *Herald* in June, 1850. "They are brought mostly from the upper Brazos and are carried to Missouri to be sold for beef or to furnish teams for California emigrants."[8]

This trailing to northern markets, which mounted steadily during the 1850's, generally followed a route that Indians, traders, and emigrants already had well established. Red Men had used it for decades. They had ridden over it in hunting buffaloes and in raiding the early white settlements in central Texas to steal horses and

[7] James R. Hanna, letter, August 18, 1856 (MS, Fort Worth Woman's Club).
[8] *Texas State Gazette*, July 6, 1850.

to capture prisoners for ransom. Many pioneer settlers, coming down through the Indian Territory in Conestoga wagons, had entered Texas by this trail. They called it the Texas Road. In the early spring of 1845, more than a thousand wagons were said to have crossed the Red River into Texas in six weeks.

This route, which some drovers came to call the Shawnee Trail, led from the ranges of southern and southwestern Texas past Austin, Waco, and Dallas. On to the north, it kept to the high prairies, skirting the post oak cross timbers. The herds swam the Red River at Rock Bluff Crossing, near Preston, in Grayson County. This crossing was popular because a natural rock formation served as a chute into the water and because a gentle slope on the opposite side made it easy for the cattle to come out.

Texas drovers who used this route in the 1850's called it the cattle trail, the Kansas Trail, or merely the trail. Just when or how some began to call it the Shawnee Trail is uncertain. That name appeared in print at least as early as 1874 and presumably was used much earlier. The name could have been suggested by an Indian village, called Shawneetown, on the Texas bank of the Red River just below the trail crossing. Or by the Shawnee Hills, which the route skirted on their eastern side before crossing the Canadian River.

In Dallas, where herds of bawling Longhorns raised clouds of dust in the streets, people knew the section of the trail from their town to the Red River as the Preston Road. This road and that into Dallas from the south had been surveyed in 1840, in the days of the Republic. In the fall of 1839, under an act the Congress of Texas had passed a year earlier, Albert Sidney Johnston, secretary of war, had sent north a company of soldiers under the command of Colonel William G. Cooke. The purpose was to lay out a military road from the Brazos to the Red River and to establish small forts for protecting the settlers against Indian raids.

Colonel Cooke joined the troops at Little River and went on to the Waco village. There he waited for the quartermaster to catch up with supplies, which included beeves on the hoof and several wagons with provisions. Five of Cooke's men, carelessly leaving their muskets when they went to get water, were killed by Indians. Soon afterward, in a cold norther, the cattle broke loose and ran away. This left the party with nothing to live on except sugar and coffee and whatever game they could kill. When the game ran out, they had to cook the meat of dogs, mules, and horses.

On the Red River, Colonel Cooke had his men build a stockade called Fort Johnson, midway between Holland Coffee's trading station and Basin Springs. He also opened a supply post that became known as Fort Preston. It took its name from that of Captain William G. Preston, who was in charge of a company of men there in 1840. Later the village that grew up about the fort was called Preston Bend or Preston.

Preston soon began to profit from its convenient Rock Bluff crossing. In the late 1830's, even before there was a Preston, James Tyson, of North Carolina birth, had begun operating a ferry at this point. Although his first ferry was little more than a log raft, it served well enough for getting wagons across the stream. In a later period, the ferry was owned by two partners, Jim Shannon and Bud Randolph. In or about 1853, to cash in on the California gold rush, Benjamin Franklin Colbert, a Chickasaw born in Mississippi, started a similar ferry service a short distance downstream, near Shawneetown. This ferry was used by the stagecoaches of the Butterfield Trail and by some of the cattle drovers.

After crossing the Red River, the Shawnee Trail entered the Choctaw country and veered a bit to the northeast. Some of the herds were trailed past Fort Washita, which had been set up in 1842 to protect the Chickasaws against wild, hostile Indians of the plains to the west. Other herds followed a more direct line a dozen miles to the east. The splits came together before reaching Boggy Depot, about fifty miles above the Red River. This settlement, on Clear Boggy Creek, had received its name from the fact that rations had been issued there to Chickasaw emigrants in the late 1830's. A stagecoach traveler in the fall of 1858 described the village as having several painted houses and a few stores.

Farther on, the trail crossed the Canadian River just below the joining of the North and South forks. After leading through the Creek country, it crossed the Arkansas just above the mouth of the Grand or Neosho River and just below the mouth of the Verdigris. From there it continued north along the west bank of the Grand.

Along the Grand River, a few miles from its mouth, the route passed the blockhouses and palisades of historic Fort Gibson, one of the oldest and best known of the frontier military outposts. Established in 1824, Fort Gibson had been influential in pacifying many of the Indian tribes. Sam Houston had lived on its outskirts from 1829 to 1832. Washington Irving, there in the latter year, had noted its neatly whitewashed buildings. Among the officers stationed there in the next few years was Lieutenant Jefferson Davis. Steamboats came up as far as Fort Gibson when the water was high. At other times the post was served by keel boats and wagon trains.

Through the Cherokee country the Shawnee Trail followed the west bank of the Grand River until it was within fifteen miles of the Kansas line. Then it crossed to the east bank and entered the southeastern corner of Kansas. A little farther north, the trail turned northeast through Missouri to the Missouri River, which it followed toward St. Louis.

The route from Fort Gibson to St. Louis had been used by explorers, Indian traders, and missionaries as early as 1802, when the powerful Osages still dominated the eastern part of the Territory. Then it was called the Osage Trace. Later it was used by some of the Santa Fe traders.

The Shawnee Trail was an unusually wide road. It needed to be to accommodate its heavy and varied traffic. Besides the long lines of settlers' wagons, there were military supply caravans and companies of freighters. On their return north, many of the freighters carried buffalo robes or other pelts. And along with the northbound cattle were occasional herds of mustang ponies and Mexican mules. As deep ruts made parts of the road impassable, teamsters and drovers went to one side or the other, thus widening the trail.

By 1854 the Shawnee Trail was a recognized and important cattle route. In early June of that year the exploring and surveying expedition of Captain Randolph B. Marcy, headed southward, passed an estimated ten thousand Longhorns, plodding in the opposite direction, between Fort Washita and Boggy Depot. The cattle were on the way to Missouri and Illinois.

The rapid increase in the trailing of Longhorns from Texas to Missouri drew comment from the *Texas State Gazette* two months later. Fifty thousand head, it reported in its issue of August 5, had crossed the Red River at Preston that season. Most of them were from the valleys of the Colorado and the Brazos.

By that time many drovers, instead of turning toward St. Louis, were continuing north through the eastern edge of Kansas. Independence, Westport, and Kansas City were becoming the chief Missouri markets for Texas cattle. The outfitting of freighters and emigrants in those towns strengthened the demand for all kinds of livestock. There was also a ready sale of steers to butchers, army quartermasters, Indian agents, and midwestern feeders. At first Independence and Westport handled most of the Texas cattle. After 1855, Westport and Kansas City took the larger share, with Kansas City in the lead.

III

On both branches of the Shawnee Trail, serious trouble had begun to overtake some of the drovers. In June, 1853, Texans had trailed three thousand cattle through Vernon County, in western Missouri, and on into the edge of Bates County. There indignant citizens, who feared that the Longhorns would give Texas fever to the Missouri cattle, turned back the invading herd and forced the drovers to retrace their route.

This livestock disease, in Texas called Spanish fever or Mexican fever and elsewhere known by many other names, had been noted in South Carolina as early as 1814. It was a scourge carried by ticks, but its means of communication was not then generally known. The tough Texas Longhorns and most other southern cattle, although carrying the ticks, seemed immune to the fever. But northern herds that were infected suffered heavy losses.

The stricken cattle began to arch their backs and droop their heads and ears. Their eyes became glassy and staring. They began to stagger from weakness in their hind legs. Their temperatures rose, and their appetites faded. The pulse became quick and weak, and the animal panted for air. The breath acquired a fetid odor, and the urine became dark or bloody. The cows gave less milk. As the disease progressed, some of the cattle slumped into a coma-like lethargy and refused to move. Others became delirious and tossed their heads about so violently that some cracked their horns.

The mortality rate was high. Those cattle not killed were left in such poor condition that months of additional feeding would be required to ready them for the market. Naturally, stockmen in the areas contaminated by the Longhorns began to clamor against allowing Texas cattle to pass through their counties.[9]

Despite this objection, considerable trailing went on until the outbreak of the Civil War. In central Texas, Captain Shapley P. Ross made up a trail herd in 1854 by buying five hundred steers at thirteen dollars each from his McLennan County neighbors. Ross, of Kentucky birth, had commanded a company of Texas Rangers and later, in 1849, had set up the first ferry service across the Brazos at Waco. He trailed his herd to Missouri, where he had lived for a time, and sold out at twenty-seven dollars a head.

Some herds traveled much farther. One of six hundred head, which had left Texas in April, 1854, arrived in Chicago in the early fall. A newspaper in the Windy City described the steers as "fine looking cattle, remarkable for their sleek appearance and long horns." But the prices they brought, it added, "would argue no superiority to those raised upon our own prairies." The drover had sold them at the Bull's Head Stockyards, at Madison and Ashland, at $2.50 to $2.75 a hundred pounds.[10]

Texans trailed several other herds to Illinois that year. In some instances, they fattened the cattle on the Illinois prairies and marketed them in Chicago in the following spring. Among the drives was that of an Illinoisan, George Jackson Squires, who had bought five hundred Longhorns near Houston. Squires was accompanied by his wife and her brother, John J. Bent, who were traveling for their health and who rode in a covered wagon. The party went through the Indian Territory, Kansas, and Missouri, crossing the Mississippi at Hannibal.[11]

In St. Louis, the arrival of that city's first Longhorns in the summer of 1854 caused a stir in the stockyards. Buyers viewed the backwoods bovines a bit critically and were willing to pay only fifteen

[9] Cox, *Historical and Biographical Record of the Cattle Industry*, 71–85; T. R. Havins, "Texas Fever," *Southwestern Historical Quarterly*, Vol. LII, No. 2 (October, 1948), 147–62.

[10] Chicago *Daily Democratic Press*, October 11, 1854.

[11] George Squires Herrington, "An Early Cattle Drive From Texas to Illinois," *Southwestern Historical Quarterly*, Vol. LV, No. 2 (October, 1951), 267–69.

to twenty dollars a head. Later, on October 27, twenty-six steers from Texas brought only fifteen dollars each. They had been trailed about five hundred miles, commented one St. Louis newspaper, "and it may be a matter of astonishment how they could be sold for so small a price. The thing is explained when we say they subsisted all the way on grass and kept in tolerable order. What is more, they never ate an ear of corn in their lives. An attempt was made to feed them with corn and provender at the stockyards, but they ran away from it. Texas cattle are about the nearest to wild animals of any now driven to market. We have seen some buffaloes that were more civilized."[12]

St. Louis continued to get some cattle trailed from Texas and the Indian Territory, though it did not value them highly. One of the stockyards men remarked that they were "not fit for people to eat. They will do to bait traps to catch wolves."[13] Those not slaughtered locally were sent to Illinois farms for fattening or shipped by boat to New Orleans.

New York, which had received a few Illinois-fed Cherokee Longhorns in 1853, saw its first ones from Texas a year later. Two young midwestern cowmen, Tom Candy Ponting and Washington Malone, had ridden horseback to Texas and gathered about seven hundred head. Trailing from Fannin County by way of Fort Gibson in 1853, they wintered the Longhorns in Illinois. From the herd they picked 150 fat beeves to take on east the next summer. The cattle went on foot to Muncie, Indiana, thence by rail to New York. At Allerton's Washington Drove Yards, at Fourth Avenue and Forty-fourth Street, they brought up to eighty dollars a head.

The New York *Tribune* noted that while it cost only two dollars a head to trail these cattle from Texas to Illinois, it required seventeen dollars a head to get them to Indiana on foot and on to New York by rail. This newspaper reported that the Longhorns generally were five to seven years old, "long-legged, with long taper horns and something of a wild look. It is said that the meat is fine-grained and close, somewhat like venison. It is apt to be a little tough when cooked in the ordinary way, and therefore not as good to eat fresh as that of cattle of a more domestic character. This will be changed

12 St. Louis *Intelligencer*, October 30, 1854.
13 *Missouri Republican*, July 20, 1857.

by purchasing them young and feeding them two years as well as this drove has been fed for one year."[14]

As New Yorkers did not care much for the Longhorns, few were shipped there before the war. Newspaper notices indicate that about 750 head reached the metropolis in 1855, probably 1,000 to 2,000 a year from 1856 through 1859, and only 99 in 1860. Most of the Texas cattle had been fed in Illinois and forwarded by rail, but a few were trailed all the way from Texas to New York.

The long journey, whatever the means, did not enhance the Longhorns in the eyes of Manhattan buyers. These cattle "were barely able to cast a shadow," observed the New York *Times*. "According to the opinion of the sellers, they would not weigh anything were it not for their horns, which were useful also in preventing them from crawling through fences."[15] A week later the same newspaper reported that among the arriving cattle were "140 from Texas, said to have been grazed in Illinois, but it must have been by the roadside as they came along. Their appearance indicated that they had tasted little even of the prairie grass."

In 1855 the Texas drovers were plagued by a new and stronger wave of opposition from stockmen in Missouri. The antagonism arose from an epidemic of Texas fever that ravaged local stock in the western and central parts of the state, killing many fine animals. All of the counties struck were ones through which Texans had trailed herds of Longhorns. Angry farmers formed vigilance committees, stopped some of the herds, and threatened to kill any Texas cattle that entered their counties.

In several county seats, stockmen held indignation meetings and called on the legislature for action. The lawmakers responded promptly. On the mistaken assumption that the Longhorns were diseased—instead of merely carrying ticks that brought infection to less hardy animals—they drew up a quarantine bill. This measure was intended to keep anyone from trailing diseased animals into or through the state. It became a law on December 15.

Under this new act, aimed particularly at animals afflicted with Texas fever, the penalty was a fine of twenty dollars for each offend-

[14] New York *Tribune*, July 4, 1854; Tom Candy Ponting, *Life of Tom Candy Ponting*, 20–41.
[15] New York *Times*, August 19, 1858.

32

ing animal. Enforcement was left to local justices of the peace.[16] Since Missouri happened to be almost free from the tick fever in 1856 and 1857, officers made little effort to enforce the quarantine law in those years. Thus it did not at first much hamper trail driving.

The trailing of Texas cattle northward in this period was still hazardous, though. The drovers were discouraged not only by the sporadic threats of midwest stockmen who feared Texas fever but by the growing trouble over slavery. This conflict was especially strong on the Kansas-Missouri border, along which many of the herds traveled.

With the opening of a federal land office in Kansas Territory in 1854, Missourians had swarmed across the border to stake out claims. But soon they were outnumbered by free-soilers from New England and elsewhere. Many of the latter carried the new breech-loading Sharps rifle, called Beecher's Bible.[17] Late in 1855, the free-soilers drafted a constitution that forbade the bringing in of slaves. Proslavery men, in May, 1856, pillaged and burned several buildings in Lawrence. In retaliation, John Brown led an attack on a settlement on Osawatomie Creek, where his band killed five proslavery men. Trouble between the belligerent Jayhawkers and the border ruffians from Missouri lasted for several years.

IV

Despite such obstacles, the cattle drives from Texas continued. In 1856 Texans trailed at least one herd to Chicago. In the following year they walked two herds to Quincy, Illinois. The outfits went by Waco, Preston, and Fort Gibson. One herd was taken by William McCutcheon and his son Willis from rolling Bastrop County. The other was the herd of Jesse Day of Hays County. Day, of Tennessee birth, was well known not only as a cowman but as a freighter. He kept several wagons and teams busy hauling goods from Gulf ports to Austin. On this drive, Day's nineteen-year-old son, James Monroe, better known as Doc, went along as one of the trail hands.

In 1857, as the nation buzzed over the current panic and the Supreme Court's unpopular decision in the Dred Scott case, most of

[16] *Revised Statutes of the State of Missouri*, II, 1004–1005.

[17] To promote settlement of the Kansas issue, the prominent clergyman Henry Ward Beecher had pledged his Brooklyn church to send twenty-five rifles and had urged others to send them.

the Texas herds headed north still had Missouri as their destination. In Kansas City, then the largest livestock market on the western frontier, as many as fifteen thousand head of stock were sold in a single week. Some of the cattle were shipped to Chicago and other cities to the east. More, along with horses and mules, were trailed to California and other sections of the West. The *Western Journal of Commerce* estimated that about fifty-two thousand stock cattle were sold in 1857 and forty-eight thousand in 1858, along with smaller numbers of horses. This stock came from Texas, the Cherokee Nation, Arkansas, and Missouri. Two-thirds of it was estimated to have come from Texas.[18]

Among the drives of 1857 was one of twelve hundred mossy-horned steers which P. R. Mitchell and three other cowmen gathered in southern Texas and headed for Chicago. One of the trail hands was a Negro who was called Big-Mouth Henry because he was a great singer and could almost charm a bunch of Longhorns. The herd was pointed through Arkansas and Missouri and swam the Mississippi twenty-five miles above St. Louis. After the beeves were contracted to Chicago butchers, Al Fields stayed to herd them on the prairie. Later, a small bunch at a time, they were driven into the slaughter pens and killed with his cap-and-ball pistol.[19]

In 1858, while Abraham Lincoln and Stephen A. Douglas engaged in their historic debates in Illinois, Texans trailed about eleven thousand Longhorns to Chicago and nearby points. Most of these cattle crossed the muddy Missouri River at Randolph Ferry, about three miles east of Kansas City.

At Hannibal, Missouri, in the summer of 1858, the Longhorns found more favor than they had in St. Louis four years earlier. "A fine drove of Texas cattle passed through this city yesterday," wrote a local newsman. "While they were being driven down to the ferry landing, they had a stampede and ran up on Holliday's Hill, where the drivers had a long chase before they succeeded in overtaking them. They were fine, large cattle and were in good order."[20]

In that year, Oliver Loving, a pioneer Texas cowman living in

[18] C. C. Spalding, *Annals of the City of Kansas*, 78; *Western Journal of Commerce*, January 9, June 20, 1859.
[19] J. Frank Dobie, "Up the Trail to Wyoming," *Western Horseman*, Vol. XVI, No. 3 (March, 1951), 8.
[20] Hannibal *Messenger*, July 10, 1858.

northeastern Palo Pinto County, joined with a neighbor, John Durkee, for a drive to Illinois. Durkee raised horses, along with cattle, on the upland prairies of northern Parker County, drained by the Clear Fork of the Trinity River. He had an unusual taste in foods that led to friendly joking in the cow camps. His favorite summer breakfast was black coffee and sliced cucumbers sprinkled with vinegar.

Loving and Durkee brought their herds together in Parker County, near the Tarrant line. After crossing the Red River at Preston, they followed the Shawnee Trail past Fort Gibson and Baxter Springs. They crossed the Mississippi at Quincy and sold their stock at good prices.

Other Texas drovers ran into serious trouble in Missouri that year. A new epidemic of Texas fever struck western and central parts of the state. More devastating than that of 1855, it left thousands of local cattle dead and many farmers in financial straits. The law that had been enacted three years earlier to cope with this situation failed to work. The means provided for enforcement was weak. Too, the Texas cattle which brought in the disease appeared to be—and were—in excellent health and thus were not subject to the penalties of the law. So again the embattled farmers handled the situation directly. They gave notice that they would turn back Texas cattle, forcibly if necessary, and did so on several occasions.

At the Grand River bridge five miles west of Clinton, in June, 1859, a committee stopped and turned back three herds of Longhorns totaling about two thousand head. No one, said the Clinton *Journal*, "can for a moment blame the citizens of Missouri for adopting summary measures to protect their stock from the fearful ravages of Spanish fever."[21]

The mounting alarm of Missouri stockmen over Texas fever led many of the drovers from the Southwest to go through the eastern edge of Kansas to Kansas City or beyond. Beginning in 1859, when a rail line was completed across northern Missouri, they could trail to St. Joseph and ship from there to Chicago.

Yet, even in Kansas, drovers from Texas were heading into trouble. In 1858, farmers in eastern Kansas, like those across the line in Missouri, had lost thousands of cattle from Texas fever. They

21 *Missouri Statesman*, June 24, 1859.

obtained from the Kansas territorial legislature, in the next February, a protective law. In addition to having provisions like those of the Missouri act of 1855, this measure barred all Texas, Arkansas, and Indian stock from entering four specified Kansas counties between June 1 and November 1.[22] As some Texas cowmen flouted this law, Kansans formed rifle companies and threatened direct action. They tried to impose the 1859 ban on April 1 instead of the June 1 date stated in the law. Kansas farmers shot some of the Longhorns and barely avoided bloody encounters with the Texans, who were well armed with six-shooters.

In 1860, Oliver Loving avoided trouble by trailing a herd to Colorado. He and three associates gathered about three thousand steers on the upper Brazos. On August 29 they headed north, through the Indian Territory, and on to Kansas. They took their herd up the Arkansas River and into Colorado, wintering the cattle on grass near Pueblo. There and in Denver they readily sold the steers in the spring of 1861.

Yet the route through Missouri continued in some use, especially since Texas fever was less prevalent in that state in 1859 and 1860. Cowmen willing to take risks continued to point their herds northward. In May, 1859, the Dallas *Herald* reported, "Yesterday a drove of two thousand beef cattle passed through Dallas en route for the North, to feed our abolition neighbors. We hope that southern diet may agree with them."[23] Three weeks later, on June 8, the same paper noted, "The great exodus of cattle northward for this season seems to have ceased. But droves of horses and sheep frequently enliven our town with clouds of dust and the musical cries of their Mexican herdsmen."

v

The trailing of Longhorns to Kansas and Missouri was slowed down in 1860 not only by troubles resulting from cattle fever but by the rumble of approaching war. Texans took several herds north that spring, however. From Hill County, Captain F. M. Harris left with a herd of fine work oxen, bound—through Dallas—for Leavenworth, Kansas Territory. From Hays County, Jesse Day started out with

[22] *General Laws of the Territory of Kansas*, 1859, 621–22.
[23] Dallas *Herald*, May 18, 1859.

a large herd of beeves. On April 22, while swimming his cattle across the swollen Brazos River at Waco, Day was drowned. After burying him at Belton, two of his sons, William and Monroe (Doc), went on with the herd. They headed the steers toward Kansas City but were blocked by a force of armed settlers. Finally they trailed the cattle to St. Louis, where they sold at good prices.

Trailing conditions that had been discouraging in 1860 became almost prohibitory in the following spring. In March, 1861, Missouri strengthened its ban against Longhorns that might bring in Texas fever. The new law authorized each county court to set up a board of cattle inspectors. It empowered the three members of the board to inspect all incoming Texas, Mexican, and Indian stock. They could order that any stock afflicted with fever or suspected of carrying it be taken back by the incoming route. If the owners refused, the cattle were subject to being driven out or killed.[24]

The outbreak of war, while delaying the testing of this Missouri law, imposed effective bans on other grounds and by other means. On April 19, President Abraham Lincoln ordered a blockade of the coasts of the seceding states. On August 16, he forbade any trade with the South. Kansas already had enacted its own trade ban on May 1. Although there was some sporadic, illicit trade between Texas and Kansas, as well as stealing of Indian and Texas cattle by Kansans, the northern markets for Longhorns were virtually cut off during the war.

With a large proportion of able-bodied Texas men serving the Confederacy, the cattle industry on the frontier fell into neglect. Calves were left unbranded, and herds strayed far across the prairies or into the brush. As normal markets were cut off, the local price of Longhorns fell rapidly. In some sections, steers were almost given away, despite the high prices prevailing in the North. Most of the trailing done from Texas during the war was to supply Confederate states to the east.

Late in 1862 the Confederate Congress, recognizing the need for beef, exempted from the military draft a limited number of stockmen, one for each five hundred head of cattle. In the following February, a Confederate commissary agent offered Texas cowmen twenty-five dollars a head for cattle which the sellers would

[24] *Laws of Missouri*, 1860–61, 25–28.

round up, or twenty-two dollars for those which the government had to gather. This stock was trailed through Louisiana or southern Arkansas and across the Mississippi River. Often the activity of federal gunboats made the river crossing hazardous.

As the war surged through its first year, many Texans continued to trail cattle to New Orleans. After that city fell to the federal forces of Captain David D. Farragut in the spring of 1862, some of the drovers still took herds to the Crescent City, exchanging them for United States gold. Confederate leaders protested against this dealing with the enemy, but it continued through the war. In June, 1864, Texas beeves brought forty to sixty dollars a head in New Orleans.

Nearly all the trailing eastward, though, was to feed the soldiers of the South. Among the Texas cowmen who helped supply the army with beef was Tennessee-born John S. Chisum, who, at the outbreak of the war, was ranching at Bolivar, in Denton County. "Jinglebob John" and his men gathered Longhorns from several counties in 1862 and 1863 and pointed them down the Red River Valley to Shreveport, where they sold them at forty dollars a head.

Oliver Loving made even longer drives, taking several herds of steers from Palo Pinto County to Confederate forces east of the Mississippi River. From the cross timbers of the same county, a pioneer cowman, Pete Narbo, walked 225 big steers east, selling at Memphis and elsewhere.

Another army supplier, for three years, was Jesse L. Driskill, who had arrived in the Texas cow country in 1849 from Tennessee by way of Missouri. He delivered beeves at New Orleans and later at points farther north. In 1862, Terrell Jackson of Washington County sent a herd of several thousand to a delivery point east of the Mississippi. In charge was young Dudley H. Snyder, who had ridden horseback from Missouri to Texas eight years earlier. By using trained lead steers, Snyder managed to swim the herd across the wide Mississippi.

Other Texans made similar wartime drives, most of them with small herds. In October, 1862, Jim Borroum and Monroe Choate left Goliad with eight hundred beeves and with W. D. H. Saunders as a trail hand. Crossing the Guadalupe River at Clinton and the Colorado at Columbus, they headed eastward. Near Orange they crossed into Louisiana. After a long drive that involved several delays from stampedes and war blockades, they sold their cattle at Woodville, Mississippi.

In the same year, George A. Haynes sent a herd of about six hundred steers from Lockhart to a Confederate post at Shreveport. H. C. Whittaker was trail boss, and Mark A. Withers, a youth of sixteen, was one of the hands. Haynes, a big fleshy man, rode along in his buggy, Withers recalled. The outfit crossed the Brazos at Port Sullivan and trailed the cattle through the pine woods. In the timber the men used pens of pine logs which Confederate officers had had built for holding trail cattle. The steers were butchered at Shreveport. The Confederate paper money received for cattle in these drives was worthless when the war ended.[25]

During the war some Texans trailed small herds into Mexico, but the prices received there were hardly enough to warrant the expense. Some drovers resorted to barter. In 1863, Captain William C. McAdams, a veteran of the Mexican War, took a herd from Palo Pinto County, on the upper Brazos, to Mexico. He traded the cattle for sugar and other supplies that were scarce in Texas. George Bell did similar swapping a year later when he trailed two hundred beeves to Mexico and brought back spurs, bits, knives, forks, and coffee.

Others in 1864 found the Mexican market a bit more attractive. W. A. Peril took a herd from the hills of Gillespie County that season. His route was by Fort McKavett and the head of the South Concho River. It led through the chaparral country to Horsehead Crossing of the Pecos River and on to Fort Stockton, then entered the mountainous Big Bend country to cross the Rio Grande at Presidio.

By this time some Confederate soldiers and officers in the cattle country were deserting and heading for Mexico with small herds. W. C. McGough, who led a military scout in search of deserters and horse thieves, followed some fugitives to Mexico in the fall. To turn his expedition into profit, he took along three hundred steers. After passing Fredericksburg, he joined a pioneer cowman, John Hittson, who was trailing southwest with a similar herd. The two joined forces, ran the blockade, got their cattle safely across the

25 Mark A. Withers, reminiscences (MS, J. Frank Dobie, Austin, Texas); J. Marvin Hunter (ed.), *The Trail Drivers of Texas*, 267–68, 723–24.

border not far from Eagle Pass, and sold them at eighteen dollars a head.[26]

The Texas cowmen were hurt not only by isolation from their better markets but by a severe drouth that struck the ranges during the war. Streams dried up, and grass withered. Thousands of cattle perished from thirst. In some localities, losses were estimated to be as high as 75 per cent. The hardest hit stockmen frantically tried to salvage their cattle by offering them at one to two dollars a head. Even at such prices, there were few buyers.

Yet, despite the drouth, uncounted Longhorns were scattered over the prairies and plains at the close of the war. To stockmen left penniless or nearly so, they offered a handy means for obtaining the cash needed to rebuild the industry. The Texas ranges, with their year-round grazing, were almost ideal for growing cattle. Until the use of blooded stock could turn out beef of higher quality, the Longhorns could be a source of profit.

A large proportion of the half-wild cattle grazed unbranded on public land. They were mavericks. They would belong to anyone who roped and branded them. If they could be rounded up in large herds and marketed without much expense, they would help Texas to recover from the wounds inflicted in four years of war. If the cowmen could not overcome the opposition of trailing Longhorns through Missouri and eastern Kansas, perhaps they could find new markets.

[26] Hunter, *The Trail Drivers of Texas*, 411–12, 428–29, 799–800; W. C. McGough, "Driving Cattle Into Old Mexico in 1864," *West Texas Historical Association Year Book*, Vol. XIII (October, 1937), 112–21.

Pointing them north

Joseph G. McCoy, who conceived the idea of trailing Texas cattle
to the railroad at Abilene

Shanghai Pierce, from *Shanghai Pierce, A Fair Likeness*,
by Chris Emmett

Photograph by Brack in 1899

"Old Champion"

III

TROUBLE AT THE BORDER

Texas showed a dismal face to the weary soldiers who plodded home-ward at the close of the Civil War. Roads and trails turned deep ruts and eroded shoulders—scars from years of neglect—toward the un-shaved, dusty men. Through the pine woods and oak thickets and across the open prairies, the veterans made slow headway. Some of them rode horses that had known the smell of gunpowder and the roar of cannons. Others trudged on in worn boots, save when some hospitable traveler offered a ride in his wagon or oxcart.

Many of the plantations they passed seemed abandoned. There and on the smaller farms, fields were overgrown with weeds. Build-ings were crumbling, fences down, and gates broken off their hinges. In the cattle country toward the western fringe of settlement, much of the stock was gone from the corrals and the home pastures. With-out fences or horsemen to keep them in, the cattle had wandered off to look for juicier grass or to join wild herds on the open range.

Even those ranches toward the southwest, at which Mexican *vaqueros* had been left to care for the stock, were in a bad state. Captain R. H. Williams, who had commanded a frontier company, found this true when he returned unheralded to his ranch on the

Frio River, seventy miles west of San Antonio. "I arrived late in the evening, to the great surprise of the Mexicans," he wrote. "I was the last person they expected, or wished, to see. Having no one to look after them, these gentry, after the manner of their kind, had been taking things easy, and everything had been neglected. Calves had been left unbranded and horses allowed to stray away on the prairie. The only wonder was that the Indians hadn't cleared out the lot."[1]

At home the Texas stockman found little comfort beyond that of a reunited family. With Confederate currency a total loss, hard money was scarce. Even though there had been little fighting on its soil, Texas was left financially flat by the war. The frontier settler could not easily find seed for new crops or breeding stock for quality herds. True, the ranges to the west and southwest were full of half-wild cattle. Those cowmen left vigorous and uncrippled after the war could rope and brand all the Longhorns they wanted. But finding a market for such beef was a baffling problem. Hardly anyone within reach wanted to buy. The whole state was cattle poor.

Despite the experience in trail driving that some Texas cowmen had gained before and during the war, the outlook was hardly bright. Delivering Longhorns to distant markets might be even more hazardous than it had been before the fighting began. Carpetbaggers and Negro soldiers were in the saddle, ready to make trouble by enforcing harsh Reconstruction measures. In the border country, bands of roving guerrillas were plundering the stockmen and trying to prolong the tragic conflict. In Missouri the 1861 law against cattle trailing still awaited a test.

The Texas stockmen, although less dependent on Negro help than were the cotton planters, could get little work from the freedmen. Many of the blacks in the cattle country were said to be "rambling about in idleness, and will either not work at all or demand four prices for what they but half do." Some were accused of getting drunk, flourishing weapons, stealing horses, and insulting the whites.[2]

The federal soldiers were another source of trouble. Some of them disarmed white civilians, raided homes without cause, and plundered smokehouses and corrals. They jailed local leaders for political

[1] Williams, *With the Border Ruffians*, 310.
[2] Galveston *News*, November 12, December 1, 1865, July 26, October 27, 1866.

reasons and occasionally shot prisoners in the back. Several officers became involved in bloody frontier feuds. Instead of healing the sectional rift, the troops gashed it deeper.[3]

Most of the southwestern cowmen didn't recover from the war in time to round up Longhorns and trail them to market in 1865. There were, though, a few drives that year. In June, Robert K. Wylie and four others trailed a herd to Mexico. Wylie obtained $500 as his share of the profit. From his ranch on the Frio, Captain R. H. Williams took a small bunch of steers across the Rio Grande and sold them at $12 a head.

Several cowmen trailed Longhorns by way of the Concho River and up the Pecos to New Mexico in 1865. Among them were G. T. Reynolds, S. Huff, and W. R. St. John, who left with a herd in October. Other Texas stockmen walked a herd of two thousand head to Arkansas that year.

At least two herds went eastward to Shreveport in 1865. Captain W. C. McAdams of Palo Pinto County, who had bartered a herd in Mexico two years earlier, sold one in the northern Louisiana market at the close of the war. Several Fort Worth stockmen made a similar drive. One of them was Ephraim M. Daggett, a pioneer stockman there. Daggett recalled this as his hardest trip with cattle.

The Longhorns, he said, stampeded nearly every night from the time the outfit left the prairies north of Fort Worth until the brutes were loaded on boats for shipment to New Orleans. East of Marshall, Negro soldiers lined the road. To avoid them, the cowmen moved their herd through the brush. In Shreveport a Negro soldier with a gun and bayonet was stationed on almost every prominent corner. The net price which the Fort Worth men received for the cattle, after payment of the freight, feed bills, commission, and yardage, was six dollars a head.[4]

From the Frio River country, Captain R. H. Williams took a more southerly route toward New Orleans in the fall. On September 15 he headed eastward with 102 prime steers, most of them four to five years old. Accompanied by Jack Vinton and four *vaqueros*, he planned to trail seven hundred miles to the Atchafalaya River, en route to the Crescent City. Before he reached San Antonio, Wil-

[3] *Ibid.*, November 4, 1866.
[4] Hunter, *The Trail Drivers of Texas*, 532–33.

43

liams was joined by Dick Lemmons, who had 118 beeves and four *vaqueros*.

One night during a thunderstorm, a few miles east of San Antonio, the steers stampeded; and not all of them could be rounded up. Early in October, while passing through thick brush near the Brazos River, the Longhorns broke loose again. On the eighteenth, after passing many desolate farms and plantations, they reached the Trinity River. There a New Orleans cattle buyer met Williams and contracted for the 190 head left in the trail herd. The price was $4,875—$500 down and the remainder on delivery of the beeves in New Orleans.

Williams then sent his *vaqueros* and horses home and, with the buyer, trailed the small herd on eastward, crossing the Sabine River into Louisiana. After a drive of fifty-seven days from the Frio, he reached the Atchafalaya River on November 11. On the next day he loaded the cattle aboard the *Titan* and, on the afternoon of the following day, landed with them at Jefferson City, on the outskirts of New Orleans.[5]

II

Other Texas cowmen were busy rebuilding their herds for drives the next spring. They were out on the range looking for their strayed cattle, branding their calves and whatever mavericks they could round up, and castrating the males. Many also were capturing remnants of wild cattle that never had been in domestic herds. Usually, as before the war, neighbors joined in the cow hunts. Sometimes they used a bunch of tame cattle as decoys. The men had hard work, whether in dust or in mud. They had to be strong and dexterous to rope, throw, and tie Longhorn calves, yearlings, and occasionally grown cattle. They had to be constantly alert to avoid being hooked by vicious horns.

In the spring the cattle hid in the brush along the creeks and often were hard to find. But in the summer the mosquitoes, whose bite could penetrate even the tough hides of the Longhorns, drove them out on the open prairie.

Some of the men on the hunt carried a cow whip. As J. B. Polly of Floresville recalled, it might be "anywhere from eight to twenty

[5] Williams, *With the Border Ruffians*, 438–45.

feet long. This whip, made of close-plaited rawhide, was attached
to a wooden handle from twelve to fifteen inches long. It tapered
from the handle end to a buckskin cracker and was kept well oiled.
In the hands of an expert, it was a weapon of both offense and defense, the longer whip being the more powerful. Woe to the rattlesnake that came in reach; and woe to the lazy, loitering cow or steer
behind which rode the man with such a whip. When not in use, it
hung in coil to the pommel of the saddle. In use it dragged along the
ground and needed but a strong arm and a dexterous twist of the
wrist to send its tail forward to cut off the head of a snake or make
a broad gash in the side or on the hip of the unlucky animal."[6]

Lee Moore, a trail driver who later was foreman of a Wyoming
outfit, described in a letter one of the Texas cow hunts held soon
after the close of the war:

Every man on this cow hunt was a cattle owner just home from the
war and went out to see what he had left to brand. I was the only boy
on this cow hunt and was looking for cattle that belonged to my father
before the war. We had no wagon. Every man carried his grub in a
wallet on behind his saddle and his bed under his saddle. I was put on
herd and carried a lot of extra wallets behind my saddle and a string of
tin cups on a hobble around my pony's neck. A wallet is a sack with both
ends sewed up, with the mouth in the middle. Whenever the boss herder
couldn't hear those cups jingling, he would come around and wake
me up.

We would corral those cattle every night at some one of the owners'
homes and stand guard around the corral. I didn't stand guard but carried
brush and cornstalks and anything I could get to make a light for those
who were on guard to play poker by. They played for unbranded cattle,
yearlings at fifty cents a head and the top price for any class five dollars
a head, so if anyone ran out of cattle and had a little money he could
get back into the game. For ten dollars he could get a stack of yearlings.
My compensation for light was twenty-five cents per night or as long
as the game lasted.

Every few days they would divide up and brand and each man
take his cattle home. The cow hunt continued all summer.[7]

[6] San Antonio *Express*, September 6, 1908.

[7] *Letters From Old Friends and Members of the Wyoming Stock Growers Association* (pamphlet), 33–34.

Nearly all the youngsters on the stockmen's frontier caught the contagion of the cow hunt. "There is not a boy of American parentage learning a trade or reading for a profession west of the Colorado," lamented a newspaper correspondent from the brush of DeWitt County. "Our youths have souls above the mechanical arts. The little children, as early as they can walk, pilfer their mother's tape and make lassos to rope the kittens and the ducks. The boys, as soon as they can climb on a pony, are off to the prairie to drive stock. As they advance toward manhood, their highest ambition is to conquer a pitching mustang or throw a wild beef by the tail."[8]

With so many youths out to brand "anything with a hide on, from a buffalo to a tambourine," a writer in the Denton *Monitor* voiced a warning that went unheeded. "Do not allow your boys to load themselves down with Mexican spurs, six-shooters, and pipes," he wrote. "Keep them off the prairies as professional cow hunters. There, in that occupation, who knows that they may forget that there is a distinction between 'mine' and 'thine'? Send them to school, teach them a trade, or keep them at home."[9]

The physical dangers of the cow hunt and the branding seemed to whet the appetite of Texas youths for the adventurous life on the range and on the trail. From Refugio County a correspondent described an incident of a kind that seemed to give zest and relish to the life of the cowboy:

It became necessary to rope a large and powerful steer, with horns long, well set for hooking, and sharp as a lance. He showed fight and would not drive to the pen. A young man galloped forth from the crowd on a fleet horse and roped him. The steer, before he could be thrown, jerked the horse down, the lasso being fast to the horn of the saddle. The fall of the horse caught the leg of the rider under him. The young man spurred with the loose foot; but the horse, stunned by the fall, could not get up. He held the rider pinned to the ground. The steer, brought up at the end of the rope by the fall of the horse and seeing both horse and rider prostrate on the prairie, turned and charged on them with all his force. With neck bowed, he was ready to strike deep into their vitals those formidable weapons which nature had furnished his head. It was an awful moment. There appeared to be no escape. Some persons in such a situation would have been paralyzed—would have lost all presence of mind. But not so with that young man. His hand was

[8] Galveston *News*, August 16, 1866.   [9] *Ibid.*, November 25, 1869.

46

instantly on his revolver; and he shot the furious animal through the brain, when the delay of an instant would have been fatal.[10]

III

In the spring of 1866, with their herds again under control and their calves branded, many Texas cowmen were ready to resume, on a larger scale, the trailing of Longhorns to markets outside the state. Scores of outfits were hastening to convert range steers into ready cash. A Belton citizen stated that at least 200,000 Longhorns were trailed out of Texas that year. Another estimate was that 260,000 were headed north.

Not yet did all the drovers point their herds north. William Earnest of San Marcos sent a herd in charge of D. S. Combs to New Iberia, Louisiana. The cattle were valued at six dollars a head, and the two men divided the profit. Combs recalled that he and his trail drivers cooked their own food, slept on the prairie, and often worked in the rain. Several herds went east to points on the Red River. They were taken down that stream by boat and up the Mississippi to Cairo or St. Louis.

From the upper Brazos, two cowmen combined their herds to follow a westward trail to New Mexico as several had done in the preceding fall. One was Oliver Loving, who before the war had trailed to Illinois and later to Colorado by way of Kansas. The other was a younger frontiersman, Charles Goodnight, who, at the age of nine years, had ridden horseback to Texas when his family moved from Illinois in 1845.

By trailing to the Rocky Mountains, the pair could avoid trouble in the North and take advantage of the new market in the mining country. After merging their herds, twenty-five miles southwest of Fort Belknap, they set out on June 6. Together they had two thousand cattle and eighteen armed men.

Because hostile Comanches and Kiowas blocked a more direct route, Loving and Goodnight followed a circuitous course that was twice as long. Taking the abandoned trail of the Butterfield stage line southwestward, they passed Camp Cooper, trailed through Buffalo Gap, and crossed the North Concho. At Horsehead Crossing, the weary Longhorns reached the winding Pecos River. There

[10] *Texas Almanac* for 1861, 150–51.

more than a hundred head were lost. Some drank poisonous water from alkali pools near the stream, some drowned, and more bogged in the treacherous quicksands.

Loving and Goodnight pointed their herd northwestward up the desolate and almost barren Pecos valley. By the time they reached Fort Sumner, in eastern New Mexico, they had lost more than three hundred head on the seven-hundred-mile trail. But there they found a ready market for their beeves at eight cents a pound on foot. After they sold the steers, they had seven to eight hundred cows and calves left. Loving took those on north to Denver and sold them, while Goodnight rode back to Texas to gather another trail herd.

That fall Goodnight and his men took another two thousand Longhorns from the Brazos over the long and dusty trail to Bosque Grande, forty miles south of Fort Sumner. There they met Loving, who was back from Denver. They wintered the herd at Bosque Grande, taking a hundred beeves each month to sell to government contractors at Santa Fe.[11]

Several other Texas cowmen trailed Longhorns to New Mexico that season. Frank Willburn went with a small herd. In the late fall, John S. Chisum risked another. Chisum, who had taken several herds to Shreveport during the war, had established a new ranch on the Concho, two miles above its mouth. He left with six hundred jingle-bob[12] steers over the Loving-Goodnight route to Bosque Grande. He arrived in December and wintered his herd about eight miles from that of Loving and Goodnight. In the following spring he sold to government contractors.

Northern markets, though, were the goal of most of the Texas drovers of 1866. Some had better luck than others. H. M. Childress took a herd to central Iowa, where he sold out at thirty-five dollars a head. Monroe Choate and B. A. Borroum, who trailed eight hun-

---

[11] San Antonio *Herald*, August 28, 1866; J. Evetts Haley, *Charles Goodnight, Cowman and Plainsman*, 121–40, 209. On a similar drive in 1867, Oliver Loving was attacked by Indians and received wounds that led to his death at Fort Sumner on September 25. The route followed has been called variously the Loving-Goodnight Trail, the Goodnight-Loving Trail, the Goodnight Trail, and—with less warrant—the Chisum Trail.

[12] In addition to being branded, most range cattle were—and are—earmarked as an added means of identification. The jingle-bob, an earmark used by Chisum and certain others, was a hideous slit that left the lower half of the ear flopping.

dred big steers from Karnes County to Iowa, had so much trouble that Choate declared he wouldn't go again. Like others who headed for Iowa, though, they pushed through without having their herd turned back. Choate and Borroum had crossed the Red River at Colbert's ferry near Preston and taken their Longhorns up the Shawnee Trail past Boggy Depot. After crossing the Arkansas River at Fort Gibson, they went around west of the Kansas settlements and thus avoided a showdown over Texas fever. Although in February, 1866, Kansas had repealed its trail-cattle ban of a year earlier, the one enacted in 1861 was still in effect.

A similar route was chosen for the herd of two Iowa cattlemen, George C. Duffield of Keosauqua and Harvey Ray of Burlington. These two, in partnership, went to Texas early in 1866, traveling by New Orleans and Galveston. On March 20, in the Colorado River country west of Austin, they contracted for a thousand steers at twelve dollars a head. Ray then departed for home, leaving Duffield to get together an outfit, brand the cattle, and trail them north.

Duffield started his drive from Salt Creek on the evening of April 29. In the first eight days, the herd stampeded three times, causing delays in getting the steers together again. Downpours of rain and later stampedes also slowed the drive. Camp kettles and other pieces of equipment were lost while being pulled across the Brazos River on a raft. Later, in crossing the Red River, one of the men was drowned.

Duffield, who kept a diary, reported that Boggy Depot was well named. "We hauled cattle out of the mud with oxen all day," he wrote. Near Fort Gibson a few beeves were stolen by Indian raiders and several mired hopelessly while trying to cross the Arkansas River. At a point near Baxter Springs, in southeastern Kansas, Duffield turned the herd westward and later headed north on the west side of the trouble spots. Crossing the southeast corner of Nebraska and then trailing eastward through southern Iowa, he reached Ottumwa on the last day of October. He had only a few hundred cattle left. Of those, he shipped one hundred by rail to Burlington, for the Ray farm, and sent the others to Chicago.[13]

[13] George C. Duffield, "Driving Cattle From Texas to Iowa, 1866," *Annals of Iowa*, Third Series, Vol. XIV, No. 4 (April, 1924), 243–62.

Some Texas drovers tried to run the Kansas and Missouri blockades, with varying success. Colonel John J. Myers of Lockhart, who in his youth had served in California under John C. Frémont, endured many outrages before he could sell his cattle. R. D. Hunter, a Missouri stockman of Scottish birth, ran into trouble in his own state. After buying a northbound herd of four hundred Texas Longhorns in the Indian Territory, at twenty-five dollars a head, he trailed them on toward Sedalia. A railhead for two years, beginning in 1861, Sedalia still was an important cattle market. Soon after Hunter had entered Barton County, Missouri, he and other drovers were met by a frontier sheriff in a coonskin cap. The sheriff seized about ten thousand Longhorns on the trail and arrested the owners and foremen.

After consulting with the other arrested men, Hunter asked the sheriff to go with him to Lamar, the county seat, about twenty miles away. There, he said, he hoped to find friends who would put up his bail. As soon as Hunter and the sheriff were out of sight, the Texas drovers, as agreed upon, headed their herds back toward the Indian Territory, about twenty miles distant. Meanwhile, in Lamar, Hunter bought the sheriff a few drinks of firewater and easily escaped from his custody.

After resting their herds a few days, Hunter and the other drovers took their cattle west for about 150 miles. Then they turned north into Kansas and later northeast, crossing the Kaw River at St. Mary's. As they approached Atchison, some German settlers began hounding them; but a large landowner, Joel Hyatt, allowed their herds haven and rest on his range. After crossing the Missouri River at St. Joseph, the cowmen trailed on to Bartlett Station, on the Chicago, Rock Island and Pacific Railroad. There most of the Texans shipped by rail to Chicago. Hunter sent his steers to Joliet for finishing and thus obtained a better price.[14]

Some drovers sold their Longhorns on the sly at Baxter Springs, Fort Scott, or other frontier towns. Others flanked these settlements by heading west, as Hunter and those with him had done. Usually they trailed along the southern border of Kansas until they reached a point near the Arkansas River. Then they headed north to the

[14] Joseph G. McCoy, *Historic Sketches of the Cattle Trade of the West and Southwest*, 30–35.

Santa Fe Trail at or near Lost Spring. Over that route they traveled back east through Diamond Spring and Council Grove and north-east to the Kaw River, crossing at St. Mary's. From there, some went on northeast to Elwood and ferried their herds across the Missouri at St. Joseph. Others trailed from St. Mary's north through Seneca and on into Nebraska, crossing into Iowa at Brownville or Nebraska City.

Many drovers, realizing that the route to Sedalia was closed, turned east from Baxter Springs. Most of them headed for railway shipping points east of Sedalia. They had to trail across rocky, hilly country and often through heavy timber. Their cattle developed sore feet and lost flesh. When finally marketed in St. Louis or Chicago, they brought poor prices. Some cowmen, instead of selling at or near St. Louis, walked their herds on to the Illinois corn country and fed them until they could be sold to advantage. Despite the blockades, St. Louis and Quincy received thousands of Longhorns. Many were trailed or shipped from those points to central or northern Illinois for feeding.

IV

Not all the Kansans and Missourians who stopped Longhorn herds were as concerned over Texas fever as they claimed to be. Some were thieves who welcomed a chance to take cattle under the guise of law enforcement. "When, by outraging and robbing and, if needs be, by murdering the unfortunate drover, they became possessed of his stock," observed one partisan of the Texans, "all fear of disease subsided."[15] Other opponents of the drovers were ruffians who were at loose ends after release from military duty and were out for devilry. Some of the latter were encountered by James M. Daugherty, a youth of sixteen years, who had come north with a herd.

Jim Daugherty, born in Missouri and taken to Texas as a baby, had grown up in Denton County and had learned the cattle business early. In the spring of 1866, Jim began trailing cattle for himself. He bought about five hundred steers from James Adams, a stockman for whom he had been working. With the help of five

[15] Joseph G. McCoy, "Historic and Biographic Sketch," *Kansas Magazine*, Vol. II, No. 6 (December, 1909), 45–55.

cowhands, he took his herd across the Red River and followed the usual route past Fort Gibson and on toward Baxter Springs. He intended to trail his steers to Sedalia and ship them by rail to St. Louis.

Riding ahead to Baxter Springs, Jim Daugherty began to hear alarming reports. He was told that a drover from the Indian Territory had been killed by an outlaw band that had stampeded his herd. This danger led him to stop his herd in the Neutral Strip, at the northern edge of the Indian Territory. While the cattle rested, Jim rode north alone to Fort Scott, where he contracted to sell his steers to Ben Keys. Then he returned to his herd and began trailing north along the Kansas-Missouri border, warning his men to keep a sharp lookout for trouble.

There was need for such alertness. About twenty miles south of Fort Scott, a band of fifteen to twenty Jayhawkers swept down upon the Daugherty herd. They made the attack in the late afternoon. The ruffians were dressed in hunting shirts, homespun pantaloons, cowhide shoes, and coonskin caps. They yelled at the cattle and ordered Daugherty not to let them go an inch farther. When John Dobbins, one of the trail drivers, who was with Daugherty in the lead, started to draw his six-shooter, the Jayhawkers shot him dead in his saddle. Meanwhile the Longhorns, frightened by the firing, rushed off in a wild stampede.

Covering young Daugherty with their guns, the mobsters disarmed him and took him to Cow Creek. There they tied him to a tree with his own picket rope and whipped him with hickory withes. Leaving him tied to the tree, they discussed his fate. They concluded, without looking for evidence, that he was driving diseased, or at least disease-carrying, cattle. Then they began arguing over what they should do with him.

"Hang him!" shouted some of the Jayhawkers. Others advised whipping him to death. Finally one of the Kansans, impressed with the youth of the victim, took his part and persuaded the others to let him go.

Freed by his captors, Jim hastened back to his herd and found that about 150 head had been lost. The Texans buried John Dobbins, cutting down a small tree to make markers for his lonely grave. Then they trailed the remainder of their herd back to the Neutral Strip to plan a new strategy.

After a brief rest, Daugherty again rode to Fort Scott and told Ben Keys what had happened. Keys sent a guide whose knowledge of the country enabled the Texans, by night drives through thinly settled areas, to get their steers to Fort Scott. Selling them there at thirty-five dollars a head, the young drover came out with a profit in spite of having lost nearly a third of his beeves in the stampede.[16]

Other Texas drovers, right behind Daugherty, ran into trouble almost as serious. Captain Eugene B. Millett of Seguin, in Guadalupe County, pointed a herd up the Shawnee Trail, planning to sell at Westport. He went up the Kansas side of the border; but when he tried to enter Missouri, he was met by an armed mob that forced him to turn back. Retracing his trail to Baxter Springs, he turned east, with other cowmen, along the Arkansas line. After much opposition and delay, he finally put his herd across the Mississippi at St. Louis. By that time, the steers were too scrawny to sell. So he trailed them north to the Springfield area, where he fattened them on corn and sold them to farmers.

The Millett share of the profit from this drive—in which Myers and Ewing had an interest—was $2,600. Although that was a big return on an investment of $850, Millett didn't feel repaid for the hardships and dangers. He decided not to try a drive in 1867.

Helping Millett swim his cattle across the swollen Red River at Colbert's ferry was W. H. Farmer, who had a herd of six thousand. Farmer had trailed from southern Texas through Austin, Waco, Dallas, and Sherman. Pointing north through the Indian country, he reached the trouble area just after the mobbing of the Daugherty outfit. But Farmer, who had lived in Missouri and had friends there, obtained conditional permission to enter that state with his cattle.[17]

Some Texas drovers that year were even less fortunate than Jim Daugherty. More than a few were attacked and beaten by Kansas settlers, and several were killed. Their cattle were stampeded and headed back into the Indian Territory. Some cowmen who persisted in trailing into Kansas had their cattle shot down by volunteer border guards. These vigilantes wiped out several small Texas herds to the

---

[16] McCoy, *Historic Sketches of the Cattle Trade of the West and Southwest,* 24–28; Cox, *Historical and Biographical Record of the Cattle Industry,* 325–53; *Prose and Poetry of the Live Stock Industry of the United States,* 282–85; Hunter, *The Trail Drivers of Texas,* 698–99.

[17] Hunter, *The Trail Drivers of Texas,* 590–92.

last animal, reported a writer in the *Prairie Farmer* of August 25. If other drovers persisted in pushing into Kansas, he warned, their cattle would meet a like fate. The Kansas homesteaders, he said, viewed a warm-weather drover as no better than a horse thief.

Of the 200,000 to 260,000 Longhorns that crossed the Red River in 1866, a large number were delayed in reaching the intended markets. Because of the reports of trouble ahead, some Texas drovers held their herds in the Cherokee country or on unsettled land in southwestern Missouri until after November 1. After that date, they could trail into Kansas without violating any law. Early in July of that year, a Kansas newspaperman estimated that between 80,000 and 100,000 cattle were being grazed in the Cherokee lands alone.[18]

Three months later, farmers in western Missouri still complained of the Longhorns. In Vernon County the Nevada *Times* said:

At present there are about ten or twelve thousand head of Texas cattle en route across this county, for different points on the Pacific Railroad, to be shipped to St. Louis or Chicago. They are generally large cattle and in fine order, having been herded for the past summer in the southern part of this county and the neutral lands, moving up this way, destined for the same markets. It remains to be seen whether or not driving Texas and Indian stock through our country at this season of the year will generate or communicate Spanish fever to our native cattle. The general impression among the citizens seems to be that they ought not to be permitted to come into or to pass through our county, as we have laws to prevent it.[19]

Although many herds of Texas cattle went through to St. Louis or Quincy, delay from the quarantines kept others from being sold that year. Some drovers stayed on the Cherokee border until spring, even though prairie fires had destroyed much of the grass. Others wintered their steers in southern Kansas, southwestern Missouri, or central Illinois. Those who could sell their stock at all were lucky. Blizzards and poor grass had left many of the steers so thin that neither Illinois feeders nor butchers would buy them.

Meanwhile, in some parts of Texas, crop failures gave an added incentive to trail driving. The Galveston *News* reported on Oc-

[18] Leavenworth *Daily Conservative*, August 11, 1866.
[19] Quoted in the *Independent Press*, November 15, 1866.

tober 27, 1866, that on account of difficulties with Negroes and soldiers, "bad crops, and fears of trouble ahead, many people are talking of emigration. The opportunity to emigrate would be seized upon by many persons, but the failure of the crops has left them without the necessary means." In the following May, stock cattle sold in DeWitt County as low as three dollars a head. The cowmen of Texas realized more than ever the need for better access to markets, but they were at a loss on how to open the bottleneck.

The early months of 1867 brought new legal barricades against the southwestern drovers. In the first half of that year, six states enacted laws barring or restricting the trailing of Texas or Indian cattle across their borders. Colorado, Nebraska, Kansas, Missouri, Illinois, and Kentucky seemed determined to keep out the disease-bearing Longhorns.[20] The Illinois law carried a fine of $1,000 for any person who brought Texas or Cherokee cattle into the state. That of Missouri strengthened the hands of the county boards of cattle inspectors. It authorized the boards to inspect, impound, and condemn cattle driven in and to order the condemned stock to be removed or killed.

The new Kansas law repealed parts of the 1861 law but barred from most of Kansas any Texas or Indian cattle between March 1 and December 1. As winter trailing was not practical, the ban might as well have been for the whole year. The geographical loophole, though, was worth examining. A southwestern area, roughly about a quarter of the state, south and west of the site of McPherson, was left open to the drovers. A further provision allowed the cowmen, under certain conditions, to take their herds on from this free region a little farther north to shipping points on the Union Pacific Railroad, then building westward. Such drovers had to give a bond of $10,000 as a guarantee of payment for damage to local stock. They also were required to keep their herds off public highways and to avoid taking them within five miles of any settler without his consent in writing. Once loaded in railway cars, the Longhorns had to be shipped to some point outside the state.

The new railroad, plus the relaxing provisions of the Kansas law,

[20] *Laws of Missouri*, 24 asm., 1 sess., 1867, 128–30; *Laws of Kansas*, 1867, 7 sess., 263–67; *Nebraska Laws*, 1867, 74; *General Laws and Private Acts of the Territory of Colorado*, 1866–67, 76–87; *Kentucky Laws*, adjourned sess. of 1867, I, 53–54; *Public Laws of Illinois*, 1867, 169.

brought an opportunity to set up new markets for Texas cattle. If the Longhorns could be trailed without molestation to some railway point in central Kansas and shipped from there to Kansas City, St. Louis, or Chicago, there should be no more serious trouble over the fever carried by the ticks on some of the cattle. But would anyone open a new market within reach of the Texas drovers in time for the 1867 season? Much depended on the answer to that question.

Making sourdough biscuits at the chuck wagon

Herd swimming a river

Drawings by A. Castaigne, from Scribner's, *June, 18*
Courtesy Denver Public Library Western Collectio

Handling a stampede

The wrangler at work with the remuda

Loading at Abilene

MAN OF ENTERPRISE

As the pastures greened again in the spring of 1867, cowmen in the Southwest hardly knew where to turn. The harsh treatment that many of them had received at the hands of Kansas and Missouri mobs in the preceding year had dashed their hopes. The painful need still was for a market that would link the growers of Longhorns with the feeders and packers in the North.

The time was ripe for a new development. The Texans had several million cattle they wanted to sell, and they were willing to walk them over a long trail. The feeders and packers wanted to buy and were willing to pay good prices. Too, railroads were pushing westward from St. Louis and Kansas City, thus lessening the distance that beeves would have to travel on foot.

The loophole in the Kansas law left an opening for setting up a new shipping point for Longhorns. All that was needed was for some man of vision, enterprise, and business ability to take the initiative. The Texas cattlemen were too far away. Most people in the frontier towns of central Kansas were not interested. Some of them viewed the Longhorns only as a nuisance that hampered the development of farming. The farther they could keep the trampling beasts away from their corn and wheat the better. Executives of the new railroads, in their plush offices in St. Louis and Chicago, seemed almost indifferent to the cattle trade. They were too busy with the problems of financing and construction to drum up freight business.

The first overture to the Texas cowmen came from Topeka. There, on March 9, the Kansas Live Stock Company issued a circular addressed to cattle raisers in the country to the south. It was signed by Chester Thomas, president, and W. W. H. Lawrence, secretary. The circular informed stockmen of the trailing provisions of the new Kansas law and said that the company was laying out a route over which the Longhorns might pass without hindrance.

The company at Topeka agreed to buy 50,000 cattle for packing and 5,000 work oxen, provided it could obtain them by June 1. It also agreed to sell all stock delivered to its yards for disposal. The circular claimed that the company was capitalized for $100,000 and said that it would build corrals and shipping yards on the railroad. It urged drovers to take their herds by way of Fort Arbuckle and Fort Holmes and on north to the southern border of Kansas. There, it promised, agents of the company would meet the cowmen and conduct them to a shipping point on the Union Pacific, the location of which apparently hadn't yet been chosen.[1]

The circular was sent through the mails and was published in Texas newspapers. A few drovers heeded its advice, the first reaching Fort Arbuckle with a herd by July. But most of them distrusted the glib promises and followed the old Shawnee Trail to Baxter Springs. One of the skeptical was J. C. Juvenall of Williamson County. From Boggy Depot, on June 2, 1867, he wrote: "The only market that Texans can rely on at present for their stock is Baxter Springs, Kansas, unless there can be a route opened from Fort Gibson to the 6th principal meridian as designated by the circular from the Kansas Live Stock Company, thence north to some point on the Pacific Railroad. This, I fear, will not be a success this year."

Juvenall had little confidence in the Topeka project. He suspected that "there are many like myself who have listened too much to the flattering reports." He was wary "of Kansas sharpers, whose soul and principle are constructed of greenbacks and who are prompted by no other motives."[2]

[1] San Antonio *Herald*, May 17, 1867, quoting the Georgetown *Watchman*.
[2] *Ibid.*, June 28, 1867.

The plan advertised in the circular soon proved abortive. The Topeka company built no stockyards and bought no cattle. The Texas drovers still were without a satisfactory Kansas market.

Meanwhile, a similar marketing idea was taking root elsewhere. In Illinois a young cattle dealer, Joseph Geiting McCoy, who lived near Springfield, had seen the need for a new shipping point for Longhorns. McCoy was from the heart of the feeder country. He was born on a farm on the north side of Spring Creek, in Sangamon County, about ten miles west of Springfield, on December 21, 1837. He grew up on the farm, not far from the big cattle ranches of John T. Alexander and Jacob Strawn in adjoining Morgan County, and spent a year in the academy of Knox College in Galesburg.

McCoy knew the livestock business from the ground up. Soon after his marriage in 1861, he took to Kentucky by rail a carload of mules he had raised. After selling his mules at a good profit, he began feeding cattle and shipping them to market. In this business two older brothers, William and James, already had begun to prosper.[3]

At the close of the Civil War, McCoy expanded his activities to satisfy pent-up civilian demands for meat and for work animals. He bought mules, cattle, sheep, and hogs in large numbers and shipped them to city markets. From several towns in central Illinois he shipped mules to Cairo and New Orleans in 1866 and 1867. In the same period he sent cattle, sheep, and hogs to Chicago and New York. Early in 1867 he joined the firm his brothers had established.

Sometimes in a single week the three brothers shipped as many as a thousand cattle, costing $80 to $140 a head. In 1867 the McCoys shipped to eastern markets eighteen thousand mature cattle, fifteen thousand fat sheep, and twelve thousand hogs. That year their business with a single bank in Springfield amounted to $2,500,000.

Soon after he became a partner in the company of William K. McCoy and Brothers, Joseph G. McCoy developed a strong interest in the possibility of setting up a new market for Texas Longhorns. The location was the crux of the problem. It would have to be a point to which drovers could trail their cattle without being attacked by mobs and one from which they could ship readily to feeders and packers.

[3] McCoy, "Historic and Biographic Sketch," *Kansas Magazine*, Vol. II, No. 6 (December, 1909), 48–49; Florence L. McCoy, information to Hortense B. C. Gibson, October 24, 1938 (MS, Kansas State Historical Society, Topeka, Kansas).

II

At that time Joseph McCoy was twenty-nine years old and had been married five years. He was thoroughly acquainted with every phase of livestock feeding and shipping. In addition, he had a clear perspective of the whole livestock industry and could see the need for better contacts between southwestern ranchmen and midwestern feeders. He had the imagination to foresee the favorable effects of a new market and the initiative to try to establish one. Looking back, years later, he described himself as an impulsive young man with a speculative turn of mind and as not content to live at home on a good-sized and finely improved farm.

McCoy's interest in opening a new outlet for Texas Longhorns had been spurred by his talks with young Charles F. Gross, who returned from the Lone Star State in the fall of 1866. Gross, who had grown up in Springfield and had gone to school with Bob Lincoln, had run off to the war while still in his teens and had become a telegraph operator in the Union forces. In the fall of 1865, General Phil Sheridan had sent him to run the survey for a new military telegraph line from Shreveport, Louisiana, to Brownsville, near the mouth of the Rio Grande.

Gross, who was only twenty, was amazed by what he saw. The survey, he recalled, "took us through the heart of the cattle ranges of Texas; and I saw buffaloes, cattle, and wild horses galore." He noted that vast numbers of cattle and horses were "running wild and waiting for someone to gather them and drive them to the northern market."

Back in Springfield, Gross had many talks with Joe McCoy. The latter, said Gross, "soon drew out of me stories of the wild cattle of Texas. I started to fire that imagination of his, which ran far ahead of me. Before I knew anything of his plans, they were half completed."[4]

In the early spring of 1867, McCoy bought some Longhorns from W. W. Sugg in Christian County, Illinois. Sugg, who had trailed these cattle from Texas in the preceding year, gave a report like that of Gross on the abundance and cheapness of cattle in the

[4] Charles F. Gross, letters to J. B. Edwards, April 13, 1922, March 31, 1925 (MS, Kansas State Historical Society, Topeka, Kansas).

Gulf Southwest. He also informed McCoy of the political and sometimes violent means that had been used to obstruct the trailing of
Texas cattle into Missouri and eastern Kansas.

These conversations, along with confirming evidence from other
sources, deeply impressed McCoy. He determined to build at some
accessible point a depot or market to which the Texas drover could
bring his stock unmolested and be reasonably sure of finding a buyer.
This project, he recalled several years later, became "a waking
thought, a sleeping dream."[5]

In casting about for a site suitable for a shipping yard, McCoy
first considered a point on the bank of the Arkansas River near
Fort Smith. From there, dealers could ship cattle by river boats to
Cairo, and thence by rail to pastures and feed lots in southern and
central Illinois. But before taking any step toward building at Fort
Smith, he made a trip to Kansas City. Arriving by a Missouri Pacific
train from St. Louis, he found the frontier town an "unsightly ag-
gregation of bluffs and almost canyon-like gorges, bisected with
deep cuts and large fills called streets."

McCoy climbed a deep cut named Main Street and made in-
quiries about the livestock business. He was directed to the office
of Marsh and Coffy, a firm that traded goods for cattle in the Indian
Territory and along the Red River in Texas. Marsh told his visitor
of the advantages of central Kansas for shipping stock. He pointed
out that the Union Pacific Railroad's eastern division had pushed
up the Kaw River as far west as Salina. He suspected that freight
charges might be more than the cattle were worth. Nevertheless,
he gave McCoy a note of introduction to the railway freight agent
in nearby Wyandotte, Kansas.

The agent at Wyandotte showed interest in McCoy's project.
To allow the Illinoisan to look over possible sites, he gave him a
round-trip pass to Salina. When the train reached the prairie village
of Abilene, it was delayed about an hour while a bridge was repaired.
McCoy made use of this wait to ask several Abilene men about the
suitability of that point for cattle yards. On the return trip, he
stopped at Junction City—which some of the buffalo hunters called
Junk Town—twenty-four miles east of Abilene. There, at the Hale

[5] McCoy, "Historic and Biographic Sketch," *Kansas Magazine*, Vol. II, No. 6
(December, 1909), 49.

House, he met Colonel John J. Myers, a prominent Texas cattle drover from Lockhart. Myers, who had had trouble a year earlier, encouraged McCoy to go ahead with his plan. He assured him that it would have strong support from cowmen in the Southwest.

To McCoy the neighborhood of Junction City seemed suitable as a shipping point. He considered building cattle yards six miles southwest of that town, at Kansas Falls. Early in June a local newspaper noted: "A gentleman named McCoy proposes erecting all the sheds and buildings for stockyards on the railroad track at Kansas Falls. Messrs Streeter and Strickler gave him five acres for that purpose, and the railroad company tendered him a side track half a mile long. He proposes making a large business of shipping all kinds of stock. His yard will be about five miles from town."[6] But the rosy picture which this news item held out soon vanished. As the price asked for the land he wanted seemed exorbitant, McCoy decided to look elsewhere.

Before doing any more prospecting, McCoy returned to Wyandotte. There the freight agent referred him to the president of the railroad, John T. Perry, in St. Louis. McCoy then set out for St. Louis, where he laid his plan before Perry and members of the executive committee of the railroad. He spoke eloquently of the vast herds of Longhorns in Texas and of advantages that might come from providing an outlet through which these cattle might reach midwestern markets.

Several days later McCoy received his answer. "I do not believe that you can, to any extent, establish or build up a cattle trade on our road," said Perry. "It looks too visionary, too chimerical, too speculative; and it would be altogether too good a thing to happen to us or to our road."

Yet Perry, while skeptical of the plan, was willing for McCoy to go ahead at the latter's risk. "But Mr. McCoy," he added, "if you think you can get cattle freighted over our road, that is just the thing we want. If you are willing to risk your money in a stockyard and other necessary appendages, we will put in a switch. If you succeed, I will pledge you shall have full and fair recompense." Although they made no written contract with him, the Union Pacific officials promised orally to pay McCoy about five dollars a

[6] Junction City *Weekly Union*, June 8, 1867.

carload for all cattle shipped over their line that year from his proposed stockyards to markets toward the east.[7]

With this concession from the Union Pacific, McCoy next looked into the freight rates that would have to be paid to connecting lines. He wanted to know, in particular, what rate he could obtain from the Kansas-Missouri border to St. Louis. As he entered the elegant office of the Missouri Pacific, McCoy was conscious of his own rough garb—his seedy coat, slouch hat, and unpolished shoes. When the stylishly dressed railroad president looked up from the papers on his desk, McCoy described his project and stated his mission. Then the head of the Missouri Pacific, as McCoy recalled, tipped his cigar at a right angle with his nose. He struck "the attitude of indescribable greatness when stooping to notice an infinitesimal object."

This official made his attitude clear without any beating about the bush. His reply, as McCoy remembered it, was, "It occurs to me that you haven't any cattle to ship and never did have any; and I, sir, have no evidence that you ever will have any. I think you are talking about freight rates for speculative purposes. Therefore, you get out of this office, and let me not be troubled with any more of your style."

Stunned but not discouraged, McCoy went to the general freight agent of the Hannibal and St. Joseph Railroad. From this official he obtained a satisfactory rate from the Missouri River to Quincy and thence to Chicago. One result of this incident was to spur the Windy City in leaving St. Louis far behind as a market for Texas cattle.[8]

After a quick visit to Illinois to attend to business there, McCoy hastened back to Kansas. He would have to act promptly to get many Texas cattle that year, as the spring drive already was almost over. On the Union Pacific he went out to Solomon City, west of Abilene. There he found a fine site for stockyards, but local citizens were not interested. Some even opposed having herds of Longhorns brought into their town. In disgust, McCoy went back to Abilene. That was about the middle of June.

[7] Martin, Burns, and Case, *Brief of the Defendant in Error, Kansas Pacific Railway Company* vs. *Joseph G. McCoy*, Supreme Court of Kansas, 10.

[8] McCoy, *Historic Sketches of the Cattle Trade of the West and Southwest*, 42–43.

III

The frontier village of Abilene had been laid out six years earlier. It occupied land which Charles H. Thompson, from Leavenworth, had bought on the east side of Mud Creek. In the summer of 1867, Abilene had only about a dozen log cabins, roofed with dirt, and a few small business houses, also built of logs. The most imposing structure was the Bratton Hotel, which had six rooms. The proprietor, John P. Simpson, had a stable near the creek for the horses of his guests. In a dugout on the east bank of the creek was Thomas McLean's blacksmith shop.

East of the hotel was the saloon of Josiah Jones, whom McCoy described as "a corpulent, jolly, good-souled, congenial old man of the backwoods pattern." In his younger days, Jones had liked to fish and hunt. In Abilene he found pleasure in feeding the prairie dogs that lived in a colony on his lots. His attachment to these little burrowing animals, though, didn't keep him from trapping them and selling them to tourists at five dollars or more a pair.

Beyond the saloon was the Frontier Store, a one-room building eighteen feet wide and thirty feet long. Like the hotel, the store had a roof of handmade shingles, called oak shakes. There William S. Moon sold groceries and dry goods and served as postmaster and recorder of deeds. Moon, who was fifty-two years old, was a native of Ohio and had studied medicine for a time before he settled in Abilene in 1864. For some reason, McCoy took a dislike to this merchant, whom he regarded as an intolerable egotist.

Life in Abilene still smacked of the frontier. To the west of the village, on the far side of Mud Creek, were Tim Hersey's log cabin and two-story stage station. Occasionally some of the pioneer settlers held a dance on the upper floor of the station. Bayard Taylor, who had stopped in Abilene on a stagecoach trip in June, 1866, complained of the meal for which he was charged a dollar. It consisted, he said, "of strong black coffee, strips of pork fat fried to a sandy crispness, and half-baked, soggy, indigestible biscuits."

Train service on the new railroad still was spasmodic west of Junction City. The Abilene passenger station was yet to be built. A post bearing a number marked the stopping place for trains. From a hook on this post was hung the mail pouch, with a board shutter above to keep off the rain.[9]

In choosing Abilene as the site for his market for Texas cattle, McCoy violated—perhaps unwittingly—the Kansas statute of February 26, 1867. The line which this law established, only west of which could Texans trail their cattle lawfully from southwestern Kansas to the Union Pacific Railroad, ran a mile west of Ellsworth and about sixty miles west of Abilene. But as the country around and below Abilene was thinly settled and as no one seemed interested in enforcing the letter of the new law, McCoy was not hampered much at the start on legal grounds.

Once he had made his decision, McCoy acted quickly. He bought the first land for his cattle yard on June 18. This was a tract of 250 acres at the northeastern edge of the village. He made the purchase from Charles H. Thompson and Mary E. Thompson, who had owned the whole site of Abilene.

With not even lumber obtainable near by, McCoy had to bring in from a distance nearly all the materials he needed. He brought hard wood from Lenape, Kansas, and shipped pine lumber from Hannibal, Missouri. Construction on the yards began about the first of July and was completed in two months. By the first of September, McCoy had a shipping yard that would hold a thousand cattle. Other equipment included a pair of ten-ton Fairbanks scales, a barn, and an office. In addition, he was building a three-story frame hotel, called the Drover's Cottage, and behind it a large livery stable. Opposite the hotel he was putting up a bank.

McCoy sent back to Springfield for Charles F. Gross to come and keep his account books. Arriving from Junction City by stagecoach, Gross spent his first night in Tim Hersey's cabin and his second in a tent. After McCoy's small office was completed, Gross bunked in it. He kept with him two double-barreled shotguns—one loaded with buckshot and the other with bird shot. One night when someone tried to open the barred window and failed to answer a call, Gross hastened the visitor's departure with a load of bird shot.[10]

By September 24, the $15,000 hotel was complete and ready for use. Matt Beckers of Junction City had just put on the last touches of paint. The main part of the hotel was thirty by forty-six

9 *Ibid.*, 44–49; Gross, letter to Edwards, April 13, 1922, MS.
10 Dickinson County, Deed Record A, 496 (MS, Recorder of Deeds Office, Abilene, Kansas); Gross, letter to Edwards, April 13, 1922, MS.

feet; and there was a wing, sixteen by thirty feet. The new hostelry, which made a big bump on the prairie, boasted such frontier luxuries as plaster walls and Venetian blinds. It could bed eighty guests and feed three times that number. A billiard room and a bar provided entertainment. McCoy engaged Jonathan B. Warfield as hotel manager.

Facilities at the new stockyards were being readied to give an equally hospitable reception to the Longhorns. The McCoy cattle yards could load a train of forty cars in two hours.[11] McCoy induced the railroad company to build at Abilene a hundred-car switch, instead of a twenty-car one, and to put in transfer and feed yards at Leavenworth.

While this construction was under way, McCoy was busy with other preparations. In the summer he visited the governor of Kansas, Samuel J. Crawford, and outlined his plan. He explained that the cattle trail to Abilene would lie west of the settlements and that the trail herds would not hurt the interests of Kansas farmers or stockmen. The governor was convinced. "I wrote a plain, vigorous letter," he recalled, "commending Mr. McCoy's scheme and the location he had selected. I approved of the undertaking in a semi-official manner."[12] This endorsement led some Kansans to criticize the governor, but he stuck to his course. "I regard the opening of that cattle trail into and across western Kansas," he said, "of as much value to the state as is the Missouri River."

To acquaint Texas cowmen with his plan in time for fall drives, McCoy sent handbills to many towns in the Southwest. In addition, he engaged a stockman friend from Illinois, W. W. Sugg, to ride south on horseback with word of the new market at Abilene. The task of Sugg, who knew the country, was to reach those drovers who had trailed herds northward in the spring and summer without definite destination. Because of the uncertainty of shipping points, many such drovers were marking time in the Indian Territory and in southwestern Kansas. Others, including Colonel John J. Myers of Lockhart, had taken their herds to Junction City, where they awaited buyers from Illinois. On July 20, the Junction City *Weekly*

[11] Junction City *Weekly Union*, August 31, 1867; New York *Tribune*, November 6, 1867. The site of the Drover's Cottage later became that of the creamery in which young Dwight D. Eisenhower worked.
[12] Topeka *State Journal*, March 8, 1913.

Union estimated that five thousand cattle were being held within twenty miles of that town.

Riding southwest from Junction City, Sugg crossed the Arkansas River at the mouth of the Little Arkansas. To the south, mainly in the Indian country, he found drovers with herds for which they were seeking markets that they could reach without running into trouble. At first, some received with suspicion the news of McCoy's project. But many of them, tired of wasting time, were willing to take the risk. They closed in their scattered Longhorns and pointed the lead steers toward Abilene. Soon they would know whether the Illinoisan was a mere dreamer or a practical businessman.

IV

Clouds of dust on the horizon told the people of Abilene that Texas herds were breaking in the new trail. Before the last nail was driven in McCoy's new stockyards, cattle were waiting to be shipped. On August 15, the Topeka *Weekly Leader* reported that seven thousand Texas cattle were being held at Abilene but said that there was no sale for them. Most of the early arrivals had come up over the old trail and had turned west along or near the southern border of Kansas. They found no ready market until the stockyards were completed.

While people in Abilene were becoming a little excited over the boom promised by McCoy's bold venture, some of the hard-bitten farmers living east of the village opposed the opening of the cattle market. Several of them wrote protesting letters to Governor Crawford, asking him to ban, under the new law, the trailing of Texas cattle to Abilene. Referring to McCoy's proposed market, William H. Lamb wrote: "As a mass, the settlers are against it. There are some fine herds of cattle in this part of Kansas, and now to have Texas fever break out among them would be bad. We are all afraid."[13]

When he heard that some of the farmers had banded to stampede the approaching herds, McCoy attended a meeting of the belligerent settlers in the cabin of their captain. His talk on the advantages they

13 William H. Lamb, letter to Governor Samuel J. Crawford, August 31, 1867, Kansas Governor's Correspondence (MS, Kansas State Historical Society, Topeka, Kansas).

would gain from the new market was persuasive. More so were the offers of several Texas drovers who were present at McCoy's invitation. When the Texans began dickering for butter, eggs, potatoes, onions, corn, oats, and hay at high prices, they won over the farmers. If the nesters could rake in cash at this rate, they could afford to take a chance on cattle fever.[14]

McCoy got along better with the incoming cowmen and with the townspeople than with surrounding farmers. "People generally liked McCoy," said one of the early Texas drovers, Mark A. Withers of Lockhart. "He was a tall, large man, a loud talker. You could hear him all over town." Abilene people welcomed McCoy and soon were calling him Joe. J. B. Edwards of Abilene recalled him as "a noble type of man, strong in character, with a large brain, but a visionary in much of his life work. I always liked him and remember him as a noble man, kind hearted, and always faithful to his friends. He built up a vast business when he opened the door and found a way to market the herds of Texas cattle."

In the judgment of his assistant from Illinois, Charles F. Gross, "McCoy was a man of advanced vision. He had what all men need but many lack—imagination. He was progressive and far ahead of most men. Joe did not see cattle only; he saw a future not only for Abilene but for Dickinson County as an agricultural section."[15]

The first herd to arrive in Abilene, McCoy recalled, was brought by Smith, McCord, and Chandler, northern cattlemen. This firm had bought a herd in the Indian Territory from a Texas cowman who had trailed the Longhorns from their home range. The first herd to come directly up the new trail was that of a California adventurer, Colonel O. W. Wheeler, and two associates. They had gone to San Antonio and bought 2,400 head of fine Longhorns. With more than a hundred cow ponies and fifty-four Texas trail hands armed with Colt six-shooters and the new Henry repeating rifles, they had taken the herd safely through the Indian country. Wheeler had intended to turn west in Kansas and walk the cattle to the Pacific Coast but decided to sell in Abilene instead.

[14] McCoy, *Historic Sketches of the Cattle Trade of the West and Southwest*, 63–65.
[15] J. B. Edwards, letter to Stuart Henry, quoted in the latter's *Conquering Our Great American Plains*, 34–35; Gross, letter to Edwards, March 31, 1925, MS; Withers, reminiscences, MS.

The initial cattle shipment left Abilene on September 5. It filled twenty stock cars and was destined for Chicago. That night, with the new hotel not yet completed, McCoy and his friends celebrated in a tent. There was feasting, toasting in wine, and much speech-making. McCoy, who was still on the under side of thirty, was in high spirits. He was confident that he had opened a new era in the cattle business.

V

OPENING THE WAY

Across the Texas ranges, in the fall of 1867, sped word of the cattle market that Joseph G. McCoy had opened at Abilene. It was good news to the cowmen. Most of them had had a lean year. Longhorns trailed north in the spring had been few in comparison with those sent up in 1866. Not many drovers were willing to risk their herds or their men where routes were barred and violence was threatened. Only a few had learned of the Abilene outlet in time to make a fall drive in 1867.

Now they again would have an open trail, one on which their outfits would be free from attack by armed farmers. Of course, there still would be the usual hazards of swollen rivers, scarcity of grass and water, stampedes, and Indian raids. The new trail would be less well marked, and the herds that plodded over it would be more vulnerable to attack by roving bands of savage Comanches and Kiowas. The drover who had his camp supplies stolen or who needed a doctor might have to ride a long way for help. But Texas cowmen were not inclined to shy from a hard task.

For the spring of 1868, the outlook was hopeful. Many drovers were eager to try the new route, which McCoy described in enticing terms. "It is more direct," he pointed out. "It has more prairie, less timber, more small streams and fewer large ones, altogether better grass and fewer flies—no civilized Indian tax or wild Indian disturbances—than any other route yet driven over. It is also much shorter because direct from the Red River to Kansas."[1]

Through most of the Indian country, the new route was about 150 miles west of the older Shawnee Trail. It led almost straight north through the central part of the Territory. If unblazed, it at least had been followed by buffaloes, Indians, and in part by the wagons of a few pioneer traders. In addition, several troop movements had followed it in part and closely paralleled it elsewhere.

In 1855, Major Enoch Steen had taken six companies of his Second Dragoons from Fort Belknap, Texas, north to Fort Riley, Kansas. He headed "about ten degrees east of north" with 213 men, 232 horses, 468 mules, and 76 wagons. Apparently he traveled through the Indian Territory a little west of the later route of the cattle herds and near or along it in southern Kansas. Water was plentiful, he reported, streams easy to cross, and the rolling prairies traversed readily by wagons.

In May, 1861, a larger body of soldiers traveled over a similar route. Guided by Black Beaver and other Delaware Indians, Lieutenant Colonel William H. Emory led the retreat of eleven companies of United States troops northward. He left from a point about thirty-five miles northwest of Fort Cobb, in the Indian Territory. Emory had with him 750 fighting men and 150 women, children, teamsters, and other noncombatants. He took "the most direct course to Leavenworth that the nature of the ground would permit," following closely the path soon to be pounded by millions of Longhorn hoofs.

At least as early as the summer of 1864, Indians began to use regularly a part of this route. Early in the Civil War, a band of Wichitas, who were loyal to the Union, had fled for safety from the Indian Territory into southern Kansas. With them were some Caddoes, Delawares, and Shawnees. At first they stayed at Belmont, where they suffered from lack of food and where many of their horses died. Late in 1863 or early in 1864, destitute and mostly afoot, they moved to a point near that at which the Little Arkansas empties

[1] McCoy, *Historic Sketches of the Cattle Trade of the West and Southwest*, 93.

into the Arkansas River. There they found buffaloes and planted beans, corn, and pumpkins in the fertile soil.

In the summer of 1864, while the Indian women tended the gardens, many of the men went south to look for horses they had left along the Washita River and elsewhere in their northward flight. Some of them brought back not only horses but cattle, buffalo robes, and furs. Finding these forays profitable, they made repeated trips into the Indian Territory and the northern borders of Texas, where they stole horses and cattle. Their cattle, although war contraband, were easily smuggled in and the surplus sold to white Kansans who asked no questions. In the fall of 1864, the Wichitas shifted their camp to the densely timbered land at the mouth of the Little Arkansas.

Living with the band of exiled Wichitas in that period was elderly Jesse Chisholm, a veteran trader and guide. Chisholm had been born in Tennessee in 1805 or 1806. His father was of Scotch ancestry, and his mother was a Cherokee. As a youth, Jesse Chisholm had gone west with the Cherokees and had settled with them in northwestern Arkansas. Later he and his mother and his aunt moved to Fort Gibson. There the aunt was married to Sam Houston, who had been governor of Tennessee.

In 1832, Chisholm and Robert Bean laid out a wagon road over rough country from Fort Smith to Fort Towson. Chisholm then became a trader at the mouth of the Little River, where he married a half-blood Creek girl. Later he had a trading post at Council Grove, on the north fork of the Canadian River.

As he knew the country and could speak many Indian languages, Chisholm was in frequent demand as an interpreter and a guide. In 1836 he guided a party of white men up the Arkansas River to the mouth of the Little Arkansas, in search of a legendary gold mine. At various times he rescued white captives from the Indians and restored them to their families. People knew him as one who could be trusted; the Indians called him "a man with a straight tongue."

From new headquarters at the mouth of the Little Arkansas, Jesse Chisholm made trading excursions in various directions. Probably as early as the fall of 1864, he loaded his wagons with trading goods and, with several helpers, followed the Indian trail southward. He went as far as Council Grove, on the North Canadian River, the site of one of his earlier trading posts. In the early spring of 1865, as the last shots of the Civil War were being fired, he returned north, bringing cattle, buffalo robes, and furs.

In that spring, Chisholm had charge of several wagons which John Stevens of Leavenworth had loaded with goods and sent southwestward for trading. In the following summer, he gathered three thousand cattle from the Kansas prairies and had them trailed to the Sac and Fox agency. Some of them were taken on to New Mexico to fill government contracts. Part of the cattle traveled over what later became a section of the Chisholm Trail. Remaining at the mouth of the Little Arkansas, Chisholm built a trading post between the two rivers and a cabin for his family in a hackberry grove below the forks of a creek.[2]

Thereafter, along with various Indians and whites, Chisholm followed this route fairly regularly for trading and other purposes. This lasted until, in 1867 and 1868, the refugee Wichitas returned south to their old homes. In January, 1866, Chisholm loaded several wagons with goods he had bought from James R. Mead in the preceding month. Then he headed southward, accompanied by Henry Donnell, who had several wagons, drawn by four-mule teams, and who stopped at the Red Fork to trade with the Osages.

Chisholm traveled on to his old trading post on the North Canadian. In April he returned to Kansas, bringing buffalo robes, furs, and 250 head of cattle. Soon other traders and travelers began using what they sometimes called Chisholm's trail. Among them were James R. Mead, William Mathewson, and William Greiffenstein. Mead had built, in the winter of 1865, a trading post in the bend of the Ninnescah River, near the trail. A year later he established another trading station at what then was called Round Pond Creek, on the trail, and left it in charge of Jack Lawton. "Mr. Chisholm's teams and my own," recalled Mead, "were the first which ever passed over that route and marked out what afterward became known as the Chisholm Trail."[3]

William Mathewson, called Buffalo Bill, started down the trail early in July, 1867. He took with him two boys he had rescued from

[2] James R. Mead, "The Chisholm Trail," Wichita *Eagle*, March 1, 1890; T. U. Taylor, *Jesse Chisholm*.
[3] Mead, "Reminiscences of Frontier Life" (MS, Kansas State Historical Society, Topeka, Kansas), 75.

the Comanches. At Fort Arbuckle he turned the youths over to the commandant for return to their parents in Texas. At the fort he met a Texas drover who was on his way north with a herd of Longhorns. Matthewson directed the cowman over the new trail and guided him as far as the North Canadian, where he could begin following the tracks of the traders' wagons.

Late in August of the same summer, Mathewson, returning from the treaty-signing at Medicine Lodge, crossed the Little Arkansas with a train of fourteen loaded wagons. He was taking equipment for a new agency to be established at Eureka Valley, on the Washita River. With him were his wife, Lizzie, and her friend Miss Fannie Cox of St. Joseph. They were the first white women to travel over the trail. At Red Fork the Mathewson party left the Chisholm route near Kingfisher Creek and made a new trail to the Washita.

William Greiffenstein, known as Dutch Bill, crossed the Arkansas River with a wagon train on December 5, 1867, and headed down the trail. Soon James R. Mead followed, with wagons loaded with goods for Chisholm, who was trading with the Indians on the North Fork of the Canadian, near the great salt spring. Mead returned north twice for trading goods during the winter and early spring.

On the last trip into the Indian Territory, Mead recalled, "we arrived March 7 at Chisholm's, where we had left less than three weeks before a great encampment, and found it deserted. Not a living thing was to be seen but a flock of wild geese occupying the deserted camp. The trails indicated hasty departure in all directions, from some sudden and exciting cause."

Mead and his men turned down the river a few miles to a hill that the Indians called Little Mountain. Just in front of this hill, where the river bent to the south, he noticed a newly built enclosure made of logs. Inside was a fresh grave. At the head stood a board on which were cut the words: "Jesse Chisholm, Died March 4, 1868." The next day, Mead drove to Chisholm's ranch, where he found Greiffenstein and others. These friends of Chisholm said he had died of cholera morbus caused by eating bear's grease that had been poisoned by being melted in a brass kettle.

With the aid of a small keg of Kentucky's best, taken from the center of a barrel of sugar, the men held what Mead called a fitting

wake, ending with a salute from their guns.[4] Later a stone marker
was placed at the grave. Its inscription read:

JESSE CHISHOLM
BORN 1805
DIED MARCH 4, 1868
*No one left his home
cold or hungry*

Thus Jesse Chisholm passed from the scene without an inkling
of the place his name would achieve in song and legend. Not many
Texas herds had followed his wagon tracks in the fall of 1867. But
for the herds of 1868 and the next dozen years, his wagon route was
part of a much longer trail that served as the best route for taking
Texas cattle to Kansas markets. Within a few years after his death,
drovers were giving the name of Chisholm to the whole trail.

In its early years, the trail had a variety of names. Many cowmen
called it merely the trail or the cattle trail. Some Texans referred to
it as the Kansas Trail or the Abilene Trail or McCoy's Trail. In Kansas it often was called the Great Cattle Trail, the Texas Cattle Trail,
the Great Texas Cattle Trail, or the Wichita Trail. Years later, after
a new trail was opened farther west, some called the older route
the Eastern Trail. Just when it became common to call it the Chisholm Trail is uncertain. Undoubtedly the Chisholm name was used
orally for some time before it crept into print.

The first known newspaper reference to the Chisholm Trail by
that name is in a letter written at Eldorado, Kansas, on May 18,
1870. It said that Osage Indians, out on their spring hunt, had
camped on the Chisholm Trail.[5] James R. Mead also used the term
in writing from Wichita on October 7 of that year. A stage line,
he reported, was proposed to operate between Wichita and Texas,
over the Chisholm Trail.[6] Early in 1871, a Kansas writer referred
to the Chisholm Trail as the favorite route of freighters and drovers.[7]

[4] Mead, "The Chisholm Trail," Wichita *Eagle*, March 1, 1890; *Oklahoman*, July
13, 1930. Chisholm was buried in what later became southeastern Blaine County,
Oklahoma, about thirty miles northwest of El Reno.

[5] *Kansas Daily Commonwealth*, May 27, 1870.

[6] *Ibid.*, October 11, 1870.

[7] *Ibid.*, January 2, 1871.

75

Within another year the route frequently was called the Chisholm Trail, especially in Kansas. By that time, many had begun to apply the name to the whole route, including its many feeder branches and several terminals. In the spring of 1874, a Texas newspaper referred to cattle going "up the famous Chisholm Trail."[8] The Chisholm name, though, was not universally used. Government maps published through the seventies show the route as the Abilene Cattle Trail, though it seldom led to Abilene after 1871. A map issued by the Kansas Pacific Railway in 1871 through 1875 called it the Great Texas Cattle Trail. In Texas the Chisholm name caught on more slowly than in Kansas, but in time it became firmly fixed.

At its Texas beginnings, the new cattle trail to Kansas followed paths already beaten by Longhorn herds headed up the Shawnee Trail. It was like a gigantic upside-down tree with many branches. The trunk extended from Brownsville, near the southern tip of the state, north to the Red River. Feeder trails came in from both sides. The trail, especially in Texas, followed no sharply defined route. As T. C. Richardson has pointed out, "We shall get rid of a good deal of geographical difficulty at once by recalling that trails originated wherever a herd was shaped up and ended wherever a market was found. A thousand minor trails fed the main routes, and many an old-timer who as a boy saw a herd of stately Longhorns, piloted by bandanaed, booted, and spurred men, lived with the firm conviction that the Dodge or Chisholm cattle trail passed right over yonder."[9]

The main stem of the Chisholm Trail began at the Rio Grande. Drovers bought—or stole—some of the southernmost herds in Mexico and swam them across the border river. Northward they trailed through brush country and past the spreading Kenedy and King ranches. One beaten path, which some called the old Beef Trail, led almost directly north, past Beeville, Gonzales, and Lockhart to Austin. An alternate route bent a little westward to San Antonio, which was a gathering point for herds trailed in from ranges in the west and southwest. San Antonio still had a frontier aspect that attracted cowmen. While the herds grazed at the edge of town, cooks could

[8] Denison Daily News, April 28, 1874.
[9] T. C. Richardson, "Cattle Trails of Texas," Texas Geographic Magazine, Vol. I, No. 2 (November, 1937), 17.

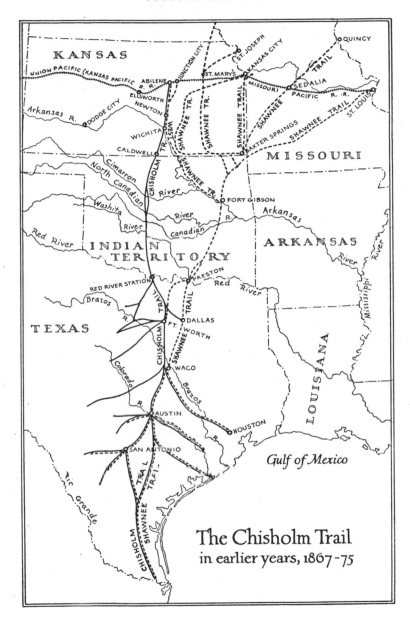

The Chisholm Trail
in earlier years, 1867-75

replenish their supplies, and drovers could find diversion in the many saloons and gambling halls.

At Austin the cowmen found easy crossings of the Colorado River. Some crossed just above the town; but most of them used a better ford a little below, near Montopolis. From Austin the strung-out herds grazed slowly northward. To the east were rolling pastures and cotton fields. To the west, above the Balcones Escarpment, was the hilly Edwards Plateau, green with live oak, mesquite, cedar, and other low growths. Past Round Rock, Georgetown, Belton, and Comanche Springs tramped the cattle. The San Gabriel River and the Lampasas they usually crossed easily.

Often the muddy, reddish Brazos River made a harder crossing. In the earlier years, many herds were swum over at Waco, after being bedded down at the edge of town on the night before crossing. Later it became customary to trail on upstream to Fort Graham or Kimball. By the time the cattle from southern Texas reached Fort Worth, many other herds had turned into the trail from the east and the west.

The frontier town of Fort Worth, still without a railroad, was becoming trail-conscious and was making use of its opportunity to outfit drovers for the long drive ahead. For the earlier Shawnee Trail, Dallas, 33½ miles to the east, was more conveniently situated as an outfitting point. But after the Chisholm Trail came into use, Fort Worth had an advantage. There the drover could buy spare saddles, six-shooters, rope, staple groceries, and other supplies.

As the trail driving mounted, Fort Worth became, too, a large market for cattle. Buyers from the north came there and persuaded some of the already weary drovers to sell out instead of going on into the dangerous Indian country. These buyers, often throwing several herds into one, trailed the Longhorns on to Kansas.

At Fort Worth the trail crossed the West Fork of the Trinity River. It then veered a bit to the northwest and led north along the Wise-Denton county line. It took the herds over billowing and generally open prairies that offered good grazing. At frequent intervals were creeks that usually were easy to ford and that brought clear water for the Longhorns. Without letting their charges linger too long on Elizabeth Creek or Oliver Creek, the drovers pointed them on north, passing east of the village of Decatur. Over more lush prairies and across Denton Creek and Clear Creek they went, holding their weight well in easy marches. Farther on, they entered the broken country in the valley of the Red River, on the northern border of Texas.[10]

Some of the earlier drovers crossed their herds at Sivell's Bend, in Cooke County. Later most of them went farther upstream to Red River Station. The latter crossing was just below the mouth of Fleetwood Branch. It took its name from an outpost that Texas Rangers had set up there during the Civil War. Soon after it came into common use by the cowmen, the place acquired an outfitting store and a saloon. The trail across Montague County to this crossing took the herds through what Tom C. Oatts of Round Rock called the most beautiful country he had seen.

Often the crossing of the Red River was made perilous by floods or quicksands that caused delays and sometimes loss of stock. Once across the river, the herds had easy traveling for a time. The trail led northwest a few miles, then north over high, rolling prairies. It skirted a patch of blackjack oak woods known as Blue Grove. The country was mostly open, except along the streams, which were heavily wooded along their banks, mainly with willows, cottonwoods, and oaks.

With an early crossing and good luck, the drover might make his first night's stop in the Indian Territory on one of the branches of Beaver Creek, about fifteen miles north of the border. This stream had a rapid flow and, in some places, high banks; but it was small enough to be forded easily. Another drive of equal length took the herds to Stinking Creek. There the camp ground was likewise good, with plenty of water, grass, and firewood.

A high point near this site soon became known as Monument Hill or Monument Rocks. This was a mesa whose almost flat top was strewn with slabs and boulders of reddish sandstone. As markers for the trail, some of the early drovers made two piles of these boulders, about three hundred feet apart. The piles were about ten feet across and twelve feet high. Many Texas cowboys used their knives or spurs to carve initials or brands on the soft rocks. Men on the trail could see the markers for ten to fifteen miles in either direction.

[10] C. V. Terrell, *The Terrells*, 33–34.

The trail continued over open prairies, skirting timber on each side. Occasionally the herds had to pass through an oak grove. After another fifteen miles, the Longhorns bedded down on the East Fork of Beaver Creek. Another long drive over high, rolling prairies brought them to the head of Rush Creek, sixty miles from the Red River. On northward the herds wound through burned jack oaks to the Little Washita, thirteen miles beyond. The drover would be lucky if, by the time he reached this point, he hadn't been met by Indians demanding a few steers as tribute for passage.

Four miles farther on was the Washita River, with willows lining its red clay banks. The ford there was called Rock Crossing, as it had a rock bottom on the north side. The outfits forded this river easily except in an occasional flood. Then the horses and cattle had to swim across, while the men ferried the camp equipment on an improvised raft. The fertile Washita Valley suited the herds. "Fine grass for cattle and horses," noted Tom Oatts, who crossed it in 1871.

Sixteen miles beyond the Washita was a good camp site on Walnut Creek, which the herds followed upstream. From there the trail crossed a nearly level prairie for ten miles to the South Canadian. Oaks, cottonwoods, and thickets of wild plum lined the banks of this stream. The south bank had good camping grounds, where herds sometimes had to wait when the water was high.

Thirteen miles farther on was the North Canadian, which most of the time could be forded easily. It had good camp sites on its north side, with plenty of grass and firewood. Beyond, the trail led over upland prairies and across Deer Creek, Kingfisher Creek, and the Cimarron River, which some called the Red Fork of the Arkansas. Those drovers who had time for hunting could vary their diet with prairie chicken, venison, and antelope tongue.

Beyond Turkey Creek, which was six miles farther north, firewood began to be scarce. Drovers had either to haul wood in their wagons or to depend on cow chips as fuel for cooking. From Turkey Creek the route led across flat country and through a prairie-dog town that was five miles long. The next stop, at Hackberry Creek, offered water and grass but no wood. There, as elsewhere on the trail, the cowmen had to keep a sharp lookout for hostile Indians, despite the reassurance of McCoy. Bronze warriors had raided near-by Buffalo Springs in July, 1867; and no one knew when a roving band of Comanches might steal horses or stampede a herd and get away with some of the best beeves.

At Shawnee or Skeleton Creek, nine miles farther on, outfits could stock up on wood for the next stop. This was on the treeless prairie along Nine Mile Creek. From that stream the route was over rolling range and through another prairie-dog town. There were good camp sites east of the trail, at the edge of timber and three miles south of the Salt Fork of the Arkansas River. Along with the South Canadian and the Cimarron, this stream was one of those most likely to give trouble in crossing. Even after a flood had subsided, there was danger of quicksand into which the cattle might disappear.

Three miles beyond the Salt Fork crossing was Pond Creek, named from a large pond on its south side, just east of the trail. Here the cattle route crossed also an old Indian warpath, Black Dog Trail, named for a gigantic Osage chief of earlier days. Near by were Indian campgrounds and burial sites.

From Pond Creek the trail veered a bit to the northeast, passing through more colonies of prairie dogs. Sometimes buffaloes were found in this section, and occasionally Indian raiders gave the drovers a fight. The trail crossed Polecat Creek and entered Kansas just below Bluff Creek and Fall Creek. If not held back by floods, stampedes, or other misfortunes, the trail herds could cross the Indian Territory in a month.[11]

In Kansas the outfits generally had easy going. The trail led north across open prairies that in the fall presented splotches of sunflowers and goldenrods and the big green *bois d'arc* balls, or Osage oranges. Sometimes herds of shaggy buffaloes shared the ranges with the Longhorns. Often small bands of Osage warriors approached the drovers, but most of them only asked for tobacco or demanded a steer or two.

Usually there was little trouble at the Kansas stream crossings— the Chikaskia River, Slate Creek, the Ninnescah River, Cow Skin Creek, and the Arkansas River. Before reaching the Arkansas, where

11 *Guide Map of the Great Texas Cattle Trail* (pamphlet); H. S. Tennant, "The Two Cattle Trails," *Chronicles of Oklahoma*, Vol. XIV, No. 1, Sec. 1 (March, 1936), 84–122.

the Wichitas had camped, the cowmen could see along Skeleton Creek the bleaching bones of Indians who had died in recent months from an epidemic of cholera.

As a rule, drovers found the hazards of the Chisholm Trail less formidable than those of the earlier Shawnee Trail. Streams, encountered a little nearer their sources, usually were easier to cross. Too, there were fewer skirmishes with troublesome tax-demanding Indians. More important, although not all troubles with Kansas farmers were ended, the herds were not met by mobs whose members threatened to kill the cattle and turn back the drovers. Colonel O. W. Wheeler and his two partners, whom McCoy credited with bringing the first herd up the Chisholm Trail from Texas, soon had many cowmen following the route their Longhorns had tramped.

Among the Texas drovers who took herds up the new trail to Abilene in 1867 was Jesse L. Driskill. Of him the Fort Worth *Democrat* said that "no shrewder cattleman ever put brand to a yearling."[12] Driskill, who during the Civil War had provided beef for some of the Confederate forces, had trailed a herd to New Orleans soon after the shooting ended.

Another pioneer on the new trail was H. M. Childress, who had grown up in the Texas cow country and at fifteen had started his own brand. Pleased with his success in trailing to Iowa in 1866, he pointed a herd to Abilene in the following year. When he did not find a ready buyer, he went east to Junction City, as Colonel John J. Myers had done, and sold his herd there. Junction City had a packing plant that slaughtered two hundred Texas beeves a day.

Most of the Texas drovers, though, found buyers in Abilene. Among the first Illinois feeders to arrive at the new market was Jay S. Smith of Springfield. He not only acquired Longhorns for his Illinois pastures and feed pens but bought a scrubby lot that he wintered on the Kansas prairies, with good results. Among the other Illinois buyers there that season was English-born Tom Ponting, of Christian County, who, with a partner, had taken the first Texas Longhorns to New York in 1854.

In Texas, drovers still could buy Longhorn cattle cheaply, the price varying with their weight, age, and condition, and the place and season of purchase. Ordinary cattle could be had at three to

[12] Fort Worth *Democrat*, March 18, 1876.

six dollars, while choice beeves sold as high as twelve dollars. In St.
Louis and Chicago markets, the better beeves brought twenty to
forty dollars.

Despite the shortness of the trailing season that remained after
the opening of McCoy's market, between thirty and forty-five thousand Texas and Indian cattle were walked into Kansas in 1867, most
of them to Abilene. McCoy estimated that thirty-five thousand head
reached Abilene that year. Between eighteen and twenty thousand
were shipped east by rail. Others were wintered on the Kansas
prairies or were trailed on to ranges farther north or west.

The cattle shipped from Abilene in the fall of 1867 filled nearly
a thousand cars, thus bringing McCoy a large bonus from the railway company. Seventeen cars went to St. Louis over the Missouri
Pacific. Many of the others were routed over the Hannibal and St.
Joseph to Chicago, where the cattle were slaughtered and the meat
packed.[13] The large shipments from Abilene, together with other
factors, brought a depression in the price of Texas beef during
the fall.

The lateness of the season was only one of several circumstances
that kept the 1867 drive from being as large as it might have been.
Excessive rains caused floods in some of the streams in the Indian
Territory and Kansas and made the grass coarse. In some places,
Indian raiders gave serious trouble. Too, cholera took a toll among
trail drivers as well as among Indians. Yet enough Longhorns went
through to the new Abilene market to give that town and the Chisholm Trail wide and effective publicity.

McCoy was favorably impressed with the Texas cowmen who
arrived in Abilene in the early fall of 1867. He described them as
"possessed of strong natural sense, well skilled in judging human
nature, close observers of all events passing before them, thoroughly
drilled in the customs of frontier life." He found them clannish and
suspicious of northerners but good riders, free spenders, full of life
and fun, and "always ready to help a comrade out of a scrape."[14]

Of the Texas drovers and their trail hands, a newspaper correspondent wrote from Abilene on September 24, 1867: "Every man
of them unquestionably was in the Rebel Army. Some of them have

13 McCoy, *Historic Sketches of the Cattle Trade of the West and Southwest*, 55.
14 *Ibid.*, 55.

not yet worn out all their distinctive gray clothing." He reported them as "keen-looking men, full of reserve force, shaggy with hair, undoubtedly terrible in a fight, yet peaceably great at cattle driving and not demonstrative in their style of wearing six-shooters."[15]

Despite the pacifying efforts which McCoy had made, sporadic opposition to the Abilene market continued to crop up during the fall. One farmer, Newton Blair, wrote to the governor that he had tried ineffectually to find in Abilene a justice of the peace or other law officer who would act on his complaints. He charged that "all the officers from whom those cattlemen thought they had anything to fear are bought up."[16]

McCoy asserted that much of this trouble was stirred up by rivals from Ellsworth, sixty miles west, who had expected the new cattle law to bring the Longhorn business to their town. Some of the Ellsworth men, he said, had traveled a hundred miles in a buggy and had spent a week trying to induce farmers near Abilene to mob the Texas drovers.[17] Their efforts were wasted. The Abilene market filled the need of the Texas cowmen. On many a Lone Star range, cattle raisers began making plans to take herds up the Chisholm Trail in the spring of 1868.

[15] New York *Tribune*, November 1, 1867.
[16] Newton Blair, letter to Governor Samuel J. Crawford, October 7, 1867, Kansas Governors' Correspondence, MS.
[17] McCoy, *Historic Sketches of the Cattle Trade of the West and Southwest*, 57–58.

Brack photograph from the N. H. Rose Collection

A Texas cowboy in the 1880's

Frontier Wichita

Gomorrah of the plains, Dodge City in 1878

Ellsworth, Kansas, 1873, from *Shanghai Pierce, A Fair Likeness,*
by Chris Emmett

Courtesy Southern Pacific Lines

An early Houston and Texas Central train, from *Rawhide Texas*,
by Wayne Gard

William Bradford Grimes, from *Shanghai Pierce, A Fair Likeness*, by Chris Emmett

Charlie Siringo, from *Shanghai Pierce, A Fair Likeness*, by Chris Emmett

VI

BEEF ON THE HOOF

As the Kansas snows melted in the spring of 1868, the growing town of Abilene took on an air of hopeful expectancy. The response of Texas drovers to the new cattle market and the Chisholm Trail was still uncertain. The small fall drive of 1867 had been encouraging but hardly decisive. Some cowmen might stick to the old Shawnee Trail in spite of its hazards. Others might blaze a new route leading to some town that would outdo Abilene as a cattle market.

Such fears did not disturb the irrepressible Joseph G. McCoy. He awaited the new trailing season with full confidence in his project. He had gambled his fortune on the success of the Abilene cattle market. After building the loading yards, hotel, and other facilities there, he had spent five thousand dollars in the late winter and early spring to let Texas drovers and northern buyers know the advantages of trading in Abilene.

McCoy also prepared a circular letter describing the new market he had established and the direct trail over which herds from the south could reach it. This he sent to the leading Texas cattle raisers and to many newspapers. Some of the papers not only published the letter but gave favorable editorial notice to the Abilene project. As an additional measure, McCoy sent two men down the trail to talk with Texas drovers. The emissaries were Colonel Samuel N. Hitt and McCoy's assistant, Charles F. Gross—both recently from Springfield, Illinois. They rode horseback into the core of the range country and told in persuasive words the advantages of the new Chisholm Trail.[1]

McCoy had an eye out for buyers, as well as for sellers. To bring feeders and packers to Abilene, he placed advertisements in several newspapers of wide circulation. In a St. Louis advertisement, he wrote: "Cattle—the best grazing cattle in the United States can be had in any number, on and after the 15th of May, 1868, at Abilene, Kansas, weighing from 1,000 to 1,200 pounds, live weight. They reach Abilene from the Southwest and will take on from 50 to 150 pounds more than native cattle, and cost less than half as much. Until the 1st of May we may be conferred with personally at Springfield, Illinois, and thereafter at Abilene, Kansas. W. K. McCoy and Brothers."[2]

With these and other preparations, McCoy had a busy spring. As he needed a new manager for his Abilene hotel, the Drover's Cottage, he looked for one in St. Louis. On the recommendation of a friend, he went to see James W. Gore, steward of the St. Nicholas. After a brief talk, he engaged Gore, who, with his wife and two young daughters, soon departed for Abilene. Mr. and Mrs. Gore, both born in New York State, quickly adjusted themselves to life in the frontier town and became two of its most valued citizens.

McCoy also made trailing easier by sending a surveying party to straighten and shorten the upper end of the route, from the Arkansas River north to Abilene. In charge of this party was Timothy F. Hersey, a pioneer who had established a farm on the west bank of Mud Creek in 1857. Hersey, a native of Maine, had been county clerk and had served in the Kansas Legislature. After surveying the trail, he had workmen throw up mounds of dirt and piles of sod as markers for the drovers. At the mouth of the Little Arkansas, where Jesse Chisholm had built his last trading post, Hersey and his

---

[1] Abilene *Weekly Reflector*, April 30, 1925; Henry, *Conquering Our Great American Plains*, 34, 44.
[2] *Missouri Republican*, March 27, 1868.

party met the season's first northbound herd of Texas Longhorns and guided the cowmen on to Abilene.[3]

Other herds were on the way. It looked as if the Texas response to McCoy's bid would be enough to keep him busy. This was a good spring for gathering trail herds in Texas. On the coastal plains, reported the Liberty *Gazette* on April 3, the range had been fine all winter, and the cattle were in excellent condition.[4]

While most drovers pointed their herds up the new trail, some still were hesitant. Colonel Dudley H. Snyder took his cattle to New Mexico instead of to Kansas. In the spring, with the help of Colonel W. C. Dalrymple, he gathered a herd of fourteen hundred in Burnet, Llano, and Mason counties and trailed them to Fort Union. There beef steers that had cost seven dollars in Texas brought thirty-five dollars. Other drovers, including Major Seth Mabry, walked their herds east to New Orleans.

There also was a large movement of cattle from the coastal ranges of Texas to New Orleans and other ports by steamer. From Indianola, then the principal Texas embarkation point for cattle, stockmen loaded 38,568 head for New Orleans and Havana in 1868. Smaller shipments went from Rockport, St. Mary's, and Galveston. Several ships also carried Longhorns from Palacios to Mobile. Beeves delivered in Indianola brought twelve to eighteen dollars a head, the price varying with the season.[5]

Some of the cattle shipped from Texas Gulf ports were taken up the Mississippi River to southern Illinois. Others were trailed to the Mississippi, usually at the mouth of the Red River, and loaded on boats. After being carried up the Mississippi to Cairo, they were transferred to freight cars and moved by rail to Tolono.

Despite heavy losses from heat, confinement, lack of water, and poor feeding, between fifteen and eighteen thousand head were unloaded at Tolono in 1868. Most of them were sold to midwest feeders at twenty to forty dollars a head. "They are the ugliest brutes we ever saw of the bovine species," observed the Cairo *Democrat*. "With horns so long that they can scarcely pass the car door, they are bully chaps for glue. But a few months on pasture will remove

[3] McCoy, *Historic Sketches of the Cattle Trade of the West and Southwest*, 121–22.
[4] Galveston *News*, April 8, 1868.
[5] *Texas Almanac* for 1870, 124–26.

from sight many of their acute angles and render them presentable."[6]

Of those Texans who trailed to Abilene or near-by Kansas points, not all used the new route all the way. Some followed the older Shawnee Trail to Fort Gibson. There they crossed and turned up the Arkansas River, following what some called the West Shawnee Trail. Pointing northwest, they hit the Chisholm Trail at the mouth of the Little Arkansas.

At Warren, fifteen miles below Preston, many large herds crossed the Red River in 1868. George T. McGehee, who left Belton with a herd that spring, went past Dallas and crossed the Red River at Colbert's ferry, a little below the old Rock Bluff crossing at Preston. In Abilene he sold his steers to McCoy, who shipped them to Illinois for feeding.

Another who followed the old route to Fort Gibson was Mark A. Withers. On April 1, he left his ranch near Lockhart with six hundred husky steers, some of which he had bought on credit at ten dollars a head. With eight hands and a cook, he crossed the Brazos River at Waco and the Trinity at Fort Worth.

As they neared the Trinity, the pointers of the Withers herd could see the abandoned fort perched on a bluff and enclosed with a picket fence. Its largest building, which had been the commissary, was made of logs, as were the soldiers' quarters. Besides these buildings, which civilians had taken over, the frontier village had little besides a supply store and a saloon. Yet many emigrant families had encamped near the settlement, in wagons and tents, for protection from the Indians.

After leaving Fort Worth, the Withers outfit bent its course northeastward to the old trail to Fort Gibson. Farther north, near the Kansas line, a band of Osage Indians threatened trouble, but Withers satisfied the braves with a gift of tobacco. The next day, though, he saw thirty warriors riding in on the camp at top speed. Fingering his six-shooter as the Negro cook crawled under the wagon sheet, the Texan thought his hour had come.

After an exchange of "How!" greetings, the chief said, "White brother have heap much cattle. Give poor John fat beef."

"Sure," replied Withers, relieved that the Indian hadn't asked for half the herd. "Ride in and take your pick."

[6] *Illinois State Journal*, May 23, 1868.

Following the West Shawnee route to Wichita and the Chisholm Trail north from there, he reached Abilene July 1. As he found the cattle market weak, he camped north of the town in the hope that prices would be higher in the fall.

Also on the Shawnee Trail, at least as far as Boggy Creek, was Dave Puckett, who trailed a thousand Longhorn steers from Helena, in Karnes County, to Abilene. He took along Steve Rogers as trail boss. Cowhands in his outfit included two brothers, E. P. and Jim Byler. Each cowboy had four horses and stood guard part of every night. The cook, in a chuck wagon drawn by a yoke of oxen, jolted along behind the herd. The Texas part of this drive led through Gonzales, Lockhart, Austin, Fort Worth, and Gainesville.

Wages were low, recalled E. P. Byler. The men drew thirty dollars a month and expenses, with a month's pay for the return trip. That was all an ordinary cowpoke could get, though some veterans drew forty dollars a month. The Puckett outfit, strung out for half a mile on the trail, tried to make fifteen miles a day.

Other drovers took the new trail all the way to Abilene. One of the early ones that spring was William G. Butler, who left Karnes County in March with a large herd and fourteen trail hands. George N. Steen started with a herd from San Marcos, with six drivers and not enough money. At Gainesville he bought groceries on credit from George Howell. In crossing the Indian Territory, he joined forces with Captain Bill George, of Seguin. Except for a stampede caused by Indians who wanted to steal their horses, they went through without trouble.

From Hays County, Mitchell and Dixon sent a herd north. One of the drivers, J. L. McCaleb, who rode up in front, recalled holding the herd along a rail fence at Red River Station while the herd just ahead completed its crossing. From Caldwell County, sturdy, sharp-eyed R. G. (Dick) Head, who had just turned twenty-one, took a herd to Abilene for Colonel John J. Myers. From their ranch in the Brazos hills of Palo Pinto County, the Rev. George W. Slaughter and one of his sons, Christopher Columbus (Lum) Slaughter, trailed eight hundred head to Kansas, where they sold them for $32,000.

Colonel James F. Ellison, of Caldwell County, walked a small Texas herd to the new McCoy market that year. He left from the

McGhee crossing of the San Marcos River, about seven miles from the town of San Marcos. Among his trail hands was his son and namesake. Two yoke of oxen drew the chuck wagon. As it was the last chance to lay in supplies, the outfit stocked up at Fort Worth with enough to last to Abilene.[7]

James Monroe (Doc) Day, who, with his brother William, had taken a herd north in the difficult year of 1860, trailed one of several thousand head to Abilene in 1868. Another on the Chisholm Trail that year was Captain Eugene B. Millett, of Seguin. He was one of the drovers who, two years earlier, had turned east along the Missouri-Arkansas line. Millett trailed 950 Longhorn steers to Abilene in 1868.[8]

Indians made trouble for Captain James T. Halsell, a pioneer ranchman of Wise County, who started north with a herd in March. Before he reached the Red River, a band of Comanches charged into his camp, letting go a volley of arrows. Although the Texans, taking cover in the brush, fired on the redskins, the raiders drove off all the horses that were loose. But Halsell obtained more mounts and continued his drive.[9]

Wild game abounded all along the Chisholm Trail. W. F. Cude, who went up from Bastrop County with a Forehand and Cockrell herd of six hundred steers, noticed many antelope and a buffalo herd. The men killed a buffalo calf, but Cude didn't find the meat as tasty as beef.

Observing the growth and business boom that Abilene enjoyed as a result of the new cattle market, people in near-by towns began to challenge this supremacy. Junction City to the east and three towns on the railroad to the west made plans to build shipping yards. Each of these towns sent one or more representatives down the trail to the Arkansas River in an effort to persuade approaching drovers to patronize it instead of Abilene.

Junction City, which had been cool to McCoy a year earlier, was especially active in trying to take cattle business away from Abilene. Its spokesmen had few scruples in belittling Abilene and

[7] Hunter, *The Trail Drivers of Texas*, 96–98, 488–89, 538–39, 779–81; *Semi-Weekly Farm News*, February 28, March 6, 1936.
[8] McCoy, *Historic Sketches of the Cattle Trade of the West and Southwest*, 70–73.
[9] H. H. Halsell, *Cowboys and Cattleland*, 62–63.

in boosting their own town. One, who signed himself G. A. W., wrote from Junction City on March 20 to the Dallas *Herald*:

The inducements held out for driving cattle to this market exceed those of any I can hear of. There will be two packing houses here this summer, and shipping stocks sufficient should persons find it advantageous to ship to St. Louis or Chicago, with which markets they are within speedy communication. Water and range unsurpassed by any in the country.

I would advise persons to avoid driving to Abilene, as the people are opposed to it in a measure. Those of this section are anxious for them, as they can see the advantages derived from it. Abilene is a small place west on the railroad. It is much farther and more costly to ship cattle to the eastern markets, should such a thing be necessary.

The writer went on to advise drovers to use the older Shawnee Trail, by way of Boggy Depot, rather than the new Chisholm Trail, which led direct to Abilene.[10]

Junction City boosters were tenacious. In July they met to hear a none too rosy report from a man they had hired to wean Texas cowmen from the Abilene market. "A cattle meeting was held at Brown's Hall last Monday forenoon," reported a local newspaper. "Mr. Booth, who was sent to the Little Arkansas to influence drovers this way, made a report. The meeting made all sorts of guarantees."[11]

To counter this rivalry, McCoy sent down the trail W. W. Sugg, the Illinois drover who had represented him earlier in Texas. Sugg, who was known and liked by many of the drovers, easily put his rivals to rout. In its ample shipping yards and cash buyers, Abilene had advantages that neighboring towns were unable to match.

By the time this near-by competition had been overcome, that of more distant places had to be faced. After arriving in Abilene—or even before—many Texas drovers were tempted to trail their herds on to Colorado, Wyoming, or Montana, where cattle were in strong demand for stocking new ranches. McCoy hired ten men at fifty dollars a month to persuade arriving drovers to sell in Abilene instead of going farther.

McCoy's overhead expenses were not limited to advertising and

[10] Dallas *Herald*, May 16, 1868.
[11] Junction City *Weekly Union*, July 25, 1868.

the hiring of men to outtalk those of his rivals. In the spring and summer of 1868 he was out $5,000 in providing free hotel and livery-stable services for his guests. He also paid $3,300 to settlers in the Abilene area to compensate them for losses from the trampling cattle.[12]

I I

Soon after the grass was green, the herds began to reach the new market. "Two herds of Texas cattle arrived at Abilene during the last week," reported the Junction City *Weekly Union* on April 25. "This is the first of the season."

Texas drovers arriving in Abilene found many arrangements made for their convenience. McCoy had engaged white-thatched W. F. Tomkins to direct the cowmen to suitable grazing grounds. At the immense Twin Livery Stables, Edward H. Gaylord was ready to care for a hundred or more cow ponies. Early arrivals from the trail met, besides McCoy, a dozen buyers with ready cash. One represented John T. Alexander of Illinois, reputed to be the biggest cattle buyer in the world.

Abilene took on the appearance of a boom town. New houses were going up. Three stores and two saloons were open for business. A small stone schoolhouse had been completed, and a frame Baptist church was under construction.

Cash talked fast to most of the weary drovers. Late in June, McCoy told a Junction City newspaperman that in the preceding two weeks, 277 carloads of cattle—about 5,500 head—had been shipped from Abilene. Most of them went to Illinois to be grazed and fed for fall slaughter. A few had gone direct to Chicago. McCoy described them as generally excellent in condition.[13]

By the end of June, cattle shipments from Abilene for the season had exceeded a thousand carloads. The railroad was unable to provide enough cars to meet the demand. It had to convert some of its flatcars into cattle cars by building a framework on them.

The boom continued through the next month. McCoy held an auction of Longhorns in Abilene on July 22. "Five hundred head

[12] *McCoy* vs. *the Kansas Pacific Railway Company* (MS, Supreme Court of Kansas), 16–17.
[13] Junction City *Weekly Union*, June 27, 1868.

92

were disposed of," reported the Junction City *Weekly Union* three days later. "The large work cattle averaged thirty dollars per head, the two-year-olds ten dollars per head. A large number of bidders were present from four states. The sales will hereafter occur semi-monthly."

At McCoy's second cattle auction of the season, on August 5, the cows and calves sold readily but there were no buyers for the beeves. Another Texas-fever scare was hurting the demand for Long-horns, and not enough of the midwestern feeders had become aware of the Abilene market. With twenty-five thousand steers grazing about Abilene, McCoy knew he must do something. So he devised a new advertising plan. He would startle Illinois feeders into an interest in Abilene.

The McCoy scheme was to send into the feeder country a Wild West show that would put Abilene on the map. To get the necessary buffaloes, he had the Union Pacific make up a special train to send forty miles west to a siding in unsettled country. As ropers he engaged two expert Mexicans from California and three Texans. McCoy asked Mark Withers if he would like to make a fourth. "Nothing would please me better," he answered. McCoy offered no money but told Withers he would buy his steers later.

The men loaded a dozen cow ponies into one of the two stock cars of the special train and put their bedding and supplies in the other. They took along plenty of stout rope and a block and tackle to use in loading the buffaloes. The cars had been reinforced with two-by-fours, and they carried extra pieces of scantling for later use.

In a week of chasing and roping, Mark Withers, Billy Campbell, and the two Mexicans captured twenty-four buffalo bulls, often after hard battles. One ferocious bull later tipped the scales at 2,200 pounds. "He was the ugliest piece of buffalo meat I ever looked at," said Withers. But the party returned to Abilene with only half the buffaloes they had captured. Some had died from overheating, fright, or rage. Others lay down and sulked, refusing to eat; they were thrown out to make room for animals that were more tractable.

In Abilene, McCoy rigged up one of the reinforced stock cars as a circus car. On August 27 he had loaded into it three buffaloes, three wild horses, and two elk. The giant buffalo bull was among those taken along. On the sides of the car were large canvas signs advertising McCoy's cattle business. A buffalo soon killed one of the elk, but the other animals rode on east.

With this Wild West show went McCoy, Withers, Campbell, the two Mexican ropers, and an attendant. McCoy took the circus first to St. Louis, where, on September 5 and 8, it gave performances before large crowds in Laclede Park. The cowboys did breathtaking stunts in riding and roping and in throwing wild steers, with and without a lariat. The Mexicans made a hit in their black velvet pants, red sashes, and bright shirts. Scarcely less novel were the Texans in wool shirts, red or blue bandanas, pants stuffed into high leather boots, leather leggings, and big-roweled spurs. A St. Louis newspaper called the show "a great success."

Later in the month, McCoy repeated the circus in Chicago, where it attracted much attention and newspaper comment. At its close, he gave the buffaloes to a veterinary surgeon who later sent their stuffed hides to London.[14] McCoy was said to have lost six thousand dollars on the circus, but it gave effective advertising to his cattle market.

While the improvised rodeo was in progress, McCoy organized a buffalo hunt for Illinois cattlemen. This excursion, which provided horses, took the party to the end of the railroad. After the hunt, McCoy entertained the cattle feeders in Abilene, where some of them bought Longhorns. Together, the show and the excursion had the desired effect. Buying again became active. McCoy paid Mark Withers twenty-eight dollars a head for his steers, for which he had been offered only twenty dollars when he arrived in the summer. Before cold weather set in, all the cattle offered at Abilene had been sold.

McCoy estimated that seventy-five thousand cattle were trailed to Abilene during the 1868 season. Of these, probably between forty-five and fifty thousand were shipped from there by rail. Some went to Kansas City, which had just opened its first packing plant. The response of Texas drovers to the new market elated McCoy. He was confident that, with this start, Abilene would get twice as many cattle the next season.

[14] *Ibid.*, September 5, 1868; McCoy, *Historic Sketches of the Cattle Trade of the West and Southwest*, 180–82; Hunter, *The Trail Drivers of Texas*, 99–101; Withers, reminiscences, MS; Withers, quoted by Cora Melton Cross in *Semi-Weekly Farm News*, March 13, 20, 1936.

Although some Texans trailed cattle north over routes that by-passed Abilene, that town was becoming the chief funnel for the trade. It handled not only feeder cattle to be shipped east by rail but cheap, scrawny animals good enough to stock new ranches to the north and west. This demand absorbed much of the Abilene stock that the railroad was unable to carry east, as well as that which Illinois feeders spurned. Of this northwestward movement, one early range historian wrote:

By 1868 many of the hostile bands of Indians in the central plains had been hunted down and taught the uselessness of further war. Many were preparing to start cattle ranches in front of the advancing line of settlement in Kansas and Nebraska. Others were arranging to go into the interior of Wyoming and Montana. To these extensive preparations for future operations on the range the great demand in 1868 for cheap range cattle was due.

By the close of the spring of 1868, the demand for stock for the new range enterprises had become so hungry that it was grasping at almost everything that looked like a cow. It threatened to cause a serious drain of stock from the Missouri River borders. Some of the trash that had been gathered in western Missouri and eastern Kansas and counted as cattle needed a passport certifying that they were the kind of creatures they were purported to be.

Early in the summer, buyers flocked to Abilene. Men from Texas met them there with thousands of cattle. Many were sold elsewhere. It was not uncommon for buyers to go south to meet the oncoming cattlemen and buy entire droves. The sellers, diverging from the trail at Abilene, often would deliver the stock on or near the purchasers' ranges, sometimes going as far as Colorado and southern Wyoming to do this.

Much of the Texas cattle taken into Kansas at that time was rough and fit only for range stock, though none too good for that. Many cows and youngsters were included in the droves. While the demand for range stock was great, the magnitude of the supply from Texas kept prices from going to extravagant figures.[15]

The new outbreak of Texas fever, which plagued McCoy and other shippers before the summer of 1868 ended, was worst in Illinois. The disease broke out in a score of Illinois counties late in July.

[15] *Prose and Poetry of the Live Stock Industry of the United States*, 437.

It was especially common among local cattle infected by Longhorns shipped from Cairo to Tolono but was carried also by some of the cattle from Abilene. In Champaign County, where the damage was heaviest, losses were estimated at $150,000. Enraged farmers formed vigilance committees to keep out offending cattle.

Farmers in Abilene and elsewhere also suffered losses from the fever. Drovers at Abilene contributed $1,200 to stockmen whose animals had died, and McCoy paid several thousand dollars to claimants near Abilene. The epidemic began to subside in September, but not before it had hurt momentarily the eastern market for cattle and had fanned the movement for further quarantines and exclusion laws. New York State imposed quarantine regulations in the summer but modified them in the fall. This situation added an element of uncertainty to prospects for the cattle movement in the year ahead.

III

Fear of shotgun quarantine, though, did not deter Texas cowmen from preparing for big drives to Kansas in the spring of 1869. The market was strong again, and hoofprints of the herds of 1868 had left the new Chisholm Trail more plainly marked. Many drovers were willing to take the risk. A wet spring had made the grass plentiful. Some cowmen said a fellow would need a rowboat to cross the prairies from Houston to Corpus Christi.

Despite the strong interest in Abilene, some Texas drovers still pointed cattle in other directions that year. From the Llano River, above Mason, Dudley H. and John W. Snyder took a herd over the Loving-Goodnight Trail to New Mexico, selling their beeves at Fort Union at thirty-five dollars a head. Several Texans made drives to California. Damon Slater of Llano headed west with 1,500 mixed cattle and a capable outfit. He trailed by Horsehead Crossing, Tucson, and Fort Yuma. In the same season, another Texan delivered a herd of 2,500 Longhorns at Los Angeles. Three Texas cowmen sent 1,200 head to California in charge of Henry Campbell. In Arizona he encountered a severe drouth. Instead of going on, he took the herd to Nevada, where he sold at twenty-five dollars a head.

Texas herds still plodded east, but in diminishing numbers. From Gonzales County, Andy Moore and A. E. Scheske trailed a mixed

96

herd of the N7-connected brand to Shreveport and on to Natchez, where they sold at $4.50 a head. From the same county, in the fall, W. F. Cude took a herd to Shreveport but found the buffalo flies so pesky that he determined to follow that route no more. "Sometimes we would get farms to put the cattle in at night," he recalled. "The farms were stocked with cockleburs. The tails of the cattle would get full of burs; and when the buffalo flies would get after them, they would lose their tails fighting flies. The tails would become entangled in small pines. There the cattle would stand and pull and bellow until they got loose. You could hear them bawl a mile."[16]

The big cattle movement, though, was up the new Chisholm Trail. Among the scores of Texas cowmen who trailed to Abilene in the spring of 1869 was Randolph Paine of Denton County. On credit, he bought three thousand four- and five-year-old steers at twelve dollars a head and assembled an outfit. Leaving in May, he easily crossed the Red River above Gainesville and the Washita at Fort Arbuckle. One of his trail hands, L. T. Clark, reported that the grass was so plentiful that the steers fattened as they grazed northward. At night Paine took his turn with the other men in guarding the herd. At Abilene he sold the steers at thirty dollars a head. After taking the money back to Texas and paying off his creditors, he pocketed a good profit.

Not all the drovers that spring had such favorable weather and easy river crossings. J. H. Smith, with a herd of fifteen hundred, had cold, rainy weather most of the time and found many of the creeks and rivers out of their banks. At the crossing of the Smoky Hill River, one of his men was drowned. W. A. Peril, who left with a small herd from near Loyal Valley, fared little better. He had to swim his herd across all the rivers from the Brazos to the Republican and had to contend with many rainstorms and stampedes.

Bill Montgomery ran into similar hazards. With a herd of 4,500 head from Lockhart, he had to take three days to put his Longhorns across the rampaging Red River. In crossing the North Fork of the Canadian, the cattle milled in the high water, and 116 of them were lost. The Arkansas also was on a spring boom, causing a delay of several days. The big herd reached Abilene late in June. The town was recovering from a flood that, earlier in the month, had pushed

16 Hunter, *The Trail Drivers of Texas*, 216, 567, 765, 848, 1,029, 1,033.

Mud Creek out of its banks, carried off several houses and barns, and drowned the prairie-dog village. Montgomery grazed his cattle for a month, then sold out to a Californian at twenty-five dollars a head.

Almost every outfit had its share of excitement. L. D. Taylor was only eighteen when he made his first trip up the Chisholm Trail from Gonzales County that spring. At Waco, where the Brazos was up to the top of its banks, young Taylor had a thrill watching the herd of a thousand beeves swim across. As the big steers went through the water, he recalled, all he could see were the tips of their horns and the ends of their noses. In crossing the Trinity at Dallas, the herd stampeded and rushed through the town. The commotion caused residents to run for cover and cost about two hundred dollars for damages. Farther north, the outfit had trouble at other crossings, lost twenty-five beeves to Comanche raiders, and had one man killed in a battle with outlaws.[17]

Also on the trail that spring were at least two of the Day brothers —sometimes called the Week boys because there were seven of them. They were the sons of Jesse Day, who had been drowned in the spring of 1860 while swimming a trail herd across the Brazos at Waco. All seven sons were Confederate veterans and pioneer cowmen. Addison J. Day made his first trip as a trail hand, leaving Belton with eight hundred beeves and crossing into the Indian Territory at Red River Station. Late in the spring, the eldest brother, Colonel William H. Day, joined his brother-in-law, Jesse M. Driskill, in gathering a trail herd of fifteen hundred head. Losing a hundred on the way, the partners sold the remaining fourteen hundred at Abilene in the summer.[18]

In his office at Abilene, McCoy was ready for the expected deluge of Longhorns from Texas. In some ways, his position was less favorable than it had been a year earlier. His two brothers had withdrawn from the Abilene enterprise, leaving him to assume the entire risk. Too, his agreement with the Union Pacific Railroad, Eastern Division—which in April changed its name to the Kansas Pacific

[17] Ibid., 42–43, 412, 498–99, 561, 565–66.
[18] William H. Day, letters (MS, James T. Padgitt, Coleman, Texas); Galveston News, April 2, 1911; James T. Padgitt, "Colonel William H. Day: Texas Ranchman," Southwestern Historical Quarterly, Vol. LIII, No. 4 (April, 1950), 347–66.

Railway[19]—was less advantageous. Instead of getting a bonus of $5 for each carload of cattle shipped from Abilene, he was to receive only $2.50 a carload for 1869. But he counted on a greatly increased volume to offset this change. On July 26, McCoy raised eight thousand dollars by selling the Drover's Cottage to his Illinois friend Colonel Samuel N. Hitt, who renewed the lease to James W. Gore.

McCoy had found a way to virtually nullify a new ban on Texas and Cherokee cattle that the Illinois Legislature had enacted in the spring. By persistent lobbying at Springfield, he had obtained a loophole in the law to exempt from the ban any cattle that had been wintered in Kansas, Missouri, or Wisconsin. All that was necessary, in shipping Texas cattle from Abilene to Illinois, was to have an easily obtained certificate saying that they had been wintered in one of the approved states.[20]

Not all the cattle had to be shipped to feeders in the Corn Belt. The booming West was still hungry for stock cattle and didn't spurn the rangy Longhorns. On May 10, the driving of a golden spike at Promontory Point, Utah, had linked the Atlantic and the Pacific by rail and had called national attention to new opportunities in the West. Farmers and stockmen were heading west from the overcrowded East and from the impoverished South, which still suffered from the injustices and hardships of Reconstruction. Nearly all of the new settlers wanted cheap cattle.

Texas cowmen were ready to supply this need. Those from the western part of the state were trailing in thousands of cattle, reported a correspondent in Austin on August 25, "Scarcely a day but a drove passes. A stranger would imagine that beef, milk, and butter would be scarce and high; but the number is not missed, and the market is not in the least affected."[21]

In southern Kansas, the village of Wichita was rising on the site of the Indian camp and Jesse Chisholm's trading post at the mouth of the Little Arkansas. It had four stores, a saloon, a blacksmith and

[19] *Republican Daily Journal*, April 6, 1869; McCoy, *Historic Sketches of the Cattle Trade of the West*, 184–85, 206–14.
[20] *Public Laws of Illinois*, 1869, 402–405; McCoy, *Historic Sketches of the Cattle Trade of the West and Southwest*, 185–89.
[21] Dallas *Herald*, June 5, 1869.

saddlery shop, and twenty families. The surrounding prairies teemed with Texas cattle. Observers estimated in August that 70,000 to 100,000 Longhorns had passed Wichita on their way north.[22]

Most of the herds were pointed toward Abilene. That town, McCoy figured, received 150,000 head during the season—twice as many as in 1868. Prices there were good. Second-class beef steers, which included most of the Longhorns, brought $22.50 to $25 a head. Extra fine ones brought $26 or more, sometimes as much as $32. Stock cattle often went for $12 or $12.50. Calves were sold for trifling sums or given away.

Neighboring towns still were trying to cut in on the Abilene market, but without success. An Ellsworth booster, sixty miles west of Abilene, wrote to Texas, soliciting cattle and saying that drovers would not be allowed to reach Abilene, Junction City, or Salina. But Ellsworth was unable to match the facilities of Abilene or to keep Texas drovers from patronizing the McCoy market.[23]

Kansas City, meanwhile, was gaining from the Abilene enterprise. It was taking advantage of its favorable location to begin building a meat-packing industry to rival those of St. Louis and Chicago. One of its packing plants advertised a capacity of four hundred head of cattle a day and solicited shipments from drovers and brokers.

IV

Although cattle often were grazed near Abilene before being shipped, the record of rail loadings there in 1869, in which the peak month was October, suggests that fall drives were larger than usual that year. One such drive, from the hills of Palo Pinto County, was headed by the Rev. George Webb Slaughter, a pioneer circuit rider and cowman. Slaughter, who preached with a six-shooter in his belt to be prepared for an Indian attack, was one of the most successful stockmen on the frontier.

More is known of this drive because one of the men who went along, J. H. Baker, kept a diary.[24] Baker, a native of Virginia, was

22 *Kansas Daily Tribune*, August 8, 1869; Junction City *Weekly Union*, September 4, 1869.
23 Dallas *Herald*, July 3, 1869. In 1871, and again in 1874, McCoy estimated the 1869 drive at 150,000. A typographical error in the United States Census of 1880, which made the figure 350,000, has led many writers astray.

thirty-seven at the time of the drive and had had military experience in protecting the frontier against Indian raids. Slaughter, Baker, and others spent most of August in gathering the Longhorns and in branding and tallying. The trail herd included about 2,250 head, of which 480 belonged to Baker. The drive started from the Slaughter ranch, north of Palo Pinto, on September 2.

As the pointers headed the cattle toward Flat Top Mountain, Baker, with J. R. Jowell and P. E. Slaughter, a son of Parson Slaughter, the trail boss, rode to Jacksboro with the tally and had it recorded. Then they followed the herd, catching up with it the next morning, five miles west of Flat Top. That night Baker stood guard from midnight until dawn. The next morning Dick Jowell and some of the other boys started back. The trail outfit crossed the West Fork in the evening and camped a mile beyond.

On the fourth day, as on the preceding one, the herd traveled about ten miles. The bed ground was on the divide between the West Fork and the Little Wichita. The cattle had wide prairies and good grass. The next morning, Baker recorded, "rain began falling about daybreak and continued until 10 a.m. We drove to Buffalo Station. Damp and cold all day. Our cattle stampeded during the afternoon, and it was several hours before we stopped them. Do not think we lost any."

The cattle were restless and troublesome during the night. On the next day, which was clear and cold, they still were hard to manage until they came to a stream, near Victoria Peak, where they satisfied their thirst. Two more days brought them to Red River Station. The men swam the herd on the morning of the tenth and crossed the wagons on a ferry. One of the hands, William Cowden, came near drowning and was rescued with difficulty. Two days later the herd crossed Muddy Creek. This took more time than had the Red River crossing, as the banks were slippery and boggy. Five head of cattle were lost.

That night a downpour made it impossible to hold the cattle in a compact herd, and the men had to spend all the next day in gathering them. On the fifteenth the herd struck timber and crossed several boggy creeks. The next day the men were glad to find some clear creeks with gravel bottoms. On the seventeenth they passed

[24] J. H. Baker, diary (MS, University of Texas Library).

Fort Arbuckle, a small post on the Washita River, garrisoned by two companies of soldiers. The drovers camped three miles east of the fort, where they had good grass and water.

The next day they crossed the Washita without difficulty and traveled ten miles toward Cherokee Town, camping on a hill covered with tall grass. Rain fell that night. On the twentieth, which was foggy and showery, they trailed into the Seminole Nation about eleven miles and crossed the South Canadian River. The night was misty. In the next two days they skirted timber and a few Seminole settlements and crossed several muddy creeks. Baker noted "considerable dissatisfaction on account of the boss' ill temper."

The outfit emerged on a prairie in the Shawnee Nation on the twenty-third and crossed the North Fork of the Canadian, camping a mile beyond. The next day's drive of ten miles took the herd across open prairie and through several muddy streams. The men made camp in the Osage country. On the twenty-fifth a norther brought cold air and rain, making the cattle a little inclined to run. But the party made twelve miles before crossing a creek and camping on the edge of the prairie.

Of the next two days, Baker's diary says:

Sunday, September 26: Calm, clear, and cool this morning. About two miles of travel brought us to the Deep Fork of the Canadian, a pretty running stream with a rock bottom. After crossing, we had dinner and put a new tongue in one of the wagons. We took the left-hand road here. We seem to be on a divide between some waters. After going eight miles, we made camp. Wide prairies and good grass.

Monday, September 27: A clear, cool night, with heavy dew this morning. We traveled along fine on a high prairie until noon. After dinner we turned the cattle off the road to get water and drove through the prairie, expecting to strike the road in the former direction. But soon after we left it, it turned to the right. Night overtook us before we found it. We were compelled to camp on the top of a high hill, without our wagons and suppers.

The men found the wagons early the next morning. They trailed twelve miles that day, crossing the Salt Fork of the Arkansas in the evening and camping two miles beyond. On the twenty-ninth, which was clear and cool, they made twelve miles over high prairies. The country was marked by poor soil, deep ravines, and lack of timber; but it had fairly good sedge grass. The next day brought cloudy skies and a cool south wind that carried drizzly rain. The cattle grazed on good mesquite grass and crossed Grapevine Creek before reaching their bed ground. During the night a heavy rain drenched cattle, horses, and men. Baker had to remain on guard all night.

The herd reached the Arkansas River on the afternoon of the next day, October 1. "We drove the herd across and forded without swimming," wrote Baker. "It is a clear, pretty stream, about six hundred yards wide. No bottoms of any consequence along the river. The bluffs come close to it. But little timber here. We made camp about a mile from the river." With frosty weather, the outfit traveled twelve miles on the second, over high prairie that had poor soil, patches of high mesquite grass, and no timber in sight. On the third the cattle had high, rolling prairies, with sedge grass and occasional patches of mesquite. The men camped on the north side of Clear Creek, a pretty stream with rock bottom. A day later the camp was six miles to the northwest, at the head of the same creek.

The drives of the next three days, each ten miles, took the herd over open prairies and across Spring Creek and Prairie Creek. The Longhorns had plenty of mesquite grass. On the following two days Baker wrote:

Friday, October 8: A cold norther, with rain, blew up just before day. Continued to rain until 9 a.m. Norther blew all day. Some of the hands drove the cattle about four miles, while the boss, myself, and four of the hands spent the day hunting for a yoke of our oxen. Found them in another herd and got them back to our camp about sunset. Made camp on Rock Creek near the Kansas line. Twenty thousand head of cattle are being grazed in this vicinity, waiting for buyers.

Saturday, October 9: A heavy frost this morning. Started early and drove three miles to Walnut Creek. Here we found several settlements and a number of men who had put up hay for wintering cattle. I sold them ninety two-year-olds for $10 gold each. Fine valley lands on Walnut Creek, and considerable timber. Traveled two miles west of the creek and made camp.

The men spent the next two and a half days in grazing the cattle and in cutting out more steers and some heifers to sell. On the thir-

teenth the outfit camped on a small stream about three miles northeast of Fort Wichita. The next day Baker made a note of rich lands
and tall sunflowers along the streams. The camp that night was about
three miles from the Little Arkansas River. There the cattle remained
for two days while the men cut out five hundred head from the herd
to be left for wintering. The drovers dickered with the buyers for
some of the other cattle. In the distance they saw a prairie fire, but
it was not blowing in their direction.

On the seventeenth Parson Slaughter split the outfit. He and
one of the hands stayed to brand the cattle that were to be wintered.
Five of the men remained with some of the other cattle, while
Baker and five others started trailing the remaining 350 head—most
of them Baker's—on to Abilene. Baker made ten miles the first day
but had to spend the morning of the next recovering strayed oxen.
For the next two days, lack of timber made it necessary to haul wood.

On the nineteenth, after a sleet storm, Baker met C. C. Slaughter,
eldest son of the parson, who was on his way back from Abilene.
Slaughter reported favorably on the market there. The next day,
with more moderate weather, Baker trailed fifteen miles, crossing
the high divide between the Arkansas and the Neosho and camping
at the head of the timber on Cottonwood Creek. He passed Smoky
Hill before noon of the twenty-second and camped that night on
the west side of Holland Creek. The next day he found many herds
waiting for buyers. Most of the cattle were shabby. That night Baker
and his men bedded down their small herd on Smoky Hill River,
two and one-half miles from Abilene. Other cowmen were saying
that the cold weather would bring a rush of cattle on the market
and thus would pull down the price.

For the next two days, Baker stayed in camp, entertaining prospective buyers. On the twenty-fifth, with a cold norther blowing
and with four of his hands gone into town, Baker let buyers drive
304 of his choice steers into town. But, unable to get them loaded,
they brought the cattle back in the evening. Baker rode into town
on the twenty-sixth. On the next day he drove the 304 head into
Abilene and shipped them.

That night a prairie fire scattered his twenty-eight remaining
cattle, and only three of them could be found the next day. Baker
received $4,664 for his cattle. After paying off his hands and meeting

other expenses, he had $4,068 in currency. He spent the twenty-ninth in Abilene, getting his business in order, and that evening drove to John Slaughter's camp on Turkey Creek, about five miles from town.

Baker had some horses shod on the thirtieth and dined at the Drover's Cottage for seventy-five cents. The next day, with John Slaughter and John McKinney, he looked for his lost cattle. The three rode up Holland Creek and across the divide to Gypsum Creek but failed to find the missing steers. On the next day, November 1, Baker had better luck, locating seven head that had wandered into McCoy's herd.

Preparation for the return trip was the next concern of Baker. In Abilene on the second, he swapped horses, paying forty dollars to boot, and bought a wagon and harness for $153. He also spent $320.17 for an elaborate outfit of clothing that included eleven suits, two overcoats, and fifteen pairs of boots. He left the camp on Turkey Creek on November fifth, heading back to Texas. On December 11 he arrived at his home at Palo Pinto, an unscarred veteran of the trail.

VII

PRAIRIE CONVOYS

Perched on the top rail of the corral, Texas cowboys talked of the Chisholm Trail as a highway to stirring exploits. Only the abler and more dependable men, as a rule, were taken along. The greenhorn who "couldn't cut a lame steer from the shade of a tree" was left to do his learning on the home range. Thus, those who had been up the trail with a herd wore an enviable distinction. Stifling dust and long, sweaty hours in the saddle brought the reward of new scenes and exciting adventures. The abstemious life on the trail carried a promise of hilarious celebration at Abilene or some other live town after the cattle were sold.

The successful drover or trail boss had to use sound judgment in putting together a herd and an outfit. The cattle must have some of their wildness worn off. The men must be rugged, reliable, and well mounted. Each hand took along two to five horses, sometimes more. He could sell his surplus ponies at a profit after he reached Kansas.

Mark Withers, who rode one horse all the way on his first drive, began taking three horses for himself and two for each of his men. In later years, he said, "I'd buy from seventy to a hundred horses, and they'd end up fat and in good condition. That way, each man would ride six or seven horses on the trail. Then I'd sell the horses where we delivered the cattle."[1]

The cow ponies varied in color and build but needed to be dependable, intelligent, and well trained. "As smart as a cutting horse" was a common saying on the range. The pony inclined to jump out of his skin or to throw the hair off his back wasn't wanted on the trail. Most of the trail horses were of mustang blood, not more than a generation or two removed from the wild herds of Spanish ancestry that roamed over the Great Plains. Some of the best, though, were quarter horses whose sires had been brought from Tennessee, Kentucky, and other states east of the Mississippi.

The quarter horse, so called because many of the breed were bred and trained to compete in quarter-mile races, was a small, chunky mount. Sometimes called the short horse or the Virginia horse, it not only was an amazing sprinter but, when trained, made a superb cow pony. Especially in demand were quarter horses of the Steel Dust strain that stemmed from a celebrated Dallas County stallion brought from Illinois.

As for the trail hand, his youthful appearance often belied his experience. His muscles were firm and his nerves steady. His hand was deft with the rein, the lariat, and the six-shooter. He rode as if he were a part of his horse, sticking on "like a lean tick to a dog's ear." He understood the instincts of the Longhorns so well that usually he could anticipate their actions. He was ready for hardships and for sudden danger.

On the trail the dusty cowhand showed little of the glamour he might try to affect when he rode into town. He had bowlegs from riding and wore his hair long. His felt hat had a wide brim to give protection from sun and rain. The red bandana about his neck could be pulled up over his mouth and nose to keep out dust, sleet, or freezing wind. His boots had two-inch heels that kept his feet from slipping through the stirrups and that gave him an awkward gait. His spurs or "grappling irons" usually were nickel-plated, though some were of silver. When riding in brushy country, he wore chaps of calfskin or goatskin to protect his legs from scratches. Usually

[1] Withers, reminiscences, MS. Some Texas stockmen trailed horses to Kansas independently of cattle. But the horse droves were few in comparison with the cattle herds, and usually they were much smaller.

he took pride in his saddle, which often cost more than his mount.

The size of the trail herd varied from a few hundred head to several thousand. Usually it was not more than three thousand, since a larger number might bring difficulty and delay in watering the animals and in crossing streams. About 2,500 to 3,000 made the best-sized herd to trail, in the opinion of Mark Withers. A large herd likely would be made up of cattle from several owners. In that case, the drover was particular to obtain and record bills of sale for the cattle he bought.

As these bunches bore different brands, the men gave them a common trail brand at the point of departure. After gathering the cattle, the trail hands drove them through a chute and imprinted a road brand with a hot iron. The usual trail brand was a light slash or bar. In early days, it might be burned on the shoulder, side, or rump. Later it was required to be on the left side, behind the shoulder.

This branding ordinarily would take about three days. Then the Longhorns were ready for the long trek northward. A herd of three thousand likely would be accompanied by twelve to eighteen cow hands, forty to eighty horses, a cook who drove the chuck wagon, and a wrangler who looked after the spare horses.

The herds were of two types—beeves and mixed cattle. The beeves were mature steers that would bring good prices in Kansas, as they would need little feeding before going to the packers. On the trail they were easier to handle than the mixed herds, since a steer walks with a steadier stride than that of a cow. This advantage was partially offset, though, by the steer's greater inclination to stampede. Beef herds were likely to be smaller than mixed herds. The latter included steers, cows, and yearlings, often many of them of inferior quality. Most of the mixed herds were sold for stocking new ranges in the northwest.

One trouble with the mixed herds was that many of the cows bore calves while on the trail. Nearly every morning, the last guards would find several calves on the bed ground. Usually the trail boss had them shot, much as he hated to do so. The calves couldn't keep up with the herd on a long, hot day's drive; and the mothers, unless removed immediately, would try to return to their offspring. Some-times, in settled country, the foreman would give the calves to

near-by farmers or trade them for vegetables. In later days, as calves
became more valuable, some drovers hauled them in a calf wagon
or "blattin' cart" for the first day or two. Others even let them try
to follow their mothers if the day's drive was not expected to be
strenuous.

Much of the success of the drive depended on the trail boss. He
needed to know even more than the men he hired. As Bill Poage
put it, the boss had as many duties as the captain of a steamboat.
"He must see that there are enough provisions, as short grub does
more toward dissatisfying the cowboy than anything else. He must
assign each man to his proper duty. He must be the first up in the
morning to wake the men. He must ride ahead to see that there is
water at the proper distance. He must know where to stop for noon.
He must count the cattle at intervals to see that none have been lost.
He must settle all difficulties among his men." For a good trail boss,
said Mark Withers, "I always tried to look out for one that was sober.
A boss rides about three or four times as far as the herd goes."[1]

The expert trail boss didn't push his Longhorns too hard. He
remembered the saying, "Look out for the cows' feet and the horses'
backs, and let the waddies and the cook look out for themselves."
The trick was to keep the cattle from knowing that they were under
restraint. Every step of every steer should be taken voluntarily—
but guided in the direction in which the drover wanted the herd
to go. The apparent freedom allowed the cattle made them easier
to manage and less likely to become troublesome.

The toughness and endurance of the Longhorns fitted them well
for the long trail. Usually they lost little weight on the drive and
could be handled cheaply. "As trail cattle, their equal never has
been known," said Charles Goodnight. "Their hoofs are superior
to those of any other cattle. In stampedes, they hold together better,
are easier circled in a run, and rarely split off when you commence
to turn the front. No animal of the cow kind will shift and take
care of itself under all conditions as will the Longhorns. They can
go farther without water and endure more suffering than others."

The first few days, in which the herd was being "road broke,"
often proved to be a crucial period. "Owing to the danger of In-

[2] William R. Poage, "Drive to Cheyenne in 1874" (MS, University of Texas
Library); Withers, reminiscences, MS; Dallas *Morning News*, July 20, 1941.

dians and stampedes, I always got out of the settlements as soon as possible," recalled Goodnight. "Cattle that were scattered were much easier traced on the trail than in the settlements."[3]

Methods varied in breaking the cattle to the trail. Some bosses pushed the herd hard at first so that the cattle would be tired at night and less inclined to become restive. Others pampered them with short, easy drives, lest they become nervous and hard to manage. In either case, the men watched the Longhorns with extra care. If they could be kept from stampeding during the first ten days, they likely would be easier to handle on the remainder of the drive.

Usually the spring drive started when the rolling Texas prairies looked their best. New grass was making the ranges green again. Flowers added splotches of color to many of the prairies and hillsides. There were patches of bluebonnets and yellow blossoms of wild mustard, along with the white of the prickly poppy and the scarlet of the Indian paintbrush. The mesquite was putting out its lacy, waving foliage; and leaf buds on the post oaks and blackjacks were beginning to swell and burst. It was a season to make the young cowboy restless and eager to go places.

The drover or his foreman picked two of the most trusted hands to ride in the lead and guide the cattle in the desired direction. These men, called pointers, usually kept their posts throughout the drive. Although there was less dust in the lead than farther back, the pointers shifted from one side of the herd to the other, so that neither would have to eat more than his share. Behind the pointers, at an interval along each side of the herd, rode the swing men. Still farther back were the flank riders, and finally the drag men.

All along the line, the men kept the cattle from spreading out too far and warded off intruders. Sometimes they had to go after a one-eyed steer or a muley that tried to leave the herd. In keeping the herd strung out, they avoided crowding and consequent overheating. A large herd usually would string out for half a mile or more.

In some outfits the riders behind the pointers kept the same posts day after day, according to rank. More often they changed places in one kind of rotation or another. Goodnight had his trail men shift each morning, since those nearer the point had lighter work

[3] Charles Goodnight, "Managing a Trail Herd in Early Days," *Southwest Plainsman*, November 21, 1925; Haley, *Charles Goodnight, Cowman and Plainsman*, 256.

and less dust. "If you were first behind the pointer on the right today, you would be second on the left tomorrow, third on the right the next day, and so on until you dropped back to the drag man on the corner. Then you began working back toward the lead again. Each man knew his place and took it each morning."[4]

Unenvied in the dusty rear were the two or three tailers or drag men. They kept the back corners from becoming too far apart and prodded the weaklings and laggards that otherwise might have slowed down the drive. Sometimes they had to push some of the stronger cattle ahead to get them out of the way of the less sturdy. A buckskin popper on the end of a rope had the desired effect. Dust made riding the drag the least pleasant of all trail tasks, but an outfit needed able men in the rear to keep the herd on schedule. J. L. McCaleb, who went up the trail in 1868, recalled that the best place to learn cuss words was in the tail of the herd.

A well-managed herd would travel eight to fifteen or even twenty miles in a day, most often ten to twelve miles. Usually the location of water determined the distance. The route often deviated from a straight line. The herd had to skirt hills and timber, reach streams at points of easy crossing, and keep the thirst of the Longhorns satisfied. The nearest way on a trail, a cowman's axiom said, is the shortest distance between water holes.

The trail boss picked the route. When his outfit was taking the herd over a new or unfamiliar trail, he would get up by daybreak and ride ahead to look for watering places. Then he would ride back toward the herd and, from a hilltop, signal the point men as to the direction they should take. The men saved time by using a system of signals, most of them taken over from the Indians. They did nearly all the signaling from horseback, usually by holding or waving a hat. In open country, a rider on an eminence could be seen several miles away.

II

With the first streak of dawn, the trail riders were out of their bedrolls. As they dashed cold water into their faces, they could hear the call of the meadow lark and see the cook already at work over

[4] Goodnight, "Managing a Trail Herd in Early Days," *Southwest Plainsman*, November 21, 1925.

his fire. Usually the first to eat breakfast were the pointers and the two who were to relieve the last pair of night guards. If there was reason to fear an Indian attack, the men would keep the herd on the bed ground until all hands were mounted and in place. Otherwise, they would rouse the cattle at dawn, allow them to graze for a short time, and put them in order for moving. As soon as breakfast was over and the dishes were washed, the wrangler helped the cook load the wagon and hitch the horses or mules.

When everything was ready, the boss gave the signal to break camp and start on the trail. This was a motion with the hat in the direction to be followed. The pointers and swing men repeated the signal and thus passed it along to the rear. Then the herd began its leisurely walk—not so much a drive as a guided drift. If it were raining or snowing, the foreman would ride ahead to show the way.

Individual cattle tended to keep about the same position in the trail herd day after day. Often one or two steers would form the habit of keeping at the head of the procession. Many drovers used these ambitious animals to advantage in managing the herd, or even brought along a work ox or two for this purpose. A lead steer was especially useful in starting a herd swimming across a river or in getting the cattle to enter a pen.

Among those who used lead steers regularly, Charles Goodnight and William B. Slaughter had bells strapped about the leaders' necks. At night they usually had the bells muffled. Famous over the cow country was Goodnight's powerful and sagacious Old Blue. Goodnight considered Old Blue worth a dozen extra hands and used him repeatedly on the trail. Refusing to associate with the herd, this big steer usually grazed with the saddle horses. Often he would come to the camp and beg food from the cook.[5]

Even in a stampede, the lead steers sometimes earned their salt. On the Shawnee Trail in 1873, a herd of twelve hundred head stampeded within the town of Dallas. That is, all but two of them did. "The two that didn't take fright," reported the *Herald* the next morning, "had led the drove from the time the owners started out with them. During the alarm of the rest of the drove, they stood motionless. The drivers had the satisfaction of seeing the frightened

[5] Hunter, *The Trail Drivers of Texas*, 869; Haley, *Charles Goodnight, Cowman and Plainsman*; J. Frank Dobie, *The Longhorns*, 267–75.

cattle eventually return and gather 'round the more composed leaders."[6]

The longer the cattle were trailed, the easier most of them were to handle. This was the experience of Tom Candy Ponting and Washington Malone, who took the first Texas Longhorns to New York in 1854. One Sunday morning in June they entered the village of Attica, Indiana, with their small herd of 150 fat beeves. They had walked these and other cattle from Texas in the preceding fall and had wintered them in Illinois. "Just as we got between two churches," wrote Ponting, "both bells began to ring. I was near the head and stopped the oxen. I talked to the cattle as if they were children. They listened a moment and then moved on."

Longhorns held together on the trail seemed to form an attachment not only for their drovers but for each other. When Ponting and Malone sold their cattle in New York, in bunches of ten to twenty, and the buyers tried to drive them to various slaughter houses, the steers refused to budge. "They didn't want to leave the other cattle," said Ponting. "I told the butcher to take all the cattle to the same slaughter house and to furnish my partner and me with a horse and we would help him. We got them there without any trouble."[7]

The gait of the steers in the strung-out column depended largely on how close the swing and flank men rode to the line. "When we had a long drive to make between watering places," explained Goodnight, "the men rode in closer to the line. Under normal conditions, the herd was fifty to sixty feet across, the width being governed by the distance we had to go before resting. Narrowing the string was called 'squeezing them down.' Ten feet was the lowest limit, for then gaps came and the cattle would begin trotting to fill the spaces. The pointers checked them in front, for they were never allowed to trot. After a herd was handled a month or two, the cattle became gentler and it was necessary to ride closer to get the same results."[8]

At about eleven o'clock, the boss gave the signal to stop the herd and allow the cattle to graze beside the trail. During this nooning

---

[6] Dallas *Herald*, September 12, 1873.

[7] Ponting, *Life of Tom Candy Ponting*, 40–41.

[8] Goodnight, "Managing a Trail Herd in Early Days," *Southwest Plainsman*, November 21, 1925.

period, the men headed for the chuck wagon for their dinner. If the cook had arrived enough ahead of the herd, he might have a freshly cooked meal. Otherwise, he would give them food he had prepared that morning while breakfast was cooking.

When the Longhorns began to lie down, the foreman knew they had grazed long enough. He then gave the signal to get them back on the trail. The afternoon part of the day's drive was easier, as the cattle were becoming thirsty and were eager to reach water. The science of trailing, Goodnight used to say, was in grazing and watering the cattle. Of the two, he considered watering the more important.[9]

As the afternoon ebbed, the punchers closed in on the Longhorns and slowly "rode them down" into a more compact herd. They liked to arrive at the camp site before sundown so they would have plenty of time to water the cattle and bed them down. In watering, they had to spread the animals far enough apart, or divide them into bunches, to avoid crowding and pushing. The foreman showed the location of the bed ground by waving his hat in a circle around his head. Usually the wagon already was there, and the cook was getting supper.

To put the cattle out of the way of others that might be following and to provide better grazing, the foreman had his men "throw" the herd off to one side of the trail. He tried to pick a spot where the animals would have fresh grass to eat, dry grass to lie upon, and, on warm nights, enough elevation to catch the breeze. He didn't want the herd near timber, which might hide Indians or predatory animals, or close to ravines or washouts, into which the cattle might plunge if they should stampede in the night. "I always tried to bed the cattle on a ridge if it wasn't too high," said Mark Withers. "We always had some steers that wouldn't bed in the herd at all. They'd go twenty or thirty feet out, and we'd let them alone."

The punchers held the herd in a circle, with the cattle far enough apart for comfort and grazing. Although they had nibbled grass all day as they marched along, the Longhorns usually showed a strong appetite in the evening. As darkness fell and the cattle chewed their

[9] Charles Goodnight, account written for, and included in, *Prose and Poetry of the Live Stock Industry of the United States*, 532–34.

cuds and began to yawn, the men quietly pushed them into a more compart circle on the bed ground.

While the cattle were grazing, the punchers, in relays, ate their supper. This was their principal meal of the day and usually had some form of beef as its mainstay. Then, before starting to rest, the men made ready for their night duty. Each evening, recalled E. P. Byler, who made five trips up the Chisholm Trail, those in his outfit would catch their night horses and stake them so that each man would be ready to go on guard when his turn came. After bringing up the horses, they took lariat ropes and tied one end of each to a wheel of the chuck wagon. A man held the other end. Thus they formed a sort of corral, into which they drove the horses. The ponies soon became used to this and would not try to get out from the rope pen.[10]

ɪ ɪ ɪ

As the evening whistle of the whippoorwill came from the woods, the cattle sank to their knees. They were ready to dream of lush ranges and the cool, clear water of spring-fed streams. At about that time, the men pulled their bedrolls from the wagon. The two men on the first night guard rode off to their duty. Usually there were three or four sets of guards for the night, with each period two hours or longer. As the men had no watches, they estimated the time by the Big Dipper.

The guards rode slowly around the sleeping herd, in opposite directions. "To ride around the big steers at night, all lying down full as a tick, chewing their cuds and blowing, with the moon shining on their big horns, was a sight to make a man's eyes pop," recalled James Benton.[11] From distant hills came the hopeful howls of coyotes that would be on hand the next day to see if a calf or two had been left on the bed ground.

As he rode, the cowboy often hummed or crooned to soothe the cattle and keep them quiet. Even if he "couldn't carry a tune in a corked jug," the Longhorns seemed to like the assurance that a man on horseback was close at hand for their protection. The tunes

10 Hunter, *The Trail Drivers of Texas*, 780.
11 Jesse James Benton, *Cow by the Tail*, 44.

the men sang might be from the church or from the dance hall. Sometimes there were ballads that told of unusual experiences on the range or on the trail.

The night guard had to keep an eye on the outside, to watch for Indians or other marauders. The other he kept on the sleeping cattle, looking for signs that might lead to a stampede. A cowboy who had trouble keeping awake might rub a little tobacco juice on his eyelids. At about midnight, the Longhorns would slowly rise, stretch themselves, yawn, browse a bit, and lie down again. After another hour or so, they likely would repeat the performance. On bright moonlit nights, they were more restless and often would graze in a desultory manner through most of the night.

The men not on guard spread their bedrolls on the ground and turned in soon after the evening meal. There would be a little talk and sometimes a tune or two from some cowboy's fiddle, guitar, or harmonica. But weariness and the need for sleep when it could be obtained led them to "hit the hay" early. In warm weather, if there seemed little danger of a stampede, the men often stripped to their underclothes. If there was a chill in the air or if danger impended, they might take off only their boots and belts and loosen their shirt collars. In a series of stampedes, they might even sleep in their boots for a whole week.

When a long rainy spell made the cattle restless and the ground boggy, the trail hand who could get a little sleep was lucky. In such cases, recalled James H. Cook, sometimes three riders, each holding his horse by the bridle rein, would lie down in the form of a triangle. By using his neighbor's ankles for a pillow, each man kept his head out of the mire.

In strange country, the cook would turn the wagon tongue toward the North Star before he went to bed. If the next morning should be cloudy, this pointer might be useful as a compass. All night a pot of coffee was kept hot over the coals for those about to go on guard or just in from guard duty. When a man had to be waked, this was done by speaking to him. No one liked to touch a sleeping man, lest he become so startled by the sudden rousing that involuntarily he would reach for his six-shooter.

Usually the bed ground was near some stream that the herd had just crossed or was about to cross. Most of the streams could be forded unless they were in flood. When a river had to be swum, it sometimes was hard to induce the cattle to enter the water. Unless lead steers were at hand for this task, a man on horseback would enter the stream to show the way. Even then, there might be a delay in putting the herd across. For the chuck wagon, sometimes the men had to build a raft. In other cases, they could lash a pair of cottonwood logs to its sides to make it float. Then the punchers would pull it across with ropes.

Most of the men thrown together on the trail got along well with each other—there wasn't much chance to find other company. Yet occasionally there were shooting scrapes, some of them fatal. Two trail hands encamped in 1870 at Mustang Pens, near the head of the Concho River, got into a fight in which one was killed. Pete Owens died in a gun fight in the Texas cross timbers, after the outfit had stopped at a ranch where liquor was sold. At a trail camp twelve miles north of Caldwell, Kansas, early in June, 1871, a pair of punchers exchanged shots while their boss was in town. One died, and the other fled.

No one knew when tempers might flare—and guns bark. When they were taking their herd across the Bosque River at Clifton in 1871, two cowboys became angry at another outfit's Mexican cook, who had let his oxen run into the tail of their herd. They shot the offender and threw his body into a clump of prickly pear. Two years later, on the night of May 30, 1873, a Texas outfit on the way to Kansas had camped on Elm Fork of the Trinity River, in Cooke County. Those not on guard were sleeping peacefully in their blankets when a Mexican trail hand who had been acting as cook went berserk. Finding an ax, he began chopping off the heads of the sleepers. He had killed four and was attacking a fifth when his intended victim awoke and gave an alarm. The killer escaped in the darkness.[12] To keep trouble down, most drovers banned firewater from their camps.

Bottom hand in the trail outfit was the wrangler. Usually he was a "fryin' size" young fellow just learning to be a cowhand—perhaps a son of the boss. In other cases, he was a "stove-up" oldster who no

12 Dallas *Herald*, June 7, 1873; G. D. Freeman, *Midnight and Noonday*, 132–36.

longer was good for much else. An unusually big drive might have two wranglers. The second, for night duty, was called the night-hawk. But ordinarily an outfit had only one.

The wrangler's job wasn't as easy as it looked. He had to trail the spare horses by day and to see that they didn't wander off at night. Early in the morning he would round up his *remuda* so that the trail riders could pick the mounts they wished to use for the day. If a puncher needed a fresh horse at noon, the wrangler had to bring it for him. In the evening he drove his band to the camp again and let each guard take his night horse.

In the first hours of darkness, while his charges grazed, the wrangler had to use a sharp eye to see that none strayed. He kept them as far as he could from woods or canyons, where a horse might quickly get out of sight. The horses slept fitfully at best and were likely to be wakeful and restless in threatening weather. If a quick inventory showed any horse missing, the wrangler had to ride out in search.

When he wasn't busy with his *remuda*, the wrangler made himself useful in the camp. He roped and dragged in dead branches for the fire or, if no wood were within reach, gathered cow chips or even sunflower stalks. He helped the cook wash the dishes and load and unload the wagon. If he were a youngster, he might have to take some twitting or practical jokes from the punchers—but all in good-natured fun. The older men looked out for him when neces-sary and, when time allowed, taught him the finer points of riding and roping.[13]

Occasionally, when the drive had to wait for a swollen stream to subside or when the cattle were weary and losing too much weight, the boss would let the herd rest for a day or two in the In-dian Territory. Then, while a few of the men watched the cattle as they grazed on forbidden but often lush grass, the others would go out to see what they could find to vary their diet. Most of the streams and buffalo wallows were full of fish. Often there were tur-keys and deer within reach, and ducks and geese in the migration seasons. Blackberries and wild plums were plentiful in the early summer. On a fall drive, the men could gather pecans from the bottom lands.

[13] Ramon F. Adams, "Hoss Wranglers," *Western Horseman*, Vol. XVI, No. 1 (January, 1951), 8–9, 32.

IV

The cook, to whom the fish and game were brought, was a key man in the trail outfit. Usually he was older than the punchers and drew higher pay. In authority he ranked next to the trail boss. Often he was a veteran cowhand who, from some accident, had been disabled for work in the saddle and had learned the art of pots and kettles. A successful drover chose his cook carefully to have one who could keep the men satisfied with good grub.

On the trail, recalled James H. Cook, "a camp cook could do more toward making life pleasant for those about him than any other man in the outfit. A good-natured, hustling cook meant a lot to a trail boss. A cheery voice ringing out at daybreak, shouting, 'Roll out there, fellers, and hear the little birdies sing their praises to God!' or 'Arise and shine and give God the glory!' would make the most crusty waddy grin as he crawled out to partake of his morning meal —even when he was extremely short of sleep."[14]

As a rule, though, the punchers viewed the trail cook as grouchy and cantankerous. "Crossin' a cook is as risky as braidin' a mule's tail," said some. Many a cook gloried in this reputation for crankiness and tried to keep the trail drivers in awe of him. In addition to cooking, he drove the chuck wagon, kept it and the harness in repair, and served as doctor for men and horses. He was custodian of the personal belongings of the trail hands and often stakesholder for bets. Sometimes he would condescend to pull a tooth, trim hair, or sew on a button.

The wagon at which the cook presided was the outcome of an evolutionary process and was a highly functional vehicle. In the earliest cattle drives from Texas, as in the cow hunts of that period, each of the few men involved had carried his own food. He might take it in a saddle bag or in a sack tied behind the cantle of his saddle. As the drives became larger, an outfit might take along a Negro slave or a Mexican to do the cooking. In that event, a pack horse or mule might carry the food. In later years, one that persisted in this method was called a "greasy sack" outfit, and the mule a "long-eared chuck wagon."[15]

As trails became longer and herds larger, the pack mule gave way

14 Cook, *Fifty Years on the Old Frontier*, 39.
15 Ramon F. Adams, *Come an' Get It*.

to the oxcart. But the cart was too clumsy, and the oxen were too slow. More speed was needed to enable the cook to arrive at the camp site early and to have a hot supper ready for the tired men. At the close of the Civil War, cowmen began adapting wagons for trail use. Some of the first ones they called commissaries. In the spring of 1866, Charles Goodnight bought the gear of a government wagon, with axles of iron instead of the usual wood. He had a Parker County woodworker rebuild the wagon of tough, seasoned *bois d'arc* and put a chuck box on the back end. The wagon carried a can of tallow for greasing the axles.[16]

Although Goodnight had this early chuck wagon pulled by six oxen, it soon became the custom to use horses or mules—usually four. Almost any good wagon could be converted for trail use. The drover preferred one with wide tires that gave better traction in rough country. The narrow-tired wagon of the farmer he disdained as a "butcher-knife" wagon. In use, the trail wagon or chuck wagon usually was referred to merely as "the wagon." It had a standard bed, often with extra sideboards, for carrying the men's bedrolls and other equipment. As a rule, it had bows over which a canvas wagon sheet could be tied as a shield against sun and rain.

The chuck box, which Goodnight had had built into his trail wagon in 1866, was several years in coming into common use. "At first we just had kegs for our supplies," said Mark Withers. "Our first mess boxes were goods boxes. We put bacon, coffee, and flour in a box in the middle of the wagon. We had hides stretched under the wagon and put utensils there. We also had a water barrel with the spout out in front of the wagon. Later we turned it so the spout was out on one side. I liked the barrel spout out in front better because it didn't get broken as often."[17]

"The outfit of a Texas drover is a scientific fit," noted one who saw the wagons being loaded in front of the grocery stores at Matagorda early in 1874. "There seldom is a cover to the wagon—it's too much trouble. The whole is exposed to public gaze. There are kegs of molasses, jugs of vinegar, boxes of bacon, sugar, and a variety of other provisions. Some things are strapped to the sides in a helter-skelter but perfectly secure manner. Sometimes bundles of kindling are tied to the hind axle."[18]

[16] Haley, *Charles Goodnight, Cowman and Plainsman*, 121–22.

The chuck box, the most distinctive feature of the later wagon, was built into the back end. This was a closed cupboard with partitions, shelves, and drawers for food and utensils. Its rear end sloped outward from top to bottom, like the front of an antique writing desk. The piece across the sloping end was hinged at the bottom so that the cook could lower it to a horizontal position. This allowed it to serve as a kitchen table in front of the cabinet. The cabinet door was held in this position by ropes or chains or, more often, by a prop resting on the ground.

The chuck box held cutlery or "eatin' irons," a five-gallon keg or jar of sourdough, a sack of flour, cans of coffee, a supply of salt, and a variety of other foods and condiments. These might include beans, salt pork, dried fruits, canned tomatoes, a few onions and potatoes, sugar, molasses, pepper, and lard. One drawer might contain a few simple remedies, such as liniment, quinine, and some kind of laxative. There might be a bottle of whisky for snake bite. If so, it would be the only intoxicant allowed with the outfit.

Some wagons had beneath the chuck box a smaller box for the heavier utensils, such as skillets, pots, and Dutch ovens. A water barrel, usually with a wooden spigot, was fastened on one side of the wagon. Balancing it on the other side was a tool box containing branding irons, horseshoeing equipment, an ax, and a shovel. Usually the wagon carried grain for its harness horses or mules. The cow ponies had to get along on grass.

Stretched under the bottom of most wagons was a rawhide hammock into which the wrangler put spare wood for fuel. Where there was no wood at hand, it carried buffalo chips or cow chips, which the punchers called prairie coal. The men called this hammock the cooney, from the Spanish *cuna*, or cradle. Some called it the 'possum belly. Occasionally, when not needed for storing fuel, it was put to other use. "It was a splendid place," said G. E. Lemmon, for a small person to crawl into on a stormy night when all hands were not required with the herd—which was seldom. I have many times crawled into the cooney and come out dry and warm the next morning."[19]

17 Withers, reminiscences, MS.

18 Denison *Daily News*, February 26, 1874, quoting the *Colorado Tribune* of Matagorda, Texas.

19 G. E. Lemmon, reminiscences (MS, J. Frank Dobie, Austin, Texas).

The cook, wakened by his alarm clock ahead of the others, tried to have meals ready on time. If, in a big outfit, he needed help, he called on the wrangler. Besides bringing in fuel, the wrangler could grind the coffee, help with the dishes, and keep the water barrel filled. Sometimes it was hard to find clear water for drinking and for use at the chuck wagon. "Our cook had to make bread with red-looking water," Tom Oatts noted in his diary. "He said it made the flour look like shorts."

When breakfast was ready, the cook yelled, "Roll out! Come an' get it! Come a-runnin'!" Or a more imaginative one might call out:

> *Bacon in the pan,*
> *Coffee in the pot!*
> *Get up an' get it—*
> *Get it while it's hot!*

The trail afforded less variety in fare than did the ranch. Pancakes were out of the question in a big trail outfit, since eggs were "as scarce as sunflowers on a Christmas tree." The cook might serve eggs and fresh vegetables, though, on those rare occasions when the men could swap a calf or a shoulder of beef to some nester.

Always there was hot coffee—hot and strong. "I have yet to see a cowboy who isn't a coffee drinker," observed Bill Poage, who went up the trail in 1874. The cook put plenty of Arbuckle's in the pot and boiled it for half an hour. Some called it six-shooter coffee. It was so strong, they said, that it would float a pistol. Almost always the punchers took it without sugar and without any of the evaporated milk that the cook might have in a can.

The breakfast that the coffee washed down might include bacon or salt pork, sourdough biscuits, and some sort of dried fruit such as prunes, raisins, or apples. The sourdough biscuits came with almost every meal. They were the main test of a cook's ability. Heavy or doughy "sinkers" might give the cook a reputation as a "belly cheater." Light, fluffy ones would draw appreciative murmurs and calls for more.

The cook made the sourdoughs without yeast. At the start of the drive, he mixed batter in a keg or jar and let it ferment a day or two. Then, each day, he took out some of the batter, added soda and lard, and worked it into dough. When he did this, he put into the jar more flour, salt, and water. Thus the fermenting continued all through the drive. The cook baked the biscuits in a Dutch oven set over coals and with other coals piled on its lid. Some trail hands boasted that their cook made sourdoughs so light that, unless he mixed in blueberries or raisins, the mosquitoes and gnats would carry them off.

The noon meal, although called dinner, usually was light. Its preparation and content depended largely on the time the cook had after reaching nooning site. Supper was the big meal for the meat-eating cowboys. There always was plenty of beef. Whenever the supply in the wagon ran low, the men could easily kill another steer or heifer. Often they would rope a stray from some other herd and thus avoid killing a steer of their own. If not, they picked a young one with poor markings or one that had been giving trouble on the trail. They did the killing at some distance from the herd, since the smell of blood excited the Longhorns. The butchers hung the meat overnight to cool, then wrapped it in slickers and placed it in the wagon.

For a day or two after each killing, the trail hands would feast on son-of-a-gun stew. It had everything in it, some said, except the horns, hide, and hoofs. It was a mixture of tongue, liver, heart, and other small parts that needed to be cooked promptly where there was no refrigeration. Its distinctive flavor came from a marrow-like substance from the tube linking the two stomachs of the cud-chewing animal. Although some cooks made the stew in water, others used only the juices of the meat. They made it from beef alone, except for salt and pepper and, in some cases, an onion or a pinch of chili powder.

With the stew out of the way, the men settled down to roasts and steaks, especially the latter. The cook cut the steaks in generous slabs, covered them with flour, and cooked them in sizzling suet in his Dutch oven. Just before they were done, he added salt. With the roasts he often served potatoes and onions. When preparing dried beans, he soaked them overnight, then cooked them over a slow fire, with pieces of dry salt pork for seasoning. Most cowmen liked the beans, which some called Pecos strawberries. Occasionally a wagon carried a keg of mixed pickles.

Canned tomatoes, often used between meals to quench thirst,

sometimes appeared as a dessert. Another dessert was "boggy top" —stewed fruit with biscuit pastry covering. A more common one was molasses, called lick, which the trail men sopped up with their sourdough biscuits. On rare occasions the cook baked pies, usually with raisins or dried apples.[20]

Dennis Collins told of the time when he and a fellow puncher, out with a mixed herd, had a hankering for custard pie. The cook, who had some turkey eggs that had been found the day before, told the cowboys they would have to get the milk. "Bill and I chose a cow that seemed to have more milk than her calf required. Bill roped her, threw her, and hog-tied her. I held her down while he was endeavoring to separate her from her milk. With much labor and some protests against her restlessness, he extracted about a pint. I proudly gave it to the cook, but he informed me that it was not enough for a pie. It took wrangling with two more of those restless creatures to persuade them to favor us with some of their milk, but we succeeded."[21]

Although the trail hand, "hungry enough to eat a saddle blanket," was not choosy about his food, sometimes he found the fare monotonous and complained in song:

> Oh, it's bacon and beans 'most every day—
> I'd as soon be eatin' prairie hay.

At meals on the trail, the men, often leaving their hats on, helped themselves to food and coffee. Then, with legs crossed, they sat on the prairie and ate their fill. When through, they dropped their tin plates, cups, and cutlery in the dishpan or tub, the "wreck pan." If they didn't like the food, they seldom dared complain within hearing of the cook. But, after a hard day in the saddle, almost any grub was likely to taste good. Most of the trail men preferred the rough cow-camp fare to the fancier food of town restaurants. The "wasp-nest" bread of the cafes they rated a poor substitute for fluffy sourdough biscuits.

[20] Tom C. Oatts, diary (MS, Mrs. W. K. Oatts, Austin, Texas); Adams, *Come an' Get It*; Ramon F. Adams, *Cowboy Lingo*, 147–53.
[21] Dennis Collins, *The Indians' Last Fight; or the Dull Knife Raid*, 133–34.

VIII

HAZARDS OF THE LONG DRIVE

Only a small part of what happened on the Chisholm Trail could be set down as rollicking adventure. Hilarity had to wait until after the Longhorns were sold and delivered. The trailing itself was tiring work that brought frequent risk of life and limb. Never was danger far away. Texans who went up the trail in the spring of 1870 found on the bank of the North Canadian a fresh grave. The headboard said simply, "Killed by Indians." The years brought more such sobering reminders of the perils of the trail. The graves were especially common at river crossings

Even the everyday riding with the herd had its hazards. No trail hand knew when a big rattler, unseen in the dust or grass, might strike his horse's leg. The cowboy himself, when he went to sleep on the prairie, couldn't be sure that he wouldn't awake with a rattler cuddled beside him for warmth and ready to strike if startled by a sudden movement. On dark nights, when a rider "couldn't find his nose with both hands," the night horse might step in a prairie-dog hole, stumble, and fall.

Occasionally disease waylaid the cowhands, who, hardy as they were, could become run down from overwork and lack of enough sleep. Seldom was a doctor within reach. In 1869, cholera, which was making heavy inroads among the Indians in southern Kansas, hit some of the trail drivers. Two Texans died, while others were nursed back to health by friendly Indians.

Storms also took their toll. In 1868, lightning struck a trail camp north of Dallas, killing one man and burning three—one of them so badly that he had to quit. Two years later Ran Spencer and another trail hand, taking refuge under a tree during a thunderstorm, died from a single lightning bolt. In 1871, just south of the Red River, lightning killed a man in another outfit.

Sometimes a spring blizzard took the drovers by surprise. In April, 1874, on Hell Roaring Creek, in the Indian Territory, two outfits had their entire *remudas* frozen to death in a night of wind-driven snow and sleet. That of which Sol West was trail boss lost seventy-eight horses. In hailstorms the stones occasionally were so big and struck with such force that they killed many of the cattle. In such a storm the cowhand had to take off his saddle and get his head and shoulders under it for protection.

Even the wind alone could leave wreckage. In one camp a cyclone turned over the chuck wagon and carried off a tent that was not recovered. Cloudbursts were more frequent and sometimes did almost as much damage. One near Abilene in 1869 washed away wagons and drowned several cowmen and many head of stock. Prairie fires, started by lightning, malicious Indians, or a cook's carelessly left coals, often made detours necessary on the trail but seldom took the lives of men or cattle.

After the herds reached Kansas, some of the drovers had trouble with the farmers. "Kansans didn't like the Texas herds," said Mark Withers, of Lockhart, a veteran of many drives. "They kept pushing the cattle drivers west all the time."[1]

Bill Poage, after going up the trail in 1874, voiced a similar complaint. "There scarcely was a day when we didn't have a row with some settler," he recalled. "The boys took delight in doing everything they could to provoke the settlers. The settlers paid us back, with interest, by harassing us in every way they could think of. The boss was arrested twice in one day for trespassing. A settler would

[1] W. D. Hornaday in San Antonio *Express*, August 7, 1910; Withers, reminiscences, MS.

plow a furrow around his claim. According to the laws of Kansas, this was a fence. Any loose stock that crossed it was trespassing, and the owner was liable for damages."

As the Kansas farmers often had skimpy crops, many tried to eke out their income by collecting damages from the Texas drovers. Most of the claims, though, were settled out of court—for sums ranging from fifty cents to a hundred dollars.[2] Yet, much as the nesters disliked the Longhorns, some on the open prairie were glad to have a herd bed in a pasture or vacant field. That would leave them cow chips to use as fuel the next winter.

White rustlers, although less common on the Chisholm Trail than on the more remote ranges of western Texas, made trouble for some of the drovers. On both sides of the Red River, they sometimes stampeded herds and drove off part of the Longhorns to some fastness in the hills. If caught with stolen stock, they would say they had gathered the cattle after a stampede and were holding them until the owners came after them.

Below the Red River, the Texas Rangers were a potent force in running down cattle thieves. In the Indian Territory, the trail outfits had to depend mainly on their own resources, although soldiers were stationed at a few posts. Sometimes, by combining forces, the drovers could give effective battle to rustlers. In Kansas, they might be able to get help from an officer or posse in a near-by town. Early in 1870, a cowman galloped into Marion for aid in recovering sixty cattle taken from him by an outlaw band headed by a Texas desperado, William (Hurricane Bill) Martin. A posse quickly struck the trail, routed the thieves, and recovered the stock.[3]

Occasionally trouble came from a bogus cattle inspector who demanded a fee, or even from some frontier law officer who wasn't above a bit of blackmail. Most drovers didn't mind having their herds inspected at the start of the drive or before crossing the Red River, but they resented meddling elsewhere. Early in 1876, when Eaton Cranfill was trailing cattle through Bell County, in central Texas, the sheriff met him at Belton and demanded an inspection fee. Cranfill showed his receipt for a fee paid in Bastrop County and refused to make a second payment that no law required. Finally he offered

2 Poage, "Drive to Cheyenne in 1874," MS.
3 Junction City *Weekly Union*, February 26, 1870.

to give the sheriff a beef in place of cash, and the officer agreed. At that, Cranfill's son Jim roped a monstrous steer and tied him to a tree for the sheriff. But he purposely used a weak rope and cut two of its strands with his pocket knife when the officer wasn't looking. The outfit barely had crossed the Leon River and shaken off the dust of Belton when the big steer was back in the herd, waving a piece of broken rope from his horns.[4]

II

All through the Indian Territory, redskin raiders and beggars were an almost constant plague. Some drovers encountered a few in Texas and Kansas, too; but they were most common between the Red River and the Cimarron. A band of warriors would come during the day to beg for beeves and to look over the outfit. If they thought the situation favorable, they would come back at night and try to stampede the herd. They wanted most the horses; but sometimes they would take the cattle, too. In Kansas in 1870, Cheyennes stampeded and drove off R. R. Savage's whole herd, valued at eighteen thousand dollars.

Most of the encounters were less costly. Addison J. Day, trailing a herd through the Indian Territory, ran into a band of between three and four hundred Osage warriors. "They made us give them about ten beeves," Day recalled. "There were three or four herds going through; but, in all, the cowboy force of these herds did not exceed fifty men. We were too weak to hold the herds and fight a force which so greatly outnumbered ours. Under the circumstances, it was better to compromise on a few beeves."

Another Texas drover, W. S. Mussett, had a worse experience. At Comanche Springs, on the Lost Fork of the Red River, he found what looked like two thousand Indians in war paint. After some argument, he gave them ten beeves. But this did not satisfy the redskins. That night they stampeded the herd and drove off 250 head.[5]

In 1869, when L. D., Dan, and George Taylor and Monte Harrell were trailing a thousand steers from Gonzales County to Abilene, they had several brushes with Indians. The first visitors wanted tobacco and took no cattle. But a few days later four hundred Co-

[4] J. B. Cranfill, *Dr. J. B. Cranfill's Chronicle*, 151–52.
[5] Galveston *News*, April 2, 1911.

manches, who were out on the warpath, blocked the outfit. The Texans, greatly outnumbered, were powerless to help themselves. Every time they would try to start the herd, the Indians would surround and hold it.

The Comanches' horsemanship impressed the cowmen. The young warriors on bareback ponies would ride all over the horses' backs—off on one side, standing up, lying down—going at full speed, recalled L. D. Taylor. As they rode, they shot arrows clear through the steers. In a few minutes they killed twenty-five of the beeves. The Indians skinned the animals on the spot and ate the flesh raw, reminding the Texans of hungry dogs. Finally the raiders allowed the outfit to move on, and the punchers were not slow in departing.

In the same season, two brothers, Dudley H. and John W. Snyder, who took up a herd from Llano County, had Indian trouble in the Territory. The bronze rustlers drove off 140 of the beeves.[6]

As the Army imposed stronger control over the Indians, attacks on the herds became fewer. The braves continued to visit the trail camps, but mainly to beg for a beef or two. Sometimes, unless they were hungry, they could be sent off with a few bright bandanas or silk Mexican sashes. If they had to be given a steer, it usually was a lame or troublesome one from the drag or a stray that had wandered in from another herd.

Yet even the most innocent-looking of the visitors needed watching. Otherwise, some of the best horses might disappear when no one was looking. "We had just about as much to fear from the friendly Indians as from the wild ones," said Bill Poage. "The wild ones would stampede our horses and try to get away with them. The friendly ones would run them off at night and come back the next day to get a reward for returning them."[7]

On one drive the foreman of a herd belonging to R. R. Savage was met by an old Indian who had handed him a note signed by a prominent drover, Ike T. Pryor. "This man is a good Indian," it said. "Treat him well. If you will give him a beef, you will have no trouble driving through his country." So the foreman promptly gave the beggar a steer—one of the Pryor brand that had been picked up along the way.

[6] Hunter, *The Trail Drivers of Texas*, 500, 501, 1030.
[7] Poage, "Drive to Cheyenne in 1874," MS.

On another occasion, old Big Bow, a Kiowa chief, appeared, with his three wives, at the trail camp of a Texas outfit and stayed on to dine. The boss, Ben Juvenall, gave the chief some tobacco but didn't invite him to eat until all members of the outfit were through. Then the Kiowas devoured with great relish everything the cook offered them—cold meat, cold rice, and other leavings.

After they had done away with the last bit, Big Bow said he had a lot of starving papooses in his camp. He asked for a wohaw—a beef —to feed them. Juvenall gave him a broken-down yearling. The chief objected. It was so poor, he said, it would make an Indian sick. But the boss insisted that he must take this or nothing. As the herd started off, the Texans saw Big Bow seated in the shade, getting ready for a leisurely smoke, while his three better halves were busy with butcher knives on the scrawny yearling.[8]

Often a bit of bluffing could trim the demands of the Indians. Once two chiefs, followed by about thirty warriors, rode up to H. H. Halsell, who was riding at the tail of his herd. One of the chiefs announced in Spanish, "Cattle eat my grass. I want thirty beeves." Halsell, who had fifteen good fighters in his outfit, replied that the Indians could have one beef but only one.

The chief, seeing the trail hands fingering their six-shooters, said *Esta bueno.*

"We cut out a cow," said Halsell, "and the chiefs chased her off about two hundred yards and killed her. The last I saw of that drove of Indians, they were flocking around that slaughtered cow like a flock of buzzards."[9]

Another trail boss, whose story has been told by Edward Everett Dale, was called on by a Kiowa chief who demanded six beeves. "I'll give you two but not six," the foreman replied.

"Two not enough," said the old Kiowa. "You give me six or I'll come with my young braves tonight and stampede your cattle."

"Well," answered the boss, "when you come tonight, be sure to bring a spade."

"Why spade?" asked the chief.

"Well," the foreman replied, "the cook broke the handle of our spade yesterday. When you come to stampede the cattle, I aim to kill you. Unless you bring a spade, we can't bury you."

[8] *Ibid.;* Dallas *Morning News,* July 20, 1941.

At that, the chief decided that two beeves would do.[10]

The Indians, who had been promised the full use of their reservations, felt justified in exacting a toll for the passage of trail herds across their lands. They wanted payment, too, for those herds that were grazed for several months in the more northern reservations to restore their flesh or to await higher prices. As the alien cattle made inroads on the grass, the Indians regarded them as a taxable nuisance.

In the period when the Shawnee Trail was dominant, some of the tribes had tried to impose a fixed tax for the passage of trail herds but had been unable to collect it regularly. The escaping of such tolls was one argument that Joseph G. McCoy had used in persuading Texas drovers to shift to the new Chisholm Trail. With some Texas cattle still being trailed to Baxter Springs and some being grazed on their ranges, the Cherokees took action. On December 16, 1867, the Cherokee National Council imposed a toll of ten cents a head on all cattle trailed across tribal land.

Other tribes took similar steps later. The Council of the Creek Nation voted a specific tax on March 6, 1871. It charged 27½ cents a head for those passing through and 25 cents a head per month for cattle grazed.[11] One effect of these new levies was to dry up the use of the old Shawnee route in favor of the Chisholm Trail.

III

Often worse than Indian raiders, as a cause of cattle losses on the trail, were treacherous stream crossings. Spring and fall drives tended to coincide with flood seasons. When Shanghai Pierce arrived in Kansas with 2,500 Longhorns, his steers had done so much swimming that he referred to them as sea lions.

Even when high water did not cause delays or drownings, quicksand often took a toll. After a flood, porous sandbars appeared at places that earlier had afforded solid footing. They caught and sucked down cattle and horses. Many disappeared, never to be seen again by the owners. In 1869, quicksand caused one outfit to follow a river twenty-five miles upstream to find a place safe for crossing.

9 Halsell, *Cowboys and Cattleland*, 113–15.
10 Edward Everett Dale, *Cow Country*, 57–58.
11 Floyd Benjamin Streeter, *Prairie Trails and Cow Towns*, 74–76.

In the spring of 1872, Major George W. Littlefield's men, while crossing the Red River, lost a horse in the quicksand. Soon after it was caught, it sank out of sight.[12]

Putting a herd of Longhorns across a wide or booming river was perilous to both cattle and horsemen. The job called for judgment, courage, and quick thinking. When a cowman wanted to pay a high compliment to one of his fellows, he called him "a man to ride the river with."

Overflows converted many an ordinarily tame stream into what the cowboy called "big swimming." The boss had to pick a place where there was solid footing on each side and an hour when the cattle would not head into the glare of a low sun. Often it was hard to start the first steers into the water, especially if the crossing looked difficult. Sometimes the men crossed the whole herd as a unit. In other cases, they divided the cattle into bunches of twenty-five or thirty. A cowboy might have to swim his horse ahead to show the way. Other punchers looked after the flanks and the rear, as on the prairie. The hands tried to keep the herd or bunch compact. If they allowed a gap to appear, they might have to make a new start into the stream.

As they swam across, the cattle made a strange and impressive sight. The bulky bodies of the steers remained under the water and unseen. The cowmen could make out only the heads, with bulging eyes, flaring nostrils, and widespread horns. One drover said they looked "like a thousand rocking chairs floating on the water."

When something went wrong in midstream, the picture was different. Startled by a floating tree, a whirlpool, or some unusual sound, the cattle might start milling in a circle in the middle of the river. Unless the punchers could break up this churning mass quickly, many of the animals would be swept downstream and drowned. In putting 4,500 Longhorns across the swollen North Canadian in 1869, Bill Montgomery's outfit had trouble from milling. They lost 116 cattle and 3 horses.

In breaking up a mill of cattle in a river, the cowhands had to work fast. Riding into the tangled mass, at heavy risk to themselves and their mounts, they struck the excited beasts, yelled at them, and tried to head them for the north bank.

[12] J. Evetts Haley, *George W. Littlefield, Texan*, 56–57.

Sometimes a cowboy was unhorsed in the melee and had to watch out for beating hoofs and sharp, tossing horns. He might be able to grab hold of the tail of a horse or a big steer and thus be pulled to the bank. Otherwise he would have to swim—no easy task if he had on his heavy leather boots.

Mosquitoes were a nuisance at many of the crossings. Worse, in some cases, were swarms of hornets that, from their nests in the bushes or cottonwoods along the banks, dropped upon the cattle and horses. Even as the lead steers climbed up on dry ground, the men could not yet begin to relax. A jackrabbit leaping suddenly from the grass might so startle the Longhorns that they would turn back and mill in midstream.

Milling herds were the cause of most of the cowboy drownings. They also gave occasion at times for heroic rescues. While Texas cowmen were getting a herd across the Arkansas River near Wichita in June, 1872, a trail hand's horse went down with its rider and accidentally kicked him as he was struggling in the water near by. The Texan went under, came up, and sank a second time. Then a man who happened to be standing on the shore and watching the cattle cross jerked off his hat and coat and plunged into the turbulent stream. Swimming out to the unlucky cowboy, he grabbed him and, after a desperate effort, brought him to the bank in time for his friends to revive him.[13]

In northern Texas a few years later, a herd was delayed for three days by a freshet in the East Fork of the Trinity at Milwood, in Collin County. When the cook's helper rode a mule into the stream after a yearling, he lost his seat and sank into the swirling water, never to rise. After the flood had subsided, the punchers found the body suspended from a tree, in a fork of which a foot had been caught.[14]

IV

Of all the dangers of the trail, the most dreaded was the stampede— or stompede, as the trail hand was likely to call it. Most often it came at night, when fast riding was hazardous. Sometimes blinding rain was a further handicap in getting the panicky steers under control.

[13] Wichita *Eagle*, June 14, 1872.
[14] Dallas *Morning News*, August 9, 1925.

The stampede brought every man in the outfit into instant action. As the cowboy song put it,

> Popped my foot in the stirrup and gave a little yell;
> The tail cattle broke, and the leaders went to hell.

Anything that startled one or more of the Longhorns could panic the whole herd into one of these wild rushes. Sometimes it was the mere crackling of a dead stick or the striking of a match. It might be the sneeze of a night herder, the snort of a horse, the firing of a gun, or the sudden howl of a wolf, a coyote, or a dog. Even a strange smell could set the steers off on a rampage. One herd stampeded after scenting a panther that was after fresh beef hanging near the chuck wagon. Other Longhorns rushed off after Indian marauders burned a sack of buffalo hair on the windward side of the herd.

The sudden flight of a flock of quail or prairie chickens from the path of the herd might frighten the cattle. Once a flock of plover set off Bill Pierce's herd of 2,500 Longhorns, causing them to run fifteen miles. "The cows were all bedded down, and we had just rolled up for the night," recalled Monroe Walters. "It was about nine o'clock when a large flock of plover settled down to roost on the ground where the cattle were. Man, they were off! That was one night we didn't get any shut-eye."[15]

An injury to the eye of a steer could start a stampede in a twinkling. Hit in the eye by a hailstone, a steer might spring to his feet, trample the tails of his neighbors, and set off the whole herd. On one occasion, four thousand cattle stampeded after one of them had a shred or two of a cowboy's tobacco blown into his eyes.

Sometimes a single steer was more nervous or obstreperous than the others and would start repeated stampedes. When the trail boss detected such a trouble-maker, he would trade off or butcher the offender. In one such instance, John S. Chisum, after a series of stampedes, looked his steers over carefully in the light of a full moon. Finally he spotted a lanky, one-eyed paint steer that was starting the commotion. After he had this animal cut out from the herd, driven down to the river, and shot, there were no more stampedes.

William Hoover, while trailing a herd to Kansas in the fall of

---

[15] Waco *Tribune-Herald*, October 30, 1949.

1869, had a similar experience. One of his punchers, Albert Branshaw, was on guard on a bitterly cold night in partly timbered country. To keep from freezing, he was walking and leading his horse. Branshaw noticed that all the cattle except one big white steer were lying down. "While I was looking at him," he said, "this steer leaped into the air, hit the ground with his nose with a heavy thud, and gave a grunt that sounded like that of a hog. That was the signal. The whole herd was up and going—and heading right for me. My horse gave a lunge, jerked loose from me, and was away. I barely had time to climb into an oak. The cattle went by like a hurricane, hitting the tree with their horns. It took us all night to round them up. When we got them quieted the next morning, we found ourselves six miles from camp." Branshaw reported the antics of the white steer to his boss. The next day Hoover swapped the troublemaker to a Choctaw Indian for two yearlings. After that, he had no more stampedes.[16]

Often a stampede started during an electrical storm. The rumble of thunder in the distance made the cattle restless and alerted the trail hands. As the storm approached, balls of phosphorescent light popped out on the tips of the curved horns. Set off in the blackness of the night, this fox fire gave the herd a ghostly and foreboding appearance. As the horsemen on night guard crooned to try to quiet the Longhorns, some of the more nervous cattle began to rise from the bed ground.

Then, as a blinding flash near by brought a frightening thunderclap, the whole herd was up and off in an instant. The terrified beasts shook the ground with the rumble of their pounding hoofs. Clashing horns popped and rattled, and the striking hoofs became a roar heard above the sound of the storm. The stampeding Longhorns generated a terrific heat. "The faces of the men riding on the leeward side of the herd would be almost blistered, as if they had been struck by a blast from a furnace," said Charles Goodnight. The odor given off by the clashing horns and hoofs, he added, was almost overpowering.[17]

Any wagon in the way of the stampeding Longhorns might be smashed to bits. One trail hand, waving a blanket from a chuck

---

[16] Dallas *Morning News*, June 22, 1924.
[17] *Prose and Poetry of the Live Stock Industry of the United States*, 534.

wagon, turned the rushing brutes away. Sometimes the crazed animals tore down a tree whose trunk was as big as a man, leaving only a shredded stump. Often the herd rushed off in a compact mass; in other cases, it divided into bunches that headed in different directions.

The trail hands not already on duty mounted quickly and took after the cattle. Their first aim was not to head them off or to stop them but to bring them back under control and to save them from plunging off some cliff. Riding alongside the leaders, the horsemen usually tried to turn them into a circle and thus put the herd into a mill. They dared not let the circling mass become too solid, lest the cattle in the center be trampled or suffocated. After running around in a circle for a time, the cattle would become weary and gradually would lose their fright.

Milling the cattle, though, was not without its drawback. "The jamming together was damaging," observed G. E. Lemmon. "The steers could work off more pounds in a twenty-minute mill than in a mile-and-a-half run." With a beef herd, some drovers used the mill only as a last resort in checking a stampede. When they did mill the cattle, they kept this up no longer than seemed necessary.[18] No matter how a stampede ended, the herd had to be watched closely for the next few hours. Herds were known to stampede as many as eighteen times in a single night.

Getting the runaway herd back in hand usually left the men dog tired and short of sleep. A minor stampede might carry the cattle only a few miles from their bed ground. A bad one might last for a week and—in extreme cases—take the cattle hundreds of miles, perhaps winding up near the starting point.

A trail hand trying to check a stampede needed a quick wit, a dependable mount, and more than an ordinary share of luck. The roar of horns and hoofs warned him not to get in front of the crazed cattle. Usually the stampeding Longhorns would try to split and go around a horse or a fallen rider. For a fellow who was unhorsed in front of a rushing herd, Mark Reeves had a bit of advice. All the fallen puncher needed to do, said Reeves, was to bend over, facing the oncoming cattle, hold his hat between his teeth, and shake his

[18] Lemmon, reminiscences, MS.

136

coattails over his back. But most cowboys were less than eager to test this advice, especially at night.

Uel Livingston of Hamilton County, who went up the trail with a herd in the late sixties, owed his life to a faithful mount. While on guard one night, he became so drowsy that he couldn't stay in his saddle. With the cattle quiet, he decided to risk a nap and lay down on the prairie. Later he awoke suddenly, with the earth shaking beneath him and stampeding Longhorns rushing past on both sides. His horse was standing over him to protect him from the trampling hoofs.[19]

One of the worst losses of cattle from a stampede came in central Texas in 1876. Preparing for a big fall drive, the Wilson brothers of Kansas City had bought more than fifteen thousand Longhorns in several counties and were heading them for Comanche Springs, in McLennan County. After fording the Leon River, they camped for the night of July 4 near the South Bosque. They expected to cross the Brazos River at Towash the next day. That afternoon the threat of an electrical storm had made the cattle nervous. But at night, bedded down under the stars, they were quiet and seemed contented. Then, at about ten o'clock, they suddenly rose and rushed off with a great clattering of horns. The punchers, with their six-guns, shot at one side of the leaders to try to turn the herd into a mill. This time they didn't succeed. The maddened brutes rushed over the brink of a ravine, thirty yards wide. Soon the bellowing, dying steers —2,700 of them—filled the ravine. Later the men recovered the horns and hides, but for many years those who lived near by knew the site of this tragedy as Stampede Gully[20]

James H. Cook, with a Texas herd that had crossed the Kansas line, had a hair-raising experience during a stampede. The cattle ran into rough ground and headed for a sharp bend of a creek, where the banks were steep and high.

A sudden flash of lightning, Cook recalled, lighted the surroundings. "My companion and his horse seemed poised in mid-air for a moment, far out over the edge of a high bank of the creek. Several

[19] John Rossel, "The Chisholm Trail" (Master's thesis, University of Wichita, 1931), 103; Malissa C. Everett, "A Pioneer Woman," *West Texas Historical Association Year Book*, Vol. III (June, 1927), 68.
[20] Cranfill, *Dr. J. B. Cranfill's Chronicle*, 154–58.

cattle were following him to certain death. My horse needed no tug at the reins to stop his headlong rush. He braced his forefeet into the earth suddenly and firmly enough to bring him to a sudden halt, not more than five or six feet from the edge of the bluff over which my companion had just disappeared. How it happened that the cattle following did not crash against my horse and send us both over the bank, I shall never know. An instant of blinding light, and then intense and inky darkness reigned again."

A search showed that Cook's friend had been crushed to death under his horse and that a dozen cattle had been killed.[21]

Robert T. Hill, while riding after part of a stampeding herd on the Cimarron, had a similar ordeal. He and another trail hand were chasing at night a small bunch of cattle that had left the main herd of 2,500. They had almost caught up with the racing Longhorns when lightning crashed so near that it stunned them.

"My horse stopped dead in his tracks, almost throwing me over the saddle horn," said Hill. "The lightning showed that he was planted hardly a foot from the edge of a steep-cliffed chasm. A little off to one side, the horse of John Gifford, the other rider, was sinking on his knees, John himself slumping limp in his saddle. Just beyond him lay old Buck, the mighty lead steer, killed by the bolt of lightning that had knocked Gifford unconscious. The rest of our bunch of cattle were down under the cliff, some of them dead."[22]

Loss of cattle from tumbling over a cliff was exceptional, but some of the terrified Longhorns might run so fast and so far that the owners couldn't recover them. Or they might be driven off by Indians or white rustlers or might be lost by mingling with a vast herd of buffaloes. More often they would mix with some other cattle herd on the trail. In such a case, recovery usually was possible; but this caused delay and entailed laborious cutting of the aliens from the herd they had joined.

Following a serious stampede, as after the crossing of a swollen river, the trail outfit that had no casualty was lucky. There was no one at hand to set a broken leg, though in some instances an injured man could be taken to an Army post or to a town that had a doctor.

[21] Cook, *Fifty Years on the Old Frontier*, 106–107.
[22] Robert T. Hill, "Cowboy Days on the Old Trail in Texas," *Semi-Weekly Farm News*, June 26, 1931. Hill became a noted geologist. He spent his last years in Dallas, where he died in 1941.

There was no one to conduct funeral rites for the cowpuncher who was drowned or crushed to death. Usually the trail hands wrapped the body in a blanket and, without ceremony, laid it in a shallow grave. Heavy boulders, if any were within reach, were placed on top to keep out coyotes. Some of the graves beside the trail had crude wooden headpieces, but most of them had no marker to tell what ill-fated cowboy had reached the end of his trail on the lone prairie.

IX

BELLOWING HERDS

Northward, in an almost endless stream, came the herds. By the spring of 1870, Texas cowmen had no more doubts about the Chisholm Trail. Nearly all of them were infected with the Kansas fever. They were out gathering and road-branding twice as many Longhorns as they had sent up in 1869. The unfenced ranges still teemed with rough cattle. Yet, although they were cheap in Texas, there was good prospect for selling them at high prices in northern markets. A mature steer that cost $11 in Texas might bring $31.50 in St. Louis or Chicago, $55 in New York.

In northern Texas, bawling herds on the Chisholm Trail were giving a boom to the village of Fort Worth. Although younger and much smaller than Dallas, on the Shawnee Trail 33½ miles to the east, Fort Worth was forging ahead as an outfitting and provisioning point for drovers. It had a courthouse, a school, a livery stable, a blacksmith shop, a bank, and a few stores and saloons. Along with other drovers, William G. Butler stopped at Daggett and Hatcher's store to stock up on supplies for his trail outfit. Among the items he bought were flour, bacon, beans, dried fruit, and coffee.

Many of the outfits had loaded at least part of their supplies at San Antonio or some other place farther down the trail. It took a big outlay to keep the men well fed and the horses equipped and shod for the long trip. Two brothers, Dudley H. and John W. Snyder, from Brushy Creek, near Round Rock, jotted down many of their expenses as they took five thousand Longhorns up the trail that spring. Their notebook recorded such items as 525 pounds of bacon, $83; thirty pounds of lard, $4.80; lard stand, $1.75; corn, $25. Other entries were for flour, sugar, coffee, salt, matches, and blankets. There were several payments for the shoeing of horses and one of $15 for the recording of brands.[1]

A battered notebook of James M. Daugherty, the young drover who had been tied to a tree and whipped in southeastern Kansas in 1866, had similar entries. They were for a beef drive he made in partnership with A. Adams in 1870. Besides those for food, the payments included $7.50 for a wagon sheet, $4.00 for a branding iron, $1.20 for a teakettle, $1.40 for a skillet, $1.80 for three canteens, $1.00 for two butcher knives, and $1.50 for a bottle of whisky. A bridle cost $1.00 to $2.00, and a pair of spurs 85 cents to $1.25. Six dollars went for the ferry charge at the Red River. Blankets, articles of clothing, and tobacco were advanced to some of the hands and charged against their wages.[2]

With so many herds on the trail, it became harder to keep all of them separated. Not only did some of the herds become mixed at river crossings and in stampedes, but many of them were joined by cattle from the ranges through which they passed. One cowman complained that three hundred of his cattle had been absorbed by passing trail herds in 1869. This situation made it necessary to impose a closer check on the herds to see that the drovers did not, intentionally or by accident, take off with their herds cattle that did not belong to them.

Toward this end, Texas officials established the office of hide and cattle inspector. An inspector for Travis County was appointed in Austin early in 1870. He made copies of recorded brands, checked passing herds, and did what he could to keep out—or take out—of

---

[1] Dudley H. and John W. Snyder, cattle book (MS, University of Texas Library).
[2] James M. Daugherty, notebook (MS, University of Texas Library).

the trail herds cattle that didn't belong in them. After several local cattle dealers had made threats against him, he filed a complaint against two of them and won his case in court.

In June the legislature authorized the governor to appoint such inspectors in all counties that needed them. As this post carried no salary, it often was held by the sheriff or some other county officer, in addition to his other duties.[3]

At the Kansas end of the trail, Abilene still had yapping competition from other towns. Especially active in bidding for cattle in 1870 was Baxter Springs, at the terminus of what was left of the old Shawnee Trail. Arrival of the Missouri River, Fort Scott and Gulf Railroad at Baxter Springs in May made that town a shipping point and gave a new spurt to the fading eastern trail.

Baxter Springs, which built cattle pens at the southwest edge of town, had a full battery of saloons, gambling rooms, and red-light houses. It quickly took on the aspects of a boom town. Its promoters reminded Texas drovers that this shipping point was closer than Abilene and that the older trail offered good grass and water. But, although Baxter Springs received eighty-five thousand head of Indian and Texas cattle that season, most of the big herds were pointed up the Chisholm Trail toward Abilene.[4]

Along with the big surge to Kansas, there still was some trailing east and west. Among Texas herds taken to New Orleans in the spring of 1870 was one that Colonel Fred Malone gathered near Beeville. At the same time, W. F. Cude, who had trailed to Shreveport a year earlier, gathered a herd in Gonzales County and headed them for the Crescent City. The Longhorns had to swim many rivers and bayous. At Brazier City a man led an ox to the edge of Burwick's Bay and drove him into the water. Then two men in canoes took the herd across. Cude shipped a carload from Brazier City and went on with the others, selling some at plantations and the remainder at the Mississippi River. Later in the year he took a herd to Natchez.

Other Texas cattle went to New Orleans by coastal steamers. In addition to carrying live steers, the steamer *Aginis* took thirty

[3] Daily Austin *State Journal*, April 21, 24, 1870; *Laws of Texas*, 1870, 17; Denison *Daily News*, May 12, 1874.
[4] Weekly Austin *Republican*, June 22, 1870, quoting the Fort Scott *Monitor*.

head of refrigerated beeves. This move led stockmen to build slaughter houses at Indianola, Galveston, and other places along the Gulf Coast. Others, at Matagorda and Indianola, continued to kill cattle for their hides and tallow.

Among the herds pointed west in the spring of 1870 was one of fifteen hundred head that thirteen men rounded up at Flag Springs. Near Grandfalls on the Pecos River, Joe S. Clark recalled, Indians tried to stampede the horses every few nights but were deterred by a strong guard. The cowmen wintered the herd on the Mimbres River in New Mexico. The next spring, while Clark and several of the other hands returned to Texas, the remaining ones took the herd on to California.

Another herd headed west in the spring of 1870 was one of more than eleven hundred head that Captain Jack Cureton of Palo Pinto County turned over to his three sons, John C., J. W., and W. E. Cureton. The brothers followed the Concho Trail to the Horsehead Crossing of the Pecos River. They went up that stream to the Hondo and across New Mexico and Arizona. After wintering the herd in California, they trailed to Reno, Nevada. There the steers that had cost ten dollars in Texas brought thirty dollars.[5]

The danger of Indian attacks on the trail to California led to appeals for military escorts. Protection was needed especially on a more northerly route that some of the drovers took. In Austin on February 22, 1870, General J. J. Reynolds ordered the Sixth United States Cavalry at Fort Richardson to provide such escorts. One company was to leave the fort on or about June 1 and the others on June 15, July 1, and July 15. The escorts were to cross the Red River near the mouth of the Little Wichita.[6]

II

The outfits headed for Kansas, although without military escorts, had some safety in numbers. At the height of the spring season the herds almost bumped into each other. Many had to go off the main trail to find enough grass, and at river crossings some had to wait their turn. High water caused worse delays. About May 20, at least

[5] Hunter, *The Trail Drivers of Texas*, 55–56, 216–17, 326.
[6] Daily Austin *State Journal*, February 20, 1870; Dallas *Herald*, March 12, 1870.

a score of herds were stalled at Red River Station by high water and had to wait for the flood to subside.

Farther up the trail, the swollen North Canadian made trouble for three outfits. One was that of Mark and Dick Withers and J. W. Montgomery, with 3,500 Longhorns, two wagons, and two cooks. The three herds had to swim across. When the Withers-Montgomery herd, in the lead, reached the far side and started out, the earth bank gave way. Before the frightened cattle could be turned back, 116 of them were drowned.[7]

Some of the Texas outfits ran into Indian troubles during the 1870 drive, but only a few were serious. Before he got out of Texas, J. H. Baker had his herd stampeded at night by redskins who drove off fifteen of his twenty horses and looted his wagon, taking all his expense money. As a result, Baker had to sell his cattle to another drover on credit and go along as a trail hand. A few nights later, about fifty Indians attacked the camp of the combined outfits. They got away with forty horses and took blankets, clothing, and money from the wagons.[8]

The William G. Butler outfit, after crossing the Red River, was met on Mud Creek by a Choctaw, Bob Love. The Indian demanded ten cents a head for a passport to let the five hundred Longhorns go through his nation. After some palaver, he compromised on a twenty-dollar gold piece. The Indians that Butler ran into farther north asked only for food.

Several drovers had their herds stampeded at night by Indians, and nearly all of them had to deal with bronze beggars. Dick Withers sent them off with coffee and tobacco. Jim Byler, who took a herd north for Monroe Choate and John Bennett, had many visitors. Most of them greeted the campers with "How, John" and asked for food and tobacco.

George Lang, who ran a butcher shop in Leavenworth, had a little trouble after passing Fort Sill with seven hundred beeves he had bought near Fort Worth. Four Indians rode up and asked for a motherless calf that had followed the herd up from Texas. Lang readily gave it to them, and in a few minutes they had the calf roped and butchered and the meat packed. Soon afterward sixteen young

---

[7] Hunter, *The Trail Drivers of Texas,* 307, 1023.
[8] Baker, diary, MS.

warriors rode up, yelling, demanding more beef, and trying to stampede the herd. Lang had to give them four big steers.

C. H. Rust, taking a herd up for two cowmen west of San Antonio, looked for a similar demand when he saw forty Comanches approaching. Each Indian carried a parasol. A spokesman said they had been up on the Arkansas, making a treaty with another tribe. Fortunately, they had been well fed and didn't molest the herd.

The Indians' love for bright colors had been observed earlier by William B. Slaughter, who used it to his advantage. Slaughter, a son of the Rev. George Webb Slaughter, pioneer cowman, was foreman of a trail outfit in 1870. After about thirty Osages stopped his herd of eighteen hundred steers on the south side of the Red Fork of the Arkansas, the war-painted chief came forward and asked for food. Slaughter turned over a supply of flour, bacon, and coffee. When the warriors began making trouble, the trail boss pulled out of his shirt some presents he had on hand for such an occasion. He gave the chief a gaudy Mexican sash that one of his men, Wash Wolf, had handed him. It was about six feet long and three or four feet wide, with tasscled ends. To each of the chief's three wives he handed a bright bandana handkerchief.

While the Indians were admiring these unexpected presents, Slaughter had his men start the herd across the river. Before the crossing was completed, the Indians made it clear that they wanted beef as well as silk. They demanded several steers, even though thousands of buffalo were in sight on the plains. To satisfy them, the foreman cut out of the herd three big steers that had acquired sore feet from the wet weather. The Osages had these beeves killed and much of the raw meat eaten before the last of the herd had crossed the Red Fork.

Their appetites satisfied, the Indians wanted to match their fleet ponies with those of the Texas punchers. Slaughter and two of his hands picked out their fastest mounts and raced with the braves all afternoon. The foreman would bet two or three silver dollars against a handsome, dressed buffalo robe. The outfit got away without any more trouble, thanks probably to the bright sash and bandanas. That night Slaughter bedded his herd ten miles farther up the trail, between two deep hollows, and didn't muffle the bells on his oxen.[9]

[9] Hunter, *The Trail Drivers of Texas*, 211, 307, 432, 482, 866–69, 891, 1023.

Buffaloes were abundant that spring and summer in the northern part of the Indian Territory and in southern Kansas. At Pond Creek the Jim Byler outfit found the plains covered with the shaggy beasts. Some of the trail hands gave chase and learned that they could bring the buffaloes down with a shot behind the shoulder. One of the punchers, George Saunders, roped a husky yearling— only to have it run away with his rope. The Butler outfit ran into so many buffaloes that some of the men had to ride ahead to keep them from cutting into the herd. The foreman's brother, Pleasant Butler, downed three with his six-shooter.

Herds of buffaloes on the trail held back the progress of seven hundred big steers being taken up the trail for W. H. Mayfield. Early one morning, just as the men were putting the herd on the trail, they were told that buffaloes were heading toward them. "I went to the top of a small hill and saw a black string," said one of the hands, W. R. Massengale. "It looked as though it were coming straight toward our herd. I went back, and we rounded our cattle so we could hold them; but the buffaloes passed just ahead of us. Our cattle got a little nervous, but we held them all right. It took the buffaloes two hours to pass. Sometimes they would be one behind the other, and then they would come in bunches of three or four hundred. Later a bunch of about three hundred ran through our herd while they were grazing."[10]

After they had crossed into Kansas, the trail drivers noticed that Wichita, like Fort Worth, was booming. "Wichita has made extraordinary progress since I was here a year ago," J. H. Baker wrote in his diary. "It begins to assume the appearance of a city." Strung out along a bluff of the Arkansas River, the town had the advantage of a good crossing, since there the stream had a wide, shallow bed. Its people hoped for a bigger advantage soon, since the Atchison, Topeka and Santa Fe Railroad was building in their direction from the north.

Wichita was served by several stage lines and had two hotels. Its main streets—muddy and dusty in turn—were lined with more than a dozen small stores that sold groceries, dry goods, hardware, and drugs. Other businesses included restaurants, saloons, harness shops, lumberyards, and blacksmith shops. The town's first barber-

10 *Ibid.*, 432, 482, 1023.

shop had a dirt floor and a chair made from boxes. Its barber pole was a fence post painted with stripes and set out in front, near the hitching rack.

Wichita already had a primitive jail, and citizens had donated five lots for building an Episcopal church. At the eastern edge of town, James R. Mead was laying out a residential addition. Two pioneer doctors, E. B. Allen and A. H. Fabrique, looked after the frontiersmen's health.

Although a rail line still was in the future, no one in Wichita lost sight of the importance of the cattle trade. "The Chisholm Trail is now a great public highway, rivaling the famous Santa Fe road of old," wrote Mead. "It is conceded by all drovers and freighters to be the best natural road in the West. Trading houses, ranches, and settlements have already been built on most of the numerous streams of the road."

Wichita people assured Texas drovers of full protection there. "Our citizens, without a dissenting vote, have determined that they shall not be molested while passing through the town." Answering the ballyhoo for other cattle routes through southern Kansas, they pointed out that the distance from Slate Creek to Abilene was thirty-five miles shorter by way of Wichita. They also claimed that the grass was much better. "The citizens of Wichita," they said, "have made arrangements with the settlers along the trail from the crossing on Cow Skin through Wichita northeast for fifteen miles, to allow you to drive your cattle unmolested; and we are ready and willing to protect you."[11]

At the end of the trail, Abilene was ready for the drovers. It had formed a town government in the fall of 1869 and had enlarged its shipping yards for the 1870 season. The town was attracting new inhabitants and expanding in business. It had acquired a weekly newspaper, the *Chronicle;* and both the Masons and the Odd Fellows had established lodges.

As the bellowing herds began to arrive on the prairies about Abilene in the early summer, the cowmen found an active market and benefited from high prices. The George Slaughter herd of three thousand fat beeves sold at thirty-five dollars a head. Ordinary

[11] Baker, diary, MS; *Kansas Daily Commonwealth,* May 27, October 11, 1870; Wichita *Vidette,* August 13, 25, 1870.

beeves brought twenty to twenty-five dollars. Booted Texans and midwestern buyers crowded the Drover's Cottage and swarmed through the narrow, dusty streets. Trainloads of Longhorns headed east almost every day, most of them going direct to Chicago. "No drover whose stock was good for anything had any trouble to find a buyer at good prices," recalled Joe McCoy. In agreement, the *Chronicle* observed that "every man who has dealt in cattle in Abilene during the season has made money."

Even into the fall, prices held firm. J. A. McLaren, who made a summer drive from Palo Pinto, was pleased with what he received. Arriving on August 15, he grazed his mixed herd for five weeks before selling. He obtained $30 each for his choice steers, $16 for the cows, $12 for the two-year-olds, and $6.50 to $7.00 for the yearlings. Among others who did well in Abilene in 1870 was Willis McCutcheon of Austin, a veteran who had helped his father trail a herd to Quincy in 1857 and had made several other drives.

The cowmen gained from a railroad rate war which broke out that summer and went on for several months. Competing roads lowered the rate for hauling cattle from Chicago to New York and other eastern cities to a dollar a carload. Before this rate war ended, some of the lines carried whole trainloads of Longhorns without charge. Certain railroads, shippers said, even paid bonuses in cash or gifts for the privilege of hauling cattle free. In addition, they provided round-trip passes for the men who went along to look after the stock. The effect of this rate war was to bring New York beef prices to Chicago, and Chicago prices to Abilene. In this period, said McCoy, "it was not uncommon for a drover to realize a profit of fifteen to twenty-five dollars per head on his herd."

Among those who visited Abilene during the cattle season was the noted showman P. T. Barnum, who was on one of his western tours. He was so pleased with the town that he invested thirty thousand dollars in the cattle business, in partnership with a local man, S. A. Catherwood.[12]

Texans trailed to Kansas in 1870 an estimated 300,000 Longhorns —double the number for 1869. About half of them went to Abilene,

[12] Abilene *Chronicle*, October 3, November 3, 17, 1870; McCoy, *Historic Sketches of the Cattle Trade of the West and Southwest*, 225–26; *Prose and Poetry of the Live Stock Industry of the United States*, 461–62.

which shipped 110,000 to 120,000 head during the season. Others went to rival markets, were wintered on Kansas ranges, or were taken on to new cow country opening up to the west and north.

The prosperity of the drovers that year was not fully shared by McCoy, who had opened the Abilene market. In the fall of 1869, he had invested all his ready cash in a herd of nine hundred Longhorns. He planned to winter them on hay along the Smoky Hill River and to fatten them on grass in the following summer. For expenses, he was counting on money from the Kansas Pacific Railroad. The company had paid him $5,872 for yarding and loading charges in 1869, but its officials denied having promised the bonus of $2.50 a car which he understood he would receive. This, on 2,017 carloads shipped in 1869, would have come to $5,042.50.

Rebuffed in efforts to collect this sum from officials of the railroad, McCoy appealed to law. On May 1, he filed a suit against the company in the District Court for Davis County, at Junction City. He asked for $5,127.50 damages, of which $85 represented costs of the suit. While the case awaited trial, creditors of McCoy became alarmed and began closing in on him, clamoring for money due them. To raise cash, he sold the Great Western Stockyards in Abilene, on May 28, to E. H. Osborne, of Quincy, Illinois, who operated them for the 1870 season.[13]

While McCoy wrestled with financial setbacks, the Texas cowmen returned home with bulging money belts. This had been the most profitable year for the drovers. They were eager to gather more and bigger herds for the 1871 season. The Texas cattle reservoir seemed as overflowing as ever with Longhorns.

III

As they began to gather herds for the 1871 drive, Texas stockmen had high hopes. Down on the coastal plains, some drovers still looked to the New Orleans market; but that trade was on the decline. In 1871, Texans sent 85,355 head of cattle to the Crescent City, most

[13] *McCoy* vs. *the Kansas Pacific Railway Company* (MS, Supreme Court of Kansas, 1–83; Junction City *Weekly Union*, May 7, 1870. McCoy's suit was tried in the court term of March, 1871. The jury decided in favor of McCoy, awarding him $5,042.50 damages and $80 costs. The railway company appealed to the Supreme Court of Kansas but lost.

of them by Morgan Line steamers. This was 4,424 fewer than in 1870. During the winter of 1870–71, as in the preceding one, about 20,000 cattle in that section were slaughtered for their hides and tallow alone. Others went to a near-by canning plant that butchered 125 head a day. Yet the big drive was to Kansas.

The spring of 1871 found twice as many cattle on the Chisholm Trail as in the preceding record year—four times as many as in 1869. In Kansas and in stock markets elsewhere, dealers and railway men were making ready for the deluge. Abilene and Kansas City had built new stockyards. Rival towns were bidding against each other for the cattle trade. Several railroads were pushing construction feverishly to tap the Chisholm Trail.

Abilene, with superior handling and shipping facilities, still dominated the trail's-end business. It had built a new two-story hotel, the Gulf House, and had changed from town to city government. In an election held on April 3, the citizens had chosen Joseph G. McCoy to be their first mayor.

The advantages of Abilene were attracting many drovers who had been selling elsewhere. Among those who shifted to the McCoy market was James D. Reed of Goliad, who had lost an arm in the Civil War. Reed, who had been trailing and shipping to New Orleans, took a large herd of beeves to Abilene in 1871.

Yet competitors were pressing from several sides. On the Kansas Pacific Railroad, Abilene had less to fear from its declining rival to the east, Junction City. But two counties to the west was the boom town of Ellsworth, bidding aggressively to drovers. In other parts of the state, new towns were trying to entice the Texas cowmen.

"Abilene has seen its best days," hopefully wrote a spokesman for one rival town. As evidence, he cited the rapid extension of new rail lines through Missouri and Kansas to the edge of the Indian Territory. Several of them would be able to cut in on the Texas cattle business for the first time this season.

Of these railroads, the most formidable threat to Abilene seemed to come from the Atchison, Topeka and Santa Fe, which was reaching southwest across the Kansas prairies. Although bothered by buffaloes getting across their lines, the Santa Fe surveyors were keeping ahead of construction crews. The surveyors carried pistols for protection against Indians, and the party had an escort of fifteen soldiers. Each day a buffalo was killed to supply the camp with fresh meat.

In the spring, two pioneers in a bull-team wagon reached a spot on the prairie east of Sand Creek, about thirty miles north of Wichita. They had heard a rumor that the Santa Fe would build past there. So they stopped, put up a shack, and called the place Newton. Their guess turned out to be correct. The railroad reached the new town in time to begin operation there on July 17. By that time, Newton had a hotel, a blacksmith shop, and a saloon; and new houses and business places were going up rapidly.

One of the other railroads building toward the cow country was the South Pacific. From St. Louis it had reached Pierce City, Missouri, 291 miles to the southwest. It advertised that it was the shortest, quickest, and cheapest route to the North and East. Its daily stock trains had a twenty-four-hour schedule to St. Louis. By early June this line, which had become the Atlantic and Pacific, had extended its rails to the border of the Indian Territory and was making a strong bid to drovers. In October it reached Vinita and, by the middle of that month, had shipped twenty-two cars of stock from there to St. Louis.

Also in the race for the cattle business was the Leavenworth, Lawrence and Galveston, pushing south through eastern Kansas. By early June it had reached the north line of the Indian Territory. This was at a point seventy-five miles north of Gano's Crossing and ninety miles from Red Fork. Officials of this line reminded Texas drovers that their railroad was 125 miles nearer than Abilene and eighty miles closer than Newton. Yet the cost of shipping was no higher than from those points. Advertisements assured good water and grass, as well as freedom from settlements.

Another railroad bidder was the Missouri River, Fort Scott and Gulf, known as the Border Tier road. Over its rails Baxter Springs had been shipping to Kansas City for a year many Indian cattle and some that had come up the old Shawnee Trail from Texas. Now this road was pushing into the Indian Territory. So was the ambitious Missouri, Kansas and Texas Railway, or Katy, which had northern terminals at Junction City and Sedalia. In October the Katy reached Three Forks, near Fort Gibson. During the fall it carried twenty to fifty carloads of cattle a day from the northeastern part of the Indian Territory to Sedalia. From there the Long-horns continued their journey over the Missouri Pacific to St. Louis.[14]

As Texas cattle began pouring into the Kansas shipping pens, people in the market towns saw that there was no need for rivalry. So many herds were coming up the Chisholm Trail that all the stock-yards were swamped with Longhorns. By day and by night, their bawling let everyone know that the flood gates had opened. The loading pens couldn't handle them fast enough, and the railroads couldn't get enough stock cars. The prairies about the trail's-end towns were a sea of grazing cattle, punctuated with the camps of the Texas outfits. Many of the drovers were waiting for buyers. Others were holding back in the hope that prices would go higher.

From the south, slowly but with the force of a coastal tide, more herds kept streaming in. Day after day they darkened the horizon. Often their clouds of dust seemed to merge, as each herd followed closely the one ahead. The trail was swelling, bursting. In open country the herds spread out—some turning to the right or to the left, beating new paths. At the streams, many drovers had to wait for earlier herds to cross. It looked as if the whole Texas cow country had pulled up stakes and headed north.

With twice as many herds on the march as ever before, the trail outfits of 1871 could join hands for better protection against rustlers and Indian raiders. Against other hazards, though, there was little added strength in numbers. Panthers and wolves still skulked about at night, ready to pounce on a stray yearling. Even on Dignowity Hill, on the outskirts of San Antonio, W. B. Foster killed a wolf that spring.

There still were flooded streams to put the herds across. Colonel W. M. Todd had trouble when a bunch of his cattle milled in the swollen Red River. One of his men rode his horse out into the circling Longhorns, mounted the biggest steer, and headed for the

[14] Dallas *Herald*, April 15, 29, May 20, June 10, 1871; Robert S. Stevens, letters, October 16, November 17, 1871 (MS, Files of Missouri-Kansas-Texas Lines); Clarksville *Standard*, November 4, 1871; Streeter, *Prairie Trails and Cow Towns*, 142–44; James Marshall, *Santa Fe, the Railroad That Built an Empire*, 48–49, 396; L. L. Waters, *Steel Trails to Santa Fe*, 44; V. V. Masterson, *The Katy and the Last Frontier*. Later the Leavenworth, Lawrence and Galveston became a part of the Santa Fe system. Both the Atlantic and Pacific and the Missouri River, Fort Scott and Gulf became parts of the St. Louis and San Francisco Railroad, called the Frisco.

north bank. In the same season, two punchers came near drowning in the Washita while snagging logs with which to build a raft.

Several who went up the Chisholm Trail that season commented on the vast herds of buffaloes in the northern part of the Indian Territory. Between the Red Fork and the Salt Fork of the Arkansas, some outfits had to stop their herds while thousands of buffaloes crossed the trail. Others sent men ahead to keep the buffaloes from stampeding the cattle. Several drovers incurred losses when some of their cattle, and even horses, joined the buffalo herds.

A few ran into trouble with Indians. Two of William B. Slaughter's men, while looking for stampeded cattle, were killed and scalped. John Wesley Hardin and Jim Clements, taking up twelve hundred head from southern Texas, had their outfit attacked by a band of Osages just as they were crossing into Kansas. One of the raiders, refused a steer, angrily pulled out his pistol and shot the animal. Wes Hardin, a cold-blooded killer and a fugitive from arrest, promptly shot the Indian and left his body tied to the carcass of the steer.[15]

Soon after they crossed the Kansas line, drovers could see the beginning of a new town on the north side of Fall Creek. This was Caldwell, situated to profit from the trail business. C. H. Stone had built in March a log cabin in which he sold groceries and liquor. By late May he had two competitors, but the trail outfits brought in enough business for all.[16]

The old Shawnee Trail, despite the new railroads that had just tapped it, did not carry many of the herds of 1871. Colonel George W. Miller walked two herds to Baxter Springs. There he sold the Longhorns, and his men washed the dust from their throats at a corner bar. A herd of fifteen hundred steers from the San Marcos River was said to have been one of the last large herds to cross the Red River at Rock Bluff. Two smaller herds, one of them owned by J. H. Baker and a partner, used this old ford on July 2.

Taxes imposed by the various Indian tribes along this route had become a deterrent. Chickasaw, Choctaw, Creek, and Cherokee—all were out to levy on the Texas herds. Some tribes tried to collect as

[15] John Wesley Hardin, *The Life of John Wesley Hardin*, 36–37; Hunter, *The Trail Drivers of Texas*, 118, 385–86, 492–93, 656–58, 870.

[16] Freeman, *Midnight and Noonday*, 21–22; Hunter, *The Trail Drivers of Texas*, 807.

much as 50 cents a head on cattle passing through. The drover who paid all the Indian taxes might be out $1.25 to $1.75 a head. But, as the collecting was lax, the smart cowman usually could escape some of the levies.

J. H. Baker, whose diary indicated that he had about nine hundred cattle, made payments to three tribes. On July 4 he paid a tax collector of the Chickasaw Nation five steers at $15 a head to settle a $75 tax bill. Ten days later he was stopped by an agent of the Creeks, who in the spring had voted a tax of 27½ cents per head, but he got off with a $40 payment. On July 31 he paid the Cherokees a levy of 10 cents a head.[17]

After crossing into Kansas, whatever the route, the trail hands could relax a little; but usually the boss tried to keep his men away from saloons until the drive ended. Then they could celebrate as long as their money lasted. People in the Kansas towns usually saw the cowmen in their more boisterous moods. While the market towns reaped big profits from the influx of Longhorns, some of the Kansans took an unflattering view of the men who brought them.

The typical trail hand, wrote one, "is unlearned and illiterate, with but few wants and meager ambition. His diet is principally Navy plug and whisky, and the occupation of his heart is gambling. His dress consists of a flannel shirt with a handkerchief encircling his neck, butternut pants, and a pair of long boots in which are always to be found the legs of his pants. His head is covered with a sombrero, which is a Mexican hat with a low crown and a brim of mammoth dimensions. He generally wears a revolver on each side, which he will use with as little hesitation on a man as on a wild animal. Such a character is dangerous and desperate, and each one generally has killed his man. There are good and even honorable men among them, but run-away boys and men who find it too hot for them even in Texas join the cattle drovers and constitute a large proportion of them. They drink, swear, and fight; and life with them is a round of boisterous gaiety and indulgence in sensual pleasure."[18]

[17] Ellsworth Collings, *The 101 Ranch*, 3–13; Baker, diary, MS.
[18] *Kansas Daily Commonwealth*, August 15, 1871.

IV

To the wife of the Texas drover, the cow trail had less appeal. For her, it meant months of waiting for an absent husband and often uneasiness over his safety. Seldom did a letter or a spoken message come to give news of the outfit. Many a wife, in her lonely bed in a frontier cabin, had to fight off visions of rampaging streams, crushing stampedes, and the scalping knives of frenzied Comanches. Yet some pioneer women wanted to go with the trail drivers and share their rugged life. A few did so.

Among the many Texans who rode up the Chisholm Trail in the spring of 1871 were two hardy women. One was young Mrs. George W. Cluck, whose husband's ranch was on Brushy Creek, in Williamson County, in central Texas. In March, George Cluck gathered a herd of a thousand steers for an April 1 start. In the same neighborhood, Colonel Dudley H. Snyder put together a similar herd. The two drovers planned to travel near each other for safety and mutual help.

Mrs. Cluck, even though she had three young children and was expecting a fourth in October, decided to go along. So her husband hitched two ponies to an old hack and loaded it with bedclothes and a camping outfit. There was just enough room left for Mrs. Cluck and the three youngsters—Allie Annie, 7, Emmet, 5, and Minnie, 2. Mrs. Cluck took along her shotgun and a spy glass.

From Round Rock the Cluck and Snyder herds grazed northward past Georgetown and Salado. They forded the Brazos River at Towash on April 23. On the next day, Mrs. Cluck celebrated on the trail her twenty-fifth birthday.

When the two outfits reached the Red River, that stream was on one of its frequent rampages. To make the hack float, the men lashed cottonwood logs to its sides. Then the ponies were able to pull it safely through the swirling waters. Mrs. Cluck mounted behind her husband on one of the most trusted horses, and each of the children was carried across in the arms of an expert rider.

In the Indian Territory, the Cluck and Snyder outfits had little trouble from the Red Men. But they pulled their shooting irons out when a band of white rustlers rode out of a mountain fastness and demanded a big cut from the herds. The sixteen trail hands were outnumbered, and some of the younger ones seemed a bit nervous as Mrs. Cluck helped load the guns.

"If any one of you boys doesn't want to fight," she bantered, "come here and drive the hack and give me your gun."

Cluck spurned the demand of the outlaws' leader. "You won't get any of our cattle," he said. "We have sixteen fighters as good as ever crossed the Red River. They were raised on rattlesnakes and wildcats, and they're all crack shots." After a glance at the stern-faced cowpunchers and at the woman who was fondling a shotgun in the hack, the bandit captain wheeled his horse and led his rustlers off without firing a shot.[19]

Mrs. Cluck's hazardous trip to Abilene was matched by that of Mrs. W. F. Burks, who lived on a ranch farther south, at Banquete, in Nueces County. From the coastal plains, her husband and Jasper Clark had gathered beef herds of a thousand head each. Like Cluck and Snyder, they planned to travel near each other for better protection. After road-branding at Pinitas, the two outfits started up the trail in April, each with a cook and ten hands, most of them Mexicans. After they were out a day or two, Burks sent his brother back with a note asking his wife to set out in a buggy and overtake the herd.

Mrs. Burks had two brown ponies hitched to her buggy and took along a Negro boy who was a good cook and who could put up the tent she made before she had gone far. She quickly caught up with the trail outfit. Near Lockhart, her husband's herd lost thirty steers in the timber, but the men had no more trouble until they reached the hills of Bosque County. There a terrific hailstorm beat down on them one evening.

As the storm hit, Burks drove his wife's buggy into the timber and then hastened to help the other men hold the frightened cattle. Mrs. Burks had to get out in the hail and torrential rain and tie the ponies to a tree. Later, sitting in the buggy—wet, cold, and hungry in the dark woods—she wished she were back in her comfortable home.

In the Indian country the Burks and Clark herds stampeded, but

[19] Dudley H. and John W. Snyder, cattle book, MS; T. U. Taylor, *The Chisholm Trail and Other Routes*, 157–62; J. B. Cranfill in the Dallas *Morning News*, April 25, 1937.

the men recovered all the steers. On another occasion, while the
cattle were resting, two rustlers came up and began throwing rocks
at them, trying to start a stampede. But some of the punchers chased
them off in time to prevent a runaway. Because prices were low
when they arrived in Kansas in July, Burks grazed his herd on
Emmet Creek, twenty-two miles from Newton, and did not sell
until December. Then he and his wife went by train to St. Louis
and New Orleans, thence by coastal steamer to Corpus Christi. As
delicacies for their friends, they took back a bucket of frozen buffalo tongues.[20]

V

South-central Kansas was almost bursting with Longhorns that summer. Estimates of the year's drive ran as high as 700,000 head, though
600,000 was the generally accepted figure. "The stream of cattle
still pours in," wrote a Wichita merchant in July. "Its line is now
continuous from the Rio Grande. If the flow continues, the prairies
will be inundated with Texas Longhorns before the close of the
season. Fully half of the beeves passing here are ready for the
butcher."[21]

Other observers told a similar story. "The entire country east,
west, and south of Salina and down to the Arkansas River is filled
with Texas cattle," reported the *Saline County Journal*. "There are
not only cattle 'on a thousand hills' but a thousand cattle on one
hill and every hill. The bottoms are overflowing with them, and the
water courses with this great article of traffic. Perhaps not fewer
than 200,000 head are in the state, 60,000 of which are within a day's
ride of Salina. And the cry is, 'Still they come!'"[22]

From the sea of Texas cattle about Abilene, herds waited their
turn at the Great Western loading pens. During 1871, Abilene
shipped by rail 2,500 carloads, or nearly 50,000 head, of Longhorns.
It forwarded on foot about three times that number to other states,
including Missouri, Iowa, Nebraska, Wyoming, Colorado, Nevada,
and New Mexico.

[20] San Antonio *Express*, March 10, 1905; Hunter, *The Trail Drivers of Texas*,
295–305; Taylor, *Chisholm Trail*, 162–64.
[21] Dallas *Herald*, July 22, 1871; *Kansas Daily Commonwealth*, November 19,
1871.
[22] *Saline County Journal*, July 20, 1871.

This high tide was more than Abilene alone could handle. Several other towns in south-central Kansas shared in the boom. Almost every place that had a railroad switch and stock pens shipped out Texas cattle. Newton, which the Atchison, Topeka and Santa Fe had just reached and which was almost astride the Chisholm Trail, lost no time in capturing a part of the business. Mayor Joseph G. McCoy of Abilene had gone to Newton to supervise the building of shipping pens there by the railroad. The stockyards, about a mile and one-half west of town, had six chutes through which cattle were driven into stock cars.

By mid-August, Newton had an estimated twelve hundred to fifteen hundred inhabitants and was being called the wickedest town in Kansas. Although grass still grew in its newly laid out streets and prairie dogs barked at persons who passed by, the town had about two hundred houses completed or under construction. It boasted twenty-seven saloons, eight gambling halls, and a flourishing red-light district known as Hide Park. Its other businesses included three small hotels, six restaurants, several grocery stores and bakeries, three dry goods stores, two drugstores, a hardware store, two blacksmith shops, three paint shops, and a real estate office. The town had a doctor but no bank, school, or church.

The most popular saloon was one called the Gold Rooms, operated by Bill Pierce and Doc Thayer. It occupied a rough building on the west side of Main Street, between Fifth and Sixth. In addition to its elaborate bar, it had six tables at which gamblers dealt monte. After the dance halls began to offer competition, it added music and side shows. Across the street was the Red Front Saloon. Others included the Alamo, the Bull's Head, Do Drop In, the Mint, the Parlor, and the Side Track.

The gambling places had almost every known device for relieving suckers of their cash. Each had a bar attached, and some offered free lunches and music. They were open day and night, including Sundays. At all hours visitors could hear the click of chips, the call of keno announcers, and the music of singers and brass bands. Trail hands who tired of poker, faro, monte, and keno could bet on dog fights and horse races.

Equally noisy were the goings on in Hide Park, south of the railroad. This section had five roughly constructed houses in the yellow grass stubble. While three served as bagnios for the "soiled doves," two larger ones were dance halls. For the benefit of visiting Texans, one was called the Alamo.

At all hours of the night and on Sundays, wrote the correspondent of a Topeka newspaper, "may be heard the music of the orchestras and the hippity-hop of the dancers. About half a dozen girls are to be found in each hall. There is a bar in each, which must be patronized by the dancers upon the conclusion of each dance. The tariff for drinks is twenty-five cents each. The girls drink regularly with their male partners. The bar realizes two dollars from each dance. Besides the patronage of the dancers, the bar is constantly besieged by applicants for poison from the crowds of spectators who are always on hand, witnessing the revolting spectacle. In one corner of each hall is a gaming table, around which are always to be found gamblers at work. The girls get drunk, shout, swear, and make exhibitions too indecent for description. A staid man would think hell had broken loose to witness one of these disgusting dances."

Newton already had had several fatal shootings but had not yet organized a town government. The county and township provided two justices of the peace, two constables, and a deputy sheriff. "One of the constables and the deputy sheriff have been appointed policemen," wrote the Topeka correspondent. "They receive their pay from a fund raised by the gamblers."

These officers had little deterrent effect on the town's wild life and crime. In the Red Front Saloon, on the night of August 11, a drunken Texas gambler attacked Mike McCluskie, who recently had quit the job of night policeman to work for the Santa Fe. After exchanging blows, the two went outside and began shooting. The gambler caught a bullet in the heart and died the next morning. McCluskie left town but was back on the nineteenth, celebrating Saturday night at Perry Tuttle's dance hall. Just before two o'clock Sunday morning, while McCluskie was seated at a gambling table in the corner, friends of the slain gambler came in and started shooting. McCluskie reached for his gun, as did some of his friends. When the smoke cleared, McCluskie and three others were dead or dying, and four others had bullet wounds.

Newton's unbridled night life did not seem to interfere much, though, with its cattle business. At least two thousand drovers and buyers were said to be in the town and neighborhood in mid-August. Two thousand head of cattle had been shipped, and total shipments for the season were expected to reach forty thousand head.[23]

Ellsworth, too, shared heavily in the 1871 cattle trade. This town was several years older and had had a railroad since July, 1867. A visitor in June, 1871, found its boxlike houses like those of other Kansas towns. He saw "one long straggling street built up on both sides of the railroad, the houses all of one type of architecture—one-story with a false front." Most of the houses, he added, "seemed to be saloons, restaurants, dance halls, and other deadfalls of equally destructive nature."[24]

By that time Ellsworth had a sheriff, and a month later it acquired a mayor and a marshal. It was building a tiny jail between its schoolhouse and its only church. Some of the outlaws that the officers couldn't cope with were taken in tow by a vigilance committee and hanged from the limb of a cottonwood tree on the bank of the Smoky Hill River. By mid-July, 30,000 Texas Longhorns were grazing on the outskirts of Ellsworth, and when the season ended an estimated 35,000 had been shipped.[25] Other towns on the Kansas Pacific made smaller shipments: Solomon, 17,100; Salina, 8,500; and Brookville, 6,520.

The overflow of Texas cattle not only engulfed Abilene and the other market towns but depressed the price. The Kansas towns, with twice as many Longhorns as in 1870, had fewer than half as many buyers from Illinois and other corn states. The feeders still were well supplied from the shipments of 1870. Too, cheap cattle were beginning to come in from the new northern ranges—Nebraska, Colorado, and Wyoming. Business activity over the country was slackening, and some people were becoming worried over the currency situation. In addition, railroad rates were less favorable than they had been in 1870. Instead of hauling cattle free or at nominal charges, the eastern roads had hiked their rates in an effort to recoup the losses they had incurred in their rate war. Buyers in the cities

[23] *Kansas Daily Commonwealth*, August 15, 1871; Streeter, *Prairie Trails and Cow Towns*, 142–60.

[24] McConnell, *Five Years a Cavalryman*, 266.

[25] *Kansas Daily Commonwealth*, July 16, 1871; Streeter, *Prairie Trails and Cow Towns*, 105–106; George Jelinek, *Ellsworth, Kansas, 1867–1947* (pamphlet), 5–12.

became choosy and sharply discounted the Texas range stock, most of which was below that of 1870 in quality.

Rather than sell at a loss, many Texas drovers grazed their herds until fall or winter. But prices in the fall were no better. Early in October the disastrous Chicago fire, although it left the stockyards unharmed, tended to further push down the market. Those drovers who took their herds to the short buffalo grass west of Ellsworth ran into blizzards that raged for days. Arctic gales brought waves of snow and sleet. A thick layer of ice buried the grass.

Hungry and numb, the cattle drifted with the wind. Without food or water, they became thin and gaunt. Glistening icicles hung from their muzzles, from their ears, even from their eyes. Some found shelter of a sort in woods or ravines. Others, on the open prairies, could only point their rumps into the wind and try to outlast the storm. Many froze stiff as they waited. Some of the wolves and jackrabbits met a like fate.

When the ice and snow melted, the prairies were strewn with dead Longhorns. In some places, men said they could walk on the carcasses for miles. An estimated 100,000 to 250,000 cattle had perished, along with hundreds of ponies. The cowmen could salvage only the hides. In the winter and spring, they and some of the homesteaders shipped thirteen thousand hides from Ellsworth alone.[26]

Most of the surviving cattle were emaciated and could not be sold at a profit until after months of grazing. Many of the owners faced financial ruin. The bigger cowmen could survive a bad market season and heavy losses of stock, but some of the smaller ones were wiped out.

Meanwhile, Abilene's welcome to the Texas drovers was cooling. Despite the financial gain from the cattle business, many local people resented the vice and crime it brought. At the same time, the surrounding country was becoming more thickly settled. The incoming farmers didn't want the Longhorn herds crossing their fields and trampling their crops. For all they cared, the upstart cow town of Ellsworth would be welcome to the Texas cattle trade. Let it take the whole caboodle.

[26] Ellsworth *Reporter*, May 6, 1872.

X

HIGH JINKS IN ABILENE

Buying and shipping Longhorn cattle wasn't the only business of Abilene. The town had to provide entertainment for the thousands of bowlegged, wind-bitten Texans who came up the Chisholm Trail with their herds. The cowboys were rarin' to celebrate. They wanted to make up, in a few nights of revelry, for the hard and austere life on the long trail. The Abilene entertainment was on a low level, but it appeared to suit the customers. If the saloons, gambling tables, and bawdy houses took all their cash, that didn't seem to matter.

The cowboy knew he might be riding into a trap, but he went on anyway. As he put it in one of his songs,

> *You strap on your chaps, your spurs, and your gun—*
> *You're goin' into town to have a little fun.*

> *You play with a gambler who's got a marked pack;*
> *You walk back to camp with your saddle on your back.*

At least Abilene's night life enabled the punchers to forget the trail dust, stampedes, and swollen rivers. "Cut loose from all the refining influences and enjoyments of life," noted one observer, "these men toil for tedious months behind their slow herds. They see scarcely a house, garden, woman, or child for nearly a thousand miles. Like a cargo of sea-worn sailors coming into port, they must have—when released—some kind of entertainment. In the absence of something better, they at once fall into liquor and gambling saloons at hand."[1]

By the summer of 1870, Abilene had—in addition to the bars in the hotels—at least seven saloons. They were the Alamo, the Bull's Head, the Elkhorn, the Pearl, the Old Fruit, Jim Flynn's, and Tom Downey's. The next year brought several others, including the Applejack, the Lone Star, the Longhorn, and the Trail. Most of them were south of the railroad, in the section called Texas Abilene. In the cattle season, Texans crowded the bars every night.

The most elaborate and most popular saloon was the Alamo. It occupied a long room with a forty-foot front on Cedar Street, facing west. It had an entrance at each end and connections with the stores on each side. The front entrance, on the west, had three double glass doors that always were open. Inside was a long bar with polished brass fixtures and rails. On the back wall of the bar were large mirrors that reflected the brightly labeled and sealed bottles of joy juice. On other walls were several large paintings of nudes in a style imitative of the Renaissance masters. Green gaming tables took most of the floor space. As a special attraction, the Alamo had a small orchestra that played in the morning, afternoon, and night. The musicians had to compete with clinking glasses, jangling spurs, ribald shouts, laughter, and the occasional bark of a six-shooter.

The Alamo never lacked patrons. "Here, in a well lighted room opening on the street," wrote one reporter, "the boys gather in crowds around the tables to play or to watch the others. A bartender with a countenance like that of a youthful divinity student, fabricates wonderful drinks. The music of a piano and a violin from a seated recess enlivens the scene and soothes the savage breasts of those who retire torn and lacerated from an unfortunate combat with the 'tiger.' The games most affected are faro and monte, the latter being greatly patronized by the Mexicans in Abilene, who sit with perfectly unmoved countenances and play for hours at a stretch. Your Mexican loses with entire indifference two things somewhat valued by other men—his money and his life."

[1] Junction City *Weekly Union*, October 29, 1870.

Another saloon, the Bull's Head, on Texas Street, had been the center of a dispute that shook the frontier town in the late summer of 1869. The owner of the saloon, a Texan, had had a painter depict on the front of his building a big red bull. This seemed harmless, as bulls appeared daily in the streets of Abilene, in full view of all the residents. Yet some of the citizens found this picture a bit too realistic and suggestive. They denounced it as degrading and immoral. They called it an insult to the virtuous women of the town and a bad influence on the children. They demanded that it be painted out.

For two weeks the controversy raged. The owner of the saloon stood his ground, consigning his critics to a place even hotter than the dusty Kansas plains. But in the end, to avoid a threatened gun battle between the local and Texas factions, he gave up. Even after the picture was painted over, though, the outlines of the offending bull still showed through.[2]

To the trail hand, life in Abilene was seldom dull. After drawing his pay, visiting a barbershop, and buying a new outfit of clothes, he was ready to kick up his heels. Usually he made the rounds of several of the bars and tried his luck at one of the games of chance. After William H. (Billy) Mitchell opened the Novelty Theater in July, 1871, the visitor there could see a show put on by a company from Kansas City. If still in a hilarious mood and able to walk, he might look in on one of the nightly orgies at the dance halls.

Many of the Texans found the dance halls hard to resist. Major Seth Mabry, whom Joe McCoy regarded as a fine conversationalist and always entertaining, liked the relaxation that dancing offered after a day in the saddle. After watching Mabry at a dance in a settler's home, another friend noted that, dressed up like a dandy, he "waltzed, pirouetted, took part in every dance, and was the beau of the ball." But at the public dance halls, many became involved in brawls in the late hours. Wash Wolf, who had come up the trail with William B. Slaughter's outfit, was killed in an Abilene dance hall in 1870.

McCoy had a low opinion of the dance halls, with what he called their "wretched music, ground out on dilapidated instruments by

[2] Daily *Kansas State Record*, August 5, 1871; Henry, *Conquering Our Great American Plains*, 82–85, 267.

beings fully as degraded as the most vile." Yet he admitted that the average cowboy plunged into their dissipation with great delight. "Few more wild, reckless scenes of abandoned debauchery can be seen on the civilized earth," he wrote, "than a dance house in full blast in one of the frontier towns."

The cowboy entered the dance hall without bothering to take off his spurs, his pistols, or even his wide-brimmed Stetson. McCoy found the dancing cowhand an odd and often comical sight. "With the front of his sombrero lifted at an angle of fully forty-five degrees, his huge spurs jangling at every step or motion, his revolvers flapping up and down like a retreating sheep's tail, his eyes lit up with excitement, liquor, and lust, he plunges into it and 'hoes it down' at a terrible rate in the most approved yet awkward country style, often swinging his partner clear off the floor for an entire circle, then 'balance all,' with an occasional demoniac yell near akin to the war whoop of the savage Indian." After each dance, the man was required to buy drinks for his partner and himself.[3]

Allied with the dance halls was the spreading red-light district, which was especially populous during the cattle trading season. Abilene, with its free-spending Texas cowmen, attracted sirens from Memphis, St. Louis, Chicago, and other cities. Many of them were fashionably dressed, with the inevitable bustle. They carried, in addition to a handbag, a jeweled pistol or a dagger. The weapon was for self-defense and for protection against being defrauded.

In the earlier cattle years of Abilene, the bagnios were situated conveniently close to the heart of the town, most of them in the Texas section. But some citizens made so much fuss against them that, on May 20, 1870, the board of trustees passed an ordinance evicting the Delilahs. The sporting women then moved outside the town limits, to the bank of Mud Creek, about a mile to the northwest. There they occupied more than a score of crude, rambling houses until early September, when local officers drove them out. On September 7, they left by train for Baxter Springs and other Kansas towns.

Before the first herds arrived from Texas in the late spring of 1871, the fancy women were back in even larger numbers. "The

[3] McCoy, *Historic Sketches of the Cattle Trade of the West and Southwest,* 139–41; John Clay, *My Life on the Range,* 110.

soiled dove," recalled a local merchant, "was bedizzened in her gaudy dress, cheap jewelry, and highly colored cosmetics. Abilene was a seething, roaring, flaming hell." The "doves" found cotes in various parts of town and were ready for a deluge of business.

Outraged by this brazen invasion, more than a hundred women residents of Abilene petitioned the recently elected council on May 27. They asked that it take "active measures for the suppression of brothels." The council, on June 16, appointed one of its number and Mayor McCoy to take action. It instructed the pair "to cause the removal from the limits of the city proper of all bawdy houses or houses of ill fame and to relocate the same upon some uninhabited portion of the city common."

The committee moved the sporting women to a site at the southeast edge of town. In this section, which some called the Devil's Half Acre, the women put up shoddy houses and did a flourishing business until the cattle shipping dried up in September. "These women built houses on this ground, and it was covered with them," said Theophilus Little, a local lumber dealer. "Some of them were more than a hundred feet long. Beer gardens, dance halls, dancing platforms, and saloons galore were there. It was called the Devil's Addition to Abilene—rightly named, for hell reigned there supreme. Hacks were run day and night to this addition. Money and whisky flowed like water down hill, and youth and beauty and womanhood and manhood were wrecked and damned in that valley of perdition."

In the Texas section, the saloons and gambling rooms were open around the clock. Brass bands and pianos competed to lure the cowboys through the open doors. At the gaming tables, stakes sometimes ran into thousands of dollars. One cowman was said to have lost thirty thousand dollars at a single sitting. "I have seen a hatful of gold lying loose in a pile on these tables," said an Abilene resident. But if anyone had tried to steal it, he added, "he would have been bored full of holes in the twinkling of an eye."

While the cowboys were celebrating, their ponies stood patiently in a line along the sidewalk. Often the rider didn't bother to tie his mount but merely tossed the rein over the pony's head. The pony would wait until his owner came back. At about three in the morning, a few pistol shots fired into the air gave the signal for most of the cowboys to depart. Mounting their ponies, they headed west, firing their six-shooters in a wild fusillade. The town was blue with smoke as the Texans raced across Mud Creek and scattered to their camps.[4]

Heavy drinking, crooked gambling, and widespread vice led inevitably to shootings and other crimes. The easy money of the cowmen attracted thugs to Abilene. In the shipping season of 1871, said the local newspaper, "there was a larger number of cutthroats and desperadoes in Abilene than in any other town of its size on the continent. Most of them were from Kansas City, St. Louis, New Orleans, Chicago, and the mountains."

In Abilene that summer was John Wesley Hardin, the notorious Texas killer who later could boast of forty notches in his gun. "I have seen many fast towns," he recalled, "but Abilene beat them all. The town was filled with sporting men and women, gamblers, cowboys, desperadoes, and the like. It was well supplied with barrooms, hotels, barber shops, and gambling houses; and everything was open."

Ben Thompson, a saloonkeeper and gambler, found Abilene full of scoundrels—pickpockets, footpads, burglars, crooked gamblers, and confidence men. Besides the professional criminals who swarmed in, many of the cowboys made trouble—especially after imbibing too freely of firewater. Almost every day and night, one could hear the popping of guns in Texas Abilene.

Young J. B. Edwards, making his rounds in delivering ice, saw much of the revelry. The ice, which had been cut from the Republican River, brought six cents a pound at the eleven saloons and the Drover's Cottage. "When a man from Texas got too much tanglefoot aboard," said Edwards, "he was liable under the least provocation to use his six-shooters. Not less than two were always hanging from his belt. If his fancy told him to shoot, he did so—into the air or at anything he saw. A plug hat would bring a volley from him at any time, drunk or sober."[5]

[4] Abilene, Kansas, Minute Book of the Board of Trustees (MS, Office of the City Clerk, 67, 68, 70, 71; Abilene, Kansas, Ordinance Book (MS, Office of the City Clerk), 56; Abilene *Chronicle*, May 12, September 8, 1870, June 1, July 6, September 14, 1871; Daily *Kansas State Record*, August 5, 1871; Junction City *Weekly Union*, September 30, 1871; Theophilus Little, "Early Days in Abilene and Dickinson County," in Adolph Roenigk, *Pioneer History of Kansas*, 35–38.

[5] Abilene *Chronicle*, October 12, 1871; W. M. Walton, *Life and Adventures of Ben Thompson, the Famous Texan*, 104; Hardin, *The Life of John Wesley Hardin*, 42; J. B. Edwards, *Early Days in Abilene* (pamphlet), 3; George L. Cushman, "Abilene, First of the Kansas Cow Towns," *Kansas Historical Quarterly*, Vol. IX, No. 3 (August, 1940), 240–58.

11

Frontier Abilene had few civilizing influences with which to combat the vice and crime attracted by the cattle trade. By the opening
of the 1870 shipping season, the town had acquired a stone schoolhouse, where young Washburne Fancher taught the three R's, and
two small churches—Baptist and Universalist. Vear Porter Wilson
edited the weekly *Chronicle*. The county was building a two-story
brick courthouse; and on Texas Street, across from the Bull's Head
Saloon, men were at work on a diminutive stone jail. When, after the
walls were almost up, exuberant cowboys demolished them, construction work was resumed under guard.

In an effort to restore order, the town trustees passed an ordinance banning the carrying of firearms. They had notices of this
action posted in public places—where the Texans promptly shot
them to bits. As the sheriff and other county officers were unable
to control the town, the Abilene trustees decided to hire a marshal.

One of the early applicants for this new job was Thomas James
Smith, of Kit Carson, Colorado. Smith, a husky Irishman, had grown
up in New York and had been a policeman there. Later he had
worked at railroad construction jobs in Nebraska and had been a
successful marshal in Wyoming. In Abilene the town fathers turned
him down in favor of a local man, but neither the one chosen
nor any of his several successors could keep order.

The cowboys quickly showed their contempt for the new jail.
When it received its first prisoner—a Negro cook, from one of the
cow camps on Mud Creek, who had taken on too much firewater
and had begun shooting at street lamps—his friends shot off the lock
and freed him. Then they galloped past the office of Theodore C.
Henry, chairman of the town trustees, and shot it full of holes.

Fed up with local marshals, the trustees asked the St. Louis chief
of police to send them two officers. He did so; but the pair he sent,
after one day in Abilene in which the cowboys hazed them with
little mercy, took the night train home. After that, Henry wired
for Tom Smith to come.

Smith reappeared at Henry's office on Saturday morning, May
30. The newcomer was a stalwart, broad-shouldered fellow of about
thirty. He was nearly five feet eleven and weighed 170. He had a
fair complexion, auburn hair, and a light mustache. His bluish-gray

eyes were expressive, his manner direct, and his talk inspired confidence.

Henry explained to Smith the troubles Abilene had had and suggested that he look over the town before he decided on taking the post of marshal. Smith agreed and went off to make an inspection. He returned just before sundown, with the report that he thought he could handle the job. The pistols would have to go, he said. "As well contend with a frenzied maniac as an armed and drunken cowboy."

Tom Smith pinned on his badge and walked off toward Texas Abilene, with news of his appointment speeding ahead of him. Soon after he arrived there, he ran into one of the town rowdies, a cowboy desperado known as Big Hank. This fellow had made trouble for earlier marshals and had boasted that no one could disarm him. With a six-shooter conspicuous in his belt, he swaggered up to Tom Smith and began to taunt him. "Are you the man who thinks he's going to run this town?" he asked.

"I've been hired as marshal," Smith replied. "I'm going to keep order and enforce the law."

"What are you goin' to do about that gun ordinance?" the bully demanded.

"I'm going to see that it's obeyed—and I'll trouble you to hand me your pistol now."

When Big Hank, with a coarse oath, refused, Smith repeated his request. As this brought only more profanity and abuse, the new marshal sprang at the bully and felled him with a terrific blow on the jaw. He then took the gun from the belt of the ruffian and ordered him to leave Abilene at once and for good. Big Hank slipped out quickly, glad to get away from the gibes of his fellows.

News of this sensational encounter traveled like a prairie fire. Before midnight it was the talk of all the Abilene saloons and of the cow camps for miles about. In one camp on a branch of Chapman Creek, northeast of town, it aroused a burly desperado called Wyoming Frank. It set him to bragging. He made a bet that he could go into town and defy any demand that he give up his six-shooter.

The next morning, Sunday, Wyoming Frank rode into town. As the new marshal hadn't yet appeared, the bully began drinking and boasting. He reckoned that the officer must have heard of his arrival and lit out. Finally Tom Smith came walking quietly down the middle of the dusty street. Wyoming Frank began chaffing him insolently, trying to engage him in a quarrel. Smith merely asked for the desperado's gun, which was refused.

Daunted a bit by the steely glint in the eye of the new marshal, Wyoming Frank began backing away from him. He maneuvered for time and space to reach for his pistol, but Smith kept too close. Finally, the bully backed into a large saloon, where a crowd quickly gathered about the pair. When Wyoming Frank answered another request for his gun with an insulting oath and a vile epithet, Tom Smith sprang at him with the speed of a gamecock. With two blows, he sent Wyoming Frank to the floor, then took the pistol from his belt. "I give you five minutes to get out of this town," he said. "And don't you ever again let me set eyes on you."

This unexpected outcome astonished the spectators in the saloon and left them, for a moment, speechless. Then the proprietor stepped from behind the bar and handed Tom Smith his gun. "That was the nerviest act I ever saw," he said. "You did your duty, and the coward got what he deserved. Here's my gun. I reckon I'll not need it as long as you're marshal of this town."

At that, others came forward, offering their six-shooters. Smith told them to leave their pistols with the bartender until they went back to camp.[6]

Thus reckless Abilene learned quickly that Tom Smith had sand in his craw. On both sides of the railroad, he was undisputed boss. On the next Wednesday, June 4, the town trustees had no hesitation in confirming Henry's appointment of him. They made his pay $150 for the first month. On August 9, they raised his salary to $225 a month, effective from July 4.

Although, on June 13, the trustees hired a policeman chosen by Smith to help him patrol the town, the new marshall did much of the dangerous work himself. All that summer his gray horse, Silverheels, was a familiar figure in Abilene streets. Tom Smith was unusual among frontier peace officers in that he neither drank nor gambled. He was able to keep order without killing anyone. He

[6] Theodore C. Henry, "Thomas James Smith of Abilene," *Collections of the Kansas State Historical Society*, Vol. IX (1905–1906), 526–32.

had little serious trouble except occasionally from some newly arrived Texas cowboy who hadn't yet learned that law had come to Abilene.

One such incident took place at night in the Old Fruit Saloon, on Texas Street. In this cheap, narrow tavern, a Texan had deliberately kept his pistol on in defiance of the law. As he was drinking with about a dozen of his cronies, Tom Smith walked in. The marshal covered the crowd with his gun, and the Texans parted as he walked toward the offender, who had backed into the rear of the room.

Two of the gun-toter's half-drunk friends grabbed pistols from behind the bar and began firing, but they wounded only other Texans. Then the culprit snatched a kerosene lamp from its bracket and hurled it at the marshal. It hit the floor at his feet but, fortunately, did not explode. This act was enough, though, to cause the other Texans to stampede for the door. They recalled that a few weeks earlier, a fire started by an exploding lamp had taken a life and destroyed several buildings on the same street.

With the bystanders out of the way, Tom Smith quickly collared and disarmed his man. After disposing of the offending pistol, the marshal tossed the Texan on his shoulder and carried him across the street to the calaboose. The other cowhands were enraged at seeing their friend thus disgraced but were afraid to shoot for fear of hitting him.[7]

For five months Tom Smith and his deputy kept Abilene in hand, but trouble always lurked around the corner. On October 23, after most of the Texans had gone, there was a killing on Chapman Creek, about ten miles northeast of town. Andrew McConnell, a farmer of Scotch ancestry, had been out hunting deer. On his return to his dugout, he saw an Irish neighbor, John Shea, driving cattle across his land. The cattle had destroyed some of McConnell's corn. In an argument that followed, Shea tried twice to shoot McConnell; but his pistol snapped and failed to go off. As he was cocking it a third time, McConnell shot him through the heart.

McConnell went for a doctor and later gave himself up. He was released on a plea of self-defense. But some of his neighbors, not

[7] Abilene, Kansas, Minute Book of the Board of Trustees, MS; Henry, *Conquering Our Great American Plains*, 151–54.

satisfied with this outcome, obtained a warrant for his arrest on a charge of murder. The sheriff, Joseph Cramer, went out with the warrant but, unable to arrest McConnell, returned to Abilene for help. Tom Smith, who had added to his coat the badge of a deputy United States marshal, volunteered to make the arrest.

On the morning of Wednesday, November 2, Smith and his deputy, James H. McDonald, rode out to the McConnell dugout. There they found the accused man and with him a friend, Moses Miles, who lived on a neighboring farm.

The marshal, hardly expecting resistance, entered the dark dug-out and told McConnell that he had a warrant for his arrest. At this, McConnell instantly shot Smith with his Winchester. Recoiling, the marshal took one shot at McConnell, piercing his hand. Then, al-though seriously wounded, he grappled with the homesteader. He dragged his man outside the dugout, where Miles was holding off the deputy. Miles then turned his attention to the wounded marshal. He struck him on the head with his gun, then picked up an ax and chopped his head almost completely from his body.

The deputy, instead of giving battle to the killers, left his horse tied and ran to another claim, half a mile away. There he obtained another mount and hastened back to Abilene with the tragic news.

In town, McDonald dismounted in front of the Drover's Cottage and strode into the barroom. "Leaning against the bar, with a drink of whisky in his hand," recalled Charles Gross, who was present, "he blubbered out his yarn. There being no one to dispute him, his story had to go. But I still recall the looks that passed between men who had been raised from birth to eat six-shooters. It was so rank that no one could say a word."

Two days after the killing, Abilene suspended business while citizens from both sides of the tracks gave Tom Smith an elaborate funeral. From the little frame Baptist Church, Silverheels, with his empty saddle, followed the hearse. The procession wound through Texas Street, across the railroad, and on to the prairie burial ground.

On the morning after the burial, law officers captured McCon-nell and Miles, who had fled on the mounts of Smith and McDonald. The killers were taken in a cabin on the Republican River north-west of Clay Center. Brought back to Abilene, they later were con-victed at Manhattan and sentenced to prison.[8]

III

During the winter of 1870–71, following the death of Tom Smith, Abilene rocked along without a marshal. With the Texans gone, night life had subsided, and there was little trouble south of the tracks. But another, and bigger, cattle season was approaching. In the spring the new city administration, headed by Mayor Joseph G. McCoy, realized that Abilene must have a strong man to keep order. Charles Gross suggested James B. Hickok, whom he had met a time or two. McCoy sent Gross to Fort Harker to see Hickok, better known as Wild Bill. The envoy brought the long-haired scout back with him, and on April 15, 1871, the council hired him as marshal.

Hickok, who had been marshal at Hays two years earlier, was a colorful frontiersman and an amazing pistoleer. Born in Illinois in 1837, he had gone at the age of eighteen to turbulent Kansas. He did farm work, joined the Free State Army, and, in 1858, served as constable at Monticello. The next year he took a job as teamster in a freight caravan to Santa Fe. There he met Kit Carson, tried the gambling games, and became a stagecoach driver.

After a serious encounter with a grizzly bear, Hickok went to Rock Creek, Nebraska, to recuperate in the summer of 1861. While there, he became involved in a quarrel with a group of settlers and killed three of them. He was acquitted on grounds of self-defense. Later in the summer he was put in charge of a government wagon train carrying supplies from Fort Leavenworth to Sedalia. While stopping at Independence, he found a mob of teamsters besieging a bartender who had taken sides in a fight and wounded a man. Hickok drew his pistols and quickly disbanded the rowdies. Townspeople were relieved. One woman shouted, "Good for you, Wild Bill!" The name stuck.

During the remainder of the Civil War, Hickok served as a federal scout and guerrilla fighter. Returning to Kansas after the shoot-

8 Abilene *Chronicle*, November 3, 10, 1870; Junction City *Weekly Union*, November 5, 1870; Henry, "Thomas James Smith of Abilene," *Collections of the Kansas State Historical Society*, Vol. IX (1905–1906), 531; Gross, letter to Edwards, August 23, 1922, MS; Henry, *Conquering Our Great American Plains*, 199–210; Streeter, *Prairie Trails and Cow Towns*, 90–93. In 1904, Abilene citizens marked the grave of Tom Smith with a granite boulder. To this was fastened a bronze plate which noted that the marshal died as a martyr to duty and described him as "a fearless hero of frontier days who, in cowboy chaos, established the supremacy of law."

ing ceased, he had a taste of Indian fighting and, for a time, served as a scout for Lieutenant Colonel George A. Custer. As marshal of Hays, a town full of bullwhackers and outlaws, Wild Bill brought a semblance of order. After leaving Hays, he spent the winter of 1869–70 in Topeka. In the spring he went to Nebraska and headed an expedition that captured six buffaloes.

By the time he appeared in Abilene, Wild Bill was a glamorous and legendary figure. He had been the subject of a touched-up account in *Harper's Magazine* four years earlier. Custer had found Hickok "a strange character, just one which a novelist might gloat over." Mrs. Custer had been impressed with his "graceful, swaying step, squarely set shoulders, and well poised head." He carried two pistols, she noted, and "wore top boots, riding breeches, and a dark blue flannel shirt, with scarlet set in front. A loose neck handkerchief left his fine, firm throat free."

A handsome six-footer, Hickok had a droopy mustache and long brown tresses that brushed his shoulders, as if to dare Indian scalpers. His piercing blue eyes could freeze to steel gray if danger neared. He was proud of his polished boots. Some of them he had had made in Leavenworth, paying as high as sixty dollars a pair. They had cowboy-style heels, two inches high. The black patent-leather tops bore designs in curves and spirals. Usually he wore a hat of dark felt, with a broad brim.

In Abilene, Wild Bill put aside the fringed and beaded buckskin of his scouting days for more gorgeous raiment. Often he paraded in a Prince Albert coat, checkered trousers, and a silk vest embroidered with flower designs. Over his shoulder he flung a cape with a flowered silk lining. Sometimes, in warm weather, he replaced his boots with soft, beaded moccasins. When he was dressed up, his double action Army pistols gave way to silver-mounted, pearl-handled revolvers.

The repute of Wild Bill as a marksman had gone ahead of him to Abilene. He could toss a coin and shoot it to bits before it hit the ground. He could perforate the brim of a hat while it spun in the air. With a pistol in each hand, he could keep a tin can dancing in the dust. Once he shot ten bullets into a fence post, making only one small hole. No one in Abilene who had seen him shoot was eager to incur his wrath.

Hired at $150 a month, plus a fourth of the money collected in fines, Hickok made his headquarters at the Alamo Saloon. Instead of regularly patroling the Texas section as Tom Smith had done, Wild Bill spent most of his time in the saloons and gambling rooms. Although he liked to gamble, he drank only sparingly. He kept himself well posted on what went on in the town. Usually he had a bowie knife hidden under his sash. In addition to his pistols, he sometimes carried a repeating rifle or a sawed-off shotgun.

Wild Bill was given more help than Tom Smith had had a year earlier. On June 16, at the unanimous request of the city council, Mayor McCoy appointed James Gainsford and James H. McDonald as policemen. For nearly two months the marshal had also as a deputy Thomas Carson, a nephew of Kit Carson. Later Carson went to Newton as marshal of that booming town. The two others served until September 2, when, with the trailing season about over, the council dismissed them as no longer needed.

Thanks to the earlier work of Tom Smith, the help of deputies, and the fear inspired by his repute as a marksman and a killer, Marshal Hickok kept Abilene in order without much trouble. Occasionally some tipsy blusterer threatened to kill him, but few dared try a shot. Once, after he had handled some cowboys a bit roughly on a summer night, they and some of their friends rode into town after him the next morning. The Texans boasted that they would capture Wild Bill and hang him from a telegraph pole. But Hickok, tipped off by a friend, met them in the street outside the Last Chance Saloon. Without firing a shot, he quickly dispersed the crowd.

Wild Bill's bossing of Abilene didn't sit well with the Texas killer Wes Hardin, who had come up the Chisholm Trail with a price on his head. Wes ignored the ban against the carrying of pistols. One day, with two six-shooters in his belt, Wes was rolling at tenpins in a saloon when Wild Bill walked in.

"What are you doing with those pistols on?" asked the marshal, who had met Wes a few days earlier.

"I'm just takin' in the town," replied the desperado.

When Wild Bill ordered Hardin to take off his guns and he refused, the crowd began getting out of the way for an expected battle. But as neither man cared to risk a gun duel, the two compromised their differences and went to the bar for a drink.

Among others who chafed under Wild Bill's domination were a pair of Texas gamblers, Ben Thompson and Phil Coe. These two had just bought the Bull's Head Saloon, with its profitable gambling room. Thompson thought that Hickok picked on Southerners, especially Texans. He tried to turn Hardin against the marshal and hinted that the Texas gunman might add Wild Bill to his long list of victims. But Hardin refused to be pushed into such a fight. "If Bill needs killing," he asked, "why don't you do it yourself?" Thompson had no relish for such a chore, but he and his partner continued to harbor a smoldering animosity toward the marshal.

Meanwhile, anyone as strikingly handsome as Wild Bill was bound to create a stir among the women. Soon after he arrived in Abilene, Bill was followed there by Suzanna Moore, a fearless girl from the Ozarks. She had ridden at his side on some of his scouting and guerrilla exploits during the war and had lived with him for awhile at Springfield, Missouri. In Abilene she and Bill lived quietly together in a cottage for a short time.

During his months in Abilene, Wild Bill had several other mistresses in turn. The marshal, who refused to sleep in the same room with another man, never fully trusted any woman. He habitually took his guns to bed with him. Usually he had a six-shooter within reach of his right hand. Near by would be a sawed-off, double-barreled shotgun. It had a strap that enabled him to swing it over his right shoulder and carry it under his coat out of sight.

Among the women who were smitten with Wild Bill's charms was Mrs. Agnes Thatcher Lake, who came to Abilene in August with her traveling circus. Mrs. Lake, widowed two years earlier, was a skilled equestrienne, tightrope dancer, and lion tamer. She was forty-five years old—eleven years older than Bill—and had a young daughter. She became acquainted with the marshal when he protected her circus from ruffians. Quickly enamored, she wanted him to marry her; but he put her off with excuses.

Another lady, one of easy virtue, may have had a part in the growing enmity between Wild Bill and Phil Coe. Friends of Coe said that the two were rivals for the favors of a girl called Jessie. When Hickok found her drinking wine with Coe in a hotel parlor, they related, he struck her on the chin and knocked her senseless. Denying this, partisans of Wild Bill said that the trouble deepened from crooked doings at the Bull's Head.

After his partner, Ben Thompson, had left town on family business, Coe sold the saloon in July to Tom Sheran but stayed on there as a professional gambler. Rumors were afloat that men had been drugged and robbed in the back room of the Bull's Head and that Coe had been fleecing some who gambled there. The marshal ordered Coe to use an honest faro box and to keep it in the front of the saloon.

Coe, who was called a man of good impulses in his better moments, often became a troublemaker after putting a few drinks under his belt. Theophilus Little found him "a red-mouthed, bawling thug —a plug-ugly—a dangerous beast." Coe owed Little forty dollars for lumber; but when the merchant asked for the money, all he received was abuse.

As the cattle business slackened, both the Texans and those who preyed on them began to pull out of Abilene. On September 2, the day it dropped Wild Bill's two remaining deputies, the city council ordered the marshal to close the dance halls. This action caused a big exodus. Almost every eastbound train, reported the *Chronicle* twelve days later, had "carried away a vast multitude of sinful humanity. Prostitutes, pimps, gamblers, cappers, and others, finding their nefarious occupations no longer remunerative," had scattered to Newton and other towns. One of the dismissed policemen, James Gainsford, found a like job at Great Bend.

The trouble between Hickok and Coe came to a head on the evening of October 5. With the cattle shipping season almost ended, Coe and other Texans were getting ready to return to the Lone Star State. In the late afternoon some of them had started out on a spree to celebrate their departure. On the street they found Jacob Karatofsky, young owner of the Great Western Store. Two of the Texans hoisted him to their shoulders, carried him to the Applejack Saloon, and ordered him to buy drinks for the crowd. Later they gave similar treatment to other citizens, including Wild Bill, who cautioned them to keep within bounds.

The roisterers paid no heed to the marshal's warning. Theophilus Little, who left his office at dusk, noticed "this band of crazy men.

They went up and down the street with a wild rush and roar, totally oblivious of anything in their path. It was a drunken mob. I hurried home, got my family into the house, locked the doors, and told my folks not to step outside."

About nine o'clock the crowd of Texans, growing larger and more hilarious, reached the big Alamo Saloon, whose glass doors were open. As the men looked about for another victim to buy them drinks, the crack of a pistol shot gave pause to the shouting. Wild Bill, who had been inside the saloon, rushed out, drawing his pistols.

"Who fired that shot?" he demanded.

Phil Coe, who had a gun in his hand in violation of the local ordinance, admitted that he had done the firing. He said he had shot at a savage dog that attacked him. Others had seen no dog; they assumed that Coe's shot was a mere expression of exuberance. At any rate, both men seemed to realize that they faced a showdown. Standing not more than eight feet apart, they fired at each other.

One of Coe's shots made a hole in Wild Bill's coat; another passed between his legs, striking the floor behind him. The marshal's bullet went lower than intended but struck Coe in the abdomen, passing out through his back.

"I've shot too low!" exclaimed Bill, disgusted with his poor aim.

As Coe fell to the ground in agony, another man came rushing to the scene, pistol in hand. Hickok, mistaking him in the darkness for a belligerent Texan, fired two bullets into his head. The man fell dead on the board sidewalk.

Turning his smoking pistols on the crowd of about fifty men, the marshal said calmly, "If any of you want the rest of these pills, come an' get 'em."

The mob, suddenly sobered, stood as if paralyzed. Not a man spoke. "Now every one of you mount his pony and ride for camp— and do it quick!" the marshal ordered. Instantly the Texans scattered, looking for their horses. In less than five minutes, every cowboy had crossed Mud Creek.

Left on the sidewalk, Wild Bill discovered that he had killed his friend Mike Williams, a special policeman hired by the Novelty Theater. Coe, still breathing, was taken to a near-by home, where he died three days later.

This double shooting had a sobering effect on the whole of Texas Abilene. It proved to be the last violence of the season. With most of the cattlemen and gamblers gone, the marshal had little more serious trouble during the fall. He had kept Abilene in fairly tight rein during its peak year, although he had not enforced the gun ordinance as strictly as had Tom Smith. He had spread his fame down the Chisholm Trail, though the permanent residents of Abilene were impressed more with his appearance and marksmanship than with his character.

The hero that Abilene ranked highest was still Tom Smith. Those who knew both marshals testified that Hickok's bravery was of a lower type than Smith's. They never had noticed Tom Smith's guns when he was on duty; they couldn't help seeing Wild Bill's.

Among those not overawed by the notches in Hickok's guns was young J. B. Edwards. Terming Smith "the most efficient officer of the frontier," he noted that "Wild Bill did not use his hands as his luckless predecessor had done; he used his hardware instead. His bravery has been described by old-timers in Abilene as cruder than Tom Smith's. Many believed that Wild Bill without his guns would have been tame."

As winter approached, Wild Bill found little to keep him busy. On December 12 the city council dismissed him, effective the next day, "for the reason that the city is no longer in need of his services."[9]

[9] Abilene, Kansas, Minute Book of the City Council (MS, Office of the City Clerk), 52, 55, 57, 65, 69, 71–73; Abilene *Chronicle*, October 12, 1871; Walton, *Life and Adventures of Ben Thompson*, 103–108; Hardin, *The Life of John Wesley Hardin*, 42–45; Gross, letter to Edwards, June 15, 1925, MS; Kansas City *Star*, November 15, 1925; Frank J. Wilstach, *Wild Bill Hickok*; Henry, *Conquering Our Great American Plains*, 89; Wilbert E. Eisele, *The Real Wild Bill Hickok*; William E. Connelley, *Wild Bill and His Era*; Little, "Early Days in Abilene and Dickinson County," in Roenigk, *Pioneer History of Kansas*.

Of the three biographies of Hickok, that by Connelley is the most reliable; but none of them has as much detail on Wild Bill's eight months in Abilene as the reader would like. After he left Abilene, Hickok returned to Hays, where he served another brief term as marshal. Then he toured the country with the theatrical troupe of Colonel William F. Cody (Buffalo Bill). Tiring of this life, he went on to Cheyenne. There, on March 5, 1876, he married Mrs. Lake, whom he had met in Abilene. After a honeymoon in Cincinnati, he left his bride with relatives there and went to Deadwood, Dakota Territory, then at the height of its gold-mining boom. On August 2, while playing poker in a Deadwood saloon, he was shot in the back and killed by Jack McCall.

IV

Despite the prosperity brought by the cattle trade, many Abilene people were tiring of the whole business. Not only did farmers object to having their fences torn down and their crops trampled, but townspeople didn't want their children to grow up in an atmosphere of vice and crime.

Although Mayor McCoy wanted Abilene to keep the cattle trade he had brought there, many citizens acted to push it away. Early in February, 1872, less than two months after Wild Bill had departed, Theodore C. Henry wrote a notice that others joined him in signing. They not only published it locally but sent it to Texas. It read, "We, the undersigned members of the Farmers' Protective Association and officers and citizens of Dickinson County, Kansas, most respectfully request all who have contemplated driving Texas cattle to Abilene the coming season to seek some other point for shipment, as the inhabitants of Dickinson County will no longer submit to the evils of the trade."[10]

The Texas drovers took these spokesmen at their word. The route from Wichita to Abilene was becoming too thickly settled for easy trailing. Other markets could handle the cattle shipments. Wichita was about to acquire a railroad and was bidding for business. Ellsworth, sixty miles west of Abilene, already had some cattle trade and wanted more. Drovers could reach that town by a cutoff that would miss the settled section south of Abilene.

As a result of this diversion, Abilene—although it still shipped a few cattle—became almost a ghost town. By summer, many of its buildings were empty. Mayor McCoy was bitter. "Four-fifths of her business houses became vacant," he wrote. "Rents fell to a trifle, and many of the leading hotels and business houses were either closed or taken down and moved to other points. Property became unsalable. The luxuriant sunflowers sprang up thick and flourished in the main streets, while the inhabitants, such as could not get away, passed the time sadly contemplating their ruin. The whole village assumed a desolate, forsaken, and deserted appearance."

A bit less downcast was the editor of the *Chronicle*. "Abilene is

[10] Abilene *Chronicle*, February 8, 15, 22, 1872; Henry, *Conquering our Great American Plains*, 307.

as quiet as any village in the land," he noted. "Business is not as brisk as it used to be during the cattle season, but the citizens have the satisfaction of knowing that hell is more than sixty miles away."[11]

With more settlers coming in, the town was able to make a new start as a local farm market. Its people learned to get along without the cattle money that, for four and one-half years, Texans who came up the Chisholm Trail had strewn about with lavish hands.

11 Abilene *Chronicle*, March 21, May 30, 1872; McCoy, *Historic Sketches of the Cattle Trade of the West and Southwest*, 231. The new market sixty miles away was Ellsworth.

XI

RIVAL COW TOWNS

Those who pointed Longhorns up the Chisholm Trail in 1872 found several Kansas towns bidding for their favor. Abilene's abdication as queen of the cow towns had spurred the rivalry of her neighbors. New markets were sending out agents to capture the Texas trade. Foremost among them were Wichita and Ellsworth.

Wichita, adding rapidly to the cluster of cabins and false-front stores on the bank of the Arkansas, had nearly two thousand inhabitants. Visitors could put up at the Munger House for two dollars a day or could live in more style at the new three-story Empire House on Main Street. Each day the Empire offered a freshly printed bill of fare. The town had four livery stables, an array of saloons, and a billiard hall. It had built sidewalks on Douglas Avenue and Main Street, which boasted almost solid rows of business buildings. Residents could buy firewood at five dollars a cord. Choice buffalo quarters and venison and antelope meat retailed at five to six cents a pound. Buffalo humps, tongues, and tenderloins brought six cents a pound.

The town government formed in July, 1870, had given way to organization as a city in April, 1871. By the opening of the 1872 cattle season, citizens had started a small school. The Presbyterians had completed a church at Wichita and Second streets. The Methodists and Episcopalians were taking turns at holding services in the new schoolhouse, but the Methodists had bought two lots at Third and Market and were preparing to build. The Catholics hoped to build in the fall.

Wichita people were keenly aware of the profits to be gained from shipping Longhorns. Their town had an advantage in being the first Kansas market that the weary drovers reached as they came up the trail. Wichita folks didn't seem to mind the dust that the herds raised as they marched right up Douglas Avenue from the river.

Joseph G. McCoy, left with little to do in Abilene, visited Wichita late in April, 1872, as a salesman for wrought-iron fencing. He advertised this as "the most durable and cheap fence ever invented," one that would not "rot, burn, or fall down." It made a fitting enclosure for the showy houses that some well-to-do Kansans were building. Yet more than an iron fence would have been needed to deflect McCoy's chief interest from the cattle business.

From Wichita's Main Street, McCoy and others could look north and see the railroad construction engine at work. It was laying rails on the spur line south from Newton. T. J. Peter, a director of the Atchison, Topeka and Santa Fe, was building this short line under the charter of the Wichita and South Western Railway Company. The Santa Fe leased it as soon as it was completed and later absorbed it.

With a railroad, Wichita could compete with any of the other Kansas cow towns. On May 11, while proud citizens watched from streets and roofs, a little locomotive with a coffeepot smokestack puffed into town with the first passenger train. Two days later, the road began regular service. That was just in time to catch the Longhorn herds coming up from the south.

To make the most of this asset, the city council hired a man to ride south and acquaint Texas drovers with the advantages of Wichita as a shipping point. He was James Bryden, a well-known Texas cowman of Scotch birth, who had spent the winter in the county. The city paid him four hundred dollars. But some of the leading businessmen realized that a cattle market must have buyers as well as sellers. So they privately raised a fund and engaged McCoy to go north and east to persuade buyers to come to Wichita. During the summer he traveled through Kansas, Missouri, Iowa, and other states, boosting the new Wichita market.

Officials of the Santa Fe railroad also were aware of the potential importance of Wichita. To look after the road's cattle interests, they hired as general livestock agent a young Texas cowman, Abel H. (Shanghai) Pierce. To help him, they engaged two of McCoy's friends, Colonel Samuel N. Hitt and Charles F. Gross.

Shanghai Pierce, born in Rhode Island, was one of the most striking figures among the drovers. He had learned the cattle business on the Texas coastal prairies. He was not quite twenty-seven; but his height—six feet four—and his booming voice quickly caught attention. McCoy, himself no whisperer, had noted Pierce's "ear-splitting voice, more piercing than a locomotive whistle, more noisy than a steam calliope." Charles A. Siringo, who had been with Pierce on the trail, said that he could be heard nearly half a mile away. His salty talk and his fund of stories made Pierce a favorite in the cow camps.

After seeing that the Wichita shipping yards were ready for use, Shanghai Pierce and two Illinoisans rode south. They aimed to meet the Texas outfits that were headed up the trail.

Meanwhile, the Wichita *Eagle* was beating the drums for the new market. It advertised Wichita as the shipping point within easiest reach of the drovers, as one free from meddling by settlers, and as well supplied with grass, water, and camping sites. "Our grazing grounds are equal to those of the Longhorn's native heath. The stockyards being erected are ample and convenient. In case of high water, the Arkansas River is spanned by a heavy wooden bridge that will carry two hundred cattle to the span."[1]

Wichita people boasted that their new stockyards, on the railroad in the southeast part of town, were the most convenient in the state. They covered a space 300 by 350 feet and had fifteen pens, seven gates, and four runways and chutes. They would hold about 2,500 cattle and could load about ten cars an hour. Attached to the yard were a driving wing and a twelve-acre enclosure for holding cattle overnight.

By the middle of May, several large herds of Texas cattle had

[1] Wichita *Eagle*, April 12, 26, May 24, 1872.

arrived and were grazing near the city's outskirts. Others were waiting along the Ninnescah River and Cow Skin Creek. Buyers were coming in, too. On June 8 the first shipment of Longhorns, eighteen carloads, left Wichita for Chicago. A shipment of twenty cars went off two days later.[2]

Among the early arrivals on the range south of Wichita were wiry L. B. Harris, of San Antonio, J. C. Juvenall from Brushy Creek, and William B. Slaughter from the Palo Pinto hills of the upper Brazos. Slaughter had nearly four thousand Longhorns. He kept this large herd on the prairies until August, then took the cattle into Wichita and sold them. Another Texas drover there in May was Captain James D. Reed, of Goliad, better known as One-Arm Reed. He bought the herds of other cowmen until he had more than twenty thousand head ready to ship.

More Texas drovers were on the way. William J. Bennett brought a herd from Uvalde. After holding his Longhorns for about three months, he sold to Shanghai Pierce. W. S. Hall trailed 4,200 head from Atascosa County and sold at Wichita. In June, L. A. Franks arrived from La Salle County with about a thousand well-fed steers.

Some of the cowmen held their Longhorns to improve their condition or to try for higher prices. One day in September, after climbing to the top of Wichita's highest building, the editor of the *Eagle* counted twenty-one herds within two miles of the town. Among the drovers then waiting was E. P. Byler, who had brought a thousand beeves from Goliad for Reed and O'Connor. He grazed them on the prairies for five and one-half months, selling early in December.[3]

In Wichita the 1872 cattle business brought quick prosperity to two landowners and developers, James R. Mead and William (Dutch Bill) Greiffenstein. Both were busy selling lots to new settlers. Greiffenstein, of Prussian birth, was building the $25,000 three-story Douglas Avenue Hotel, at the southwest corner of Douglas Avenue and Water Street. He also was erecting a handsome home. Mead, who had been an associate of Jesse Chisholm in Indian trading and had served in the legislature, had many business interests and was

---

[2] *Ibid.*, June 14, 1872.
[3] *Ibid.*, May 24, 1872; Hunter, *The Trail Drivers of Texas*, 122, 213, 387, 783.

vice-president of a bank. The two men raised $28,000 to build a wooden bridge across the Arkansas River.[4]

Many Wichita residents profited from entertaining the cow-punchers. The hotels, bars, and gambling rooms were crowded. In the tough Delano district, on the west side of the river, dives were ready to snatch the Texans' dollars. Rowdy Joe Lowe, who had killed Jim Sweet in a gun fight in Newton in 1871, put up a dance hall on the west bank. Joe, a short, heavy-set fellow, had rough manners but dressed fashionably, as did his wife, Kate. Their joint soon became known among Texas cowhands as the swiftest in Kansas.

At Rowdy Joe's, as at other such dives in frontier towns, the men were expected to buy drinks for their partners and themselves after each dance. This brought the owners more than one hundred dollars a night during the cattle season. A newsman described a dance at Joe's as "unique as well as interesting. The Texan with mammoth spurs on his boots, which are all exposed, and a broad-brimmed sombrero on his head, is seen dancing by the side of a well-dressed, gentlemanly appearing stranger from some eastern city, both having painted and jeweled courtesans for partners. In the corner of the hall are seen gamblers playing at their favorite game of poker. Jests and conversations suitable to the place and occasion are heard."

The Delano section had its share of shooting affrays. In one of them, on a Sunday night in September, Charley Jennison, a local tough, engaged in a gun fight back of a saloon with Jackson Davis, a young Virginian. Jennison, who received shots in the neck and right arm, put a bullet into the body of Davis, who died a few minutes later.

Just north of Wichita, in plain view of the town, was a track on which ponies were matched on Saturday afternoons. On July 6, reported the *Eagle* six days later, "the race was between a Texas horse and a Wichita mare. The mare won, and it is said that more than a thousand dollars changed hands. It was estimated that more than one thousand men were present, besides five carriage loads of soiled doves. So great was the rush that Main Street for an hour or so seemed almost deserted."

[4] Wichita *Eagle*, October 4, 1872.

186

To the north, Ellsworth didn't take this new competition lying down. Already a rip-roaring cow town of about one thousand inhabitants, it had made a good start in shipping cattle. After a profitable business in 1871, it prepared for a boom season in 1872. Its enlarged stockyards, of which R. D. Hunter was superintendent, were said to be the biggest in the state. They could ship two hundred cars of cattle a day.

Ellsworth took over much business directly from Abilene. It acquired that city's largest hotel, the three-story Drover's Cottage. Moses B. George had it dismantled and sections moved to the new site. He set up this frame building on Main Street, in the west end of town, near the stockyards. James W. and Louisa Gore continued to manage the hostelry, which had eighty-four rooms. Young Jake Karatofsky, who had operated the Great Western Store in Abilene, moved his business to Ellsworth.

John W. (Brocky Jack) Norton, who had been a peace officer in Abilene in 1871, found a similar job in Ellsworth. He had plenty of work. The tough part of the town, which catered to the Texas cow hands, was on the east side, in the river bottoms. People called it Nauchville. In addition to the usual saloons, gambling halls, and brothels, it had a track for horse races.

One who visited Ellsworth in the summer of 1872 described it thus:

This little border town of Ellsworth is not the most moral one in the world. During the cattle season, which lasts only during the summer and fall, it presents a scene seldom witnessed in any other section. It reminds one of a town in California in its early days when gambling flourished and vice was at a premium. Here you see in the streets men from every state and from almost every nation—the tall, long-haired Texas herder, with his heavy jingling spurs and pair of six-shooters; the dirty, greasy Mexicans, with unintelligible jargon; the gambler from all parts of the country, looking for unsuspecting prey; the honest emigrant in search of a homestead in the great free West; the keen stock buyers; the wealthy Texas drovers; deadbeats; cappers; pickpockets; horse thieves; a cavalry of Texas ponies; and scores of demimonde.

Gambling of every description is carried on without any attempt of privacy. I am told that there are seventy-five professional gamblers in town. Every day we hear of some of their sharp tricks. Whisky selling seems to be the most profitable business. But there are many honorable businessmen here, who are doing a heavy business.[5]

Ellsworth, although not as well situated as Wichita for the Texas drovers, had an advantage in being on the Kansas Pacific Railroad. Cattle buyers were used to traveling over this road, and it had better facilities and longer experience in handling the trail cattle. "No other road in Kansas," wrote its general freight agent, T. F. Oakes, "can give as positive assurance of a large and regular supply of stock cars." The Kansas Pacific, like the Santa Fe, sent agents south to drum up cattle business.

The first Texas herds reached Ellsworth late in May. Three more, of about 1,000 head each, arrived early in June. Two weeks later twenty-eight herds, of 1,000 to 6,000 each, were on hand; and many others were coming up the trail. These arrivals, with more than 40,000 head that had been wintered in the country, made more than 100,000 head available for the Ellsworth market.[6]

Among those who sold at Ellsworth was W. T. Avery of Hutto. Leaving Brushy Creek on April 15, he had pointed two thousand steers up the older and longer Shawnee Trail. After crossing the Red River, his outfit had trouble from heavy rains, stampedes, and Indian raids. Avery grazed his herd for a month near Baxter Springs before going on to Ellsworth.

Most of the drovers reached Ellsworth more directly by the Chisholm Trail. From Pond Creek they left the trail to Wichita and Abilene and took a short cut, crossing the Arkansas east of the dismantled Fort Zarah. This route reduced the distance from the Red River to Ellsworth to about 350 miles.

Many Texans were in Ellsworth that summer. Among those staying at the Drover's Cottage, which fed 100 to 150 men every day, was Colonel Dudley H. Snyder. Tall and black haired, Snyder was a shrewd cowman and a veteran drover. In 1854, at the age of twenty-one, he had ridden horseback from his native Mississippi to Texas and later had settled on a farm near Round Rock. Beginning in the Civil War, he had become a familiar figure on several trails. A strict

[5] Ellsworth *Reporter*, July 25, 1872.
[6] Abilene *Chronicle*, May 23, 1872; Ellsworth *Reporter*, June 6, 20, 1872.

Methodist, he did not allow his cowhands to drink whisky, play cards, or swear in his presence.

From Ellsworth, on July 6, 1872, Snyder wrote a letter to his wife. Mrs. Snyder, lonely and not entirely well, had asked when her husband would come back to their home on Brushy Creek. "I shall come back as soon as I can," he answered. "I am making arrangements to come back the last of this month."

Yet, solicitous as he was of his family and eager to see them, his mind ran ahead to cattle deals. He referred to a prospective trip to Cheyenne and added: "I am thinking about wintering in Salt Lake if only you will go with me. I wouldn't go out there for all the cattle in the country, but I am firmly of the opinion that it will be beneficial to your health to spend the fall and winter in the western country. This we can talk over when I get home. I have bought 3,060 head of cattle at this place and bought them so that I can make money on them, if no hard luck. Cattle are high out west and low here."

Later that year Snyder trailed cattle to Cheyenne. He and his younger brother, John W. Snyder, also sold a herd to John Tierman, Ingram and Company of Salt Lake and delivered the Longhorns on Goose Creek in Nevada.[7]

III

Despite the trailing of many herds on north and west, the Kansas cattle trade continued brisk. Ellsworth and Wichita had competition from other frontier towns. On the Kansas Pacific, Brookville shipped 12,240 head, Salina 10,940, and Solomon 8,040. Abilene, despite its repudiation of the Texas trade, handled a few herds of trail cattle in 1871. One dealer, Colonel O. W. Wheeler, shipped forty-seven carloads from there and eight from Junction City.

Other railroads were busy, too. The Santa Fe, while developing its cattle business at Wichita, was pushing its tracks west along the Arkansas River. In August it reached Great Bend, which shipped a few cattle in the fall. Among them was a Choate and Bennett herd trailed by John Henry Choate from the Nueces River. Baxter

[7] Dudley H. Snyder, letter to his wife, Mary Snyder, dated Ellsworth, Kansas, July 6, 1872, MS; Hunter, *The Trail Drivers of Texas*, 518, 726, 1030. Snyder acquired large ranches in western Texas, one of them spreading over about 130,000 acres. He died in Georgetown in 1921.

Springs, on the old Shawnee Trail, continued to send Longhorns north by rail. Some of its cattle had arrived from the Indian Territory and others from Texas. Jim Saul sold there a thousand head that he and his outfit had trailed from Brushy Creek in Williamson County.

Texans trailed more than 350,000 cattle north in 1872, compared with 600,000 for the peak year of 1871. Someone at Caldwell kept a record of the Texas herds passing that town between May 1 and November 1. He listed 292 herds, totaling 349,275 head, or an average of 1,195 to the herd. This list did not include the herds that went up the Shawnee Trail or the many that left the beaten path of the Chisholm Trail at Pond Creek or some other point below Caldwell. Thus the total drive may have been considerably larger than the generally accepted estimate of 350,000 head.

Wichita, making full use of its new rail connection, took top honors as a shipping point for the 1872 season. It sent off 3,530 carloads of cattle, or about 70,600 head. Ellsworth, in second place with 40,161 head, accounted for about one-fourth of the 163,140 carried east by the Kansas Pacific.[8]

Besides shipping cattle by rail, Ellsworth and other Kansas towns served as markets for Texas herds that were trailed on to distant ranges, as were the herds the Snyders had handled. Some went to Nebraska, Wyoming, Utah, California, and other states. In June and July, more than 100,000 head of cattle were reported to have changed hands at Ellsworth. V. J. Carvajal had trailed a herd to Ellsworth for Colin Campbell, who ran the F and 66 brands on Ecleto Creek in Karnes County. He took the Longhorns on to the North Platte with the aid of a compass, a map of Nebraska, and the North Star. J. W. Jackson went with a herd of 2,290 head from Tom Lane's ranch in Milam County to Ellsworth and on to Cheyenne. Sam Garner and Mack Stewart delivered a herd at Salt Lake for Colonel John J. Myers, of Lockhart.[9]

For nearly all the Texas drovers, 1872 was a prosperous year. The falling off in the number of trail cattle from 1871 was largely

[8] *Texas Almanac* for 1873, 30–32; *Kansas Daily Commonwealth*, January 8, 1873; Wichita *Eagle*, January 23, 1873; *Guide Map of the Great Texas Cattle Trail* (pamphlet), 1875 edition, 8.

[9] Ellsworth *Reporter*, April 17, 1873; Hunter, *The Trail Drivers of Texas*, 375, 523, 549, 839.

offset by higher prices, lush grass, and lack of blizzards such as the ones that had struck many herds in the preceding season. Between 60 and 70 per cent of the cattle sent north in 1872 were mixed herds rather than beeves. That meant that most of them were used for stocking new ranches instead of being shipped east.

Trailing east and west from Texas continued to dwindle. Some cattle, though, were walked to Alexandria, Louisiana, and loaded on Red River boats for New Orleans. Others went by coastal ships from Texas Gulf ports.

The 1872 season brought hints of new developments that might affect the whole cattle industry. Salina made its first shipment of meat in refrigerated cars, thus pointing to the rise of a large decentralized packing industry in the Middle West and the Southwest. Another change was a noticeable shortening of the horns of some of the Texas trail cattle. Writing from Wichita in midsummer, Joseph G. McCoy called attention to the fact that many of the arriving Longhorns showed that they had been graded upward by the use of Durham bulls on the home range. This was true especially of herds from northern and northwestern Texas. The resultant steers were squarely built, and their horns were not quite so long.[10] Already the famous Texas breed was beginning to lose some of its wild look and to take on a more civilized appearance.

[10] Wichita *Eagle*, August 2, 1872.

XII

PROSPERITY AND PANIC

No matter how large the drives to Kansas, they did not appear to lessen the supply of Longhorns on the Texas ranges. As the herds plodded off to northern markets, their places were taken by calves that grew rapidly in the mild climate that afforded year-round grazing. The spring of 1873 found another big crop of steers and mixed cattle ready for the long trek.

Texas was recovering at last from the devastating blows of the Civil War. Railroads were extending their lines and were bringing in new settlers, mainly from the Old South. The state was becoming less isolated from the rest of the country. Many Texans showed renewed interest in national affairs. While the men talked about the bribery of congressmen by a railway construction company, the Crédit Mobilier, the women buzzed in back-fence gossip over the Beecher-Tilton scandal.

Those Texans who had fought for the Confederacy had won back the right to vote. They had taken control of the legislature and were preparing to oust their carpetbag governor. Farmers and ranchmen were arguing over whether the state needed a new law to keep livestock from roaming at large.

Some Texans on the coastal prairies were probing new methods of packing meat and of keeping it fresh. One sent to Liverpool a test shipment of beef that had been treated chemically and packed in casks. Another began monthly shipments of beef to Philadelphia on steamers that kept it cool with currents of air which had been forced across ice. On Tres Palacios Creek, W. B. Grimes canned beef, which he sold to planters. In the same section, the Stabler Patent Beef Packing Company obtained a contract to sell canned beef to the United States Navy. Yet the main interest of Texas cowmen still was in sending beef to market on the hoof.

In the early spring of 1873, conditions were favorable for a bigger trail drive than that of the preceding year. Drovers who had profited in 1872 were eager to send more and bigger herds up the trail. From Matagorda, on the coastal plains, the *Colorado Citizen* reported in mid-March that cattle in that section had not suffered as seriously as was feared from the severe winter. "They are looking well after their hardships, and the fresh grass soon will bring them out." A large number already had been shipped by rail to Galveston and Houston.[1]

Yet people in the Kansas cow towns, while getting ready for a banner year, were a bit apprehensive. Texas stockmen at last had a railroad over which they could ship cattle to Kansas City or St. Louis and beyond. They expected to have by midsummer a second line to St. Louis. Building north from the Gulf Coast, the Houston and Texas Central had reached Dallas in July, 1872, and had pushed on to Denison, near the Red River. On Christmas Day the Missouri, Kansas and Texas Railroad, rushing south along the Shawnee Trail, reached Denison. Meanwhile, the Texas and Pacific, building from a St. Louis connection westward toward Dallas, was expected to reach that city in July. Would Texas cowmen use the new railroads instead of the old trails?

Many in Dallas and Denison were confident that the railroads would quickly take over the task of transporting Texas cattle to markets. In Dallas the *Herald* pointed out that, from neighboring Hutchins, two cowmen had shipped about five hundred corn-fed beeves by rail to Houston, thence by Morgan Line steamers to New Orleans. With the cost of the steers figured at eighteen dollars a head

[1] Quoted in the Denison *Daily News*, March 19, 1873.

and transportation at twenty-nine dollars, the shippers had a good profit from the sixty-five dollars a head received in the Crescent City.[2]

During the spring, Denison quickly took on the aspects of a cow town and became one of the toughest on the frontier. The tents and shacks of Skiddy Street—later Chestnut—housed some of the most depraved saloons, gambling dives, and "dovecotes" that anyone could find. For every cowhand who wanted entertainment, Denison was ready.

The *Daily News* pictured glowing prospects for the new town as a cattle loading point. Shipments from Denison would be large, it predicted. "The driving to Kansas is about at an end. Some few dealers will probably operate on the old plan this year, as it is hard to convince some men that their way is not the best. But the advantages of shipping by rail are so apparent that driving across the Nation may be considered virtually at an end."[3]

Denison and other Katy points did ship many cattle that season—about eighty thousand head. At the height of the loadings, in late June and through July, shipments sometimes reached forty-five cars a day. As there were not enough loading pens to hold all the cattle brought in, some drovers had to wait their turns. Yet the cattle shipped from Denison were largely from near-by ranges. Most of the experienced drovers stuck to the hoof-marked trails. When they compared railway freight rates with the cost of trailing, they figured that they could make more profit by walking their cattle. In spite of the competition of the railroads, trailing in 1873 was heavier than in 1872. Some of the drovers went past Denison and up the old Shawnee Trail to Baxter Springs or Coffeyville, much of the time within view of the new railroad. But nine-tenths of them took their herds up the Chisholm Trail.

Texans pointed an estimated 500,000 Longhorns to Kansas during the season. This compared with 600,000 for the peak year of 1871 and more than 350,000 for 1872. About 450,000 of the 1873 drive went to the central and western sections of the state and 50,000 to the Baxter Springs and Coffeyville area in the southeast. At least three-fifths of the herds were of mixed cattle, and many of the ani-

[2] Dallas *Herald*, April 5, 1873.
[3] Denison *Daily News*, April 6, 1873.

mals were of poor quality. The Texans wanted to sell every scrawny critter they could while prices were high.

In Fort Worth, J. T. Litton, who had dealings with many of the drovers, kept a count of the herds which passed through the town that spring. At the end of April he reported that fifty-six herds had gone north. They ranged from 550 head to 6,000. Together they had 62,235 cattle, an average of 1,111 to the herd. From the south, more Longhorns were on the way.[4]

Fort Worth, growing and prospering from the cattle trade, was as rough and bawdy as ever. For the cowmen it offered more frontier entertainment than civilized comfort. When some citizens asked that hogs no longer be allowed to run at large in the streets, the city council refused to impose such a ban.

Some drovers complained of extortion on the part of the cattle inspectors. In Fort Worth a deputy inspector made so many demands for money that one newspaper called the practice a "genteel system of blackmail." This situation was remedied soon after it was aired, but sporadic cases of injustice cropped up elsewhere. At Red River Station two inspectors looked over thirteen herds and found two unbranded beeves. They told the drover he would have to pay them fifty dollars. Instead of complying, he had his men capture the inspectors and put them in a wagon. The outfit hauled the inspectors across most of the Indian Territory to Pond Creek. When turned loose there, they had to swim the creek to start their long trip home.[5]

Trailing conditions generally were favorable, although some of the early drovers ran into cloudbursts and booming streams. Dick Withers, who had to swim his herd across the Red River and every large stream beyond, said that this was the wettest year he ever saw on the trail. Indian troubles were not serious. Most of the buffaloes had retreated to the west, but several trail drivers proved their marksmanship by downing a shaggy or two.

Yet the Indian Territory still held danger for the drovers. The cattle trail, noted a Fort Smith editor, was "infested with murderers, robbers, and horse thieves gathered from all parts of the country."

4 Fort Worth *Democrat*, May 3, 1873; Denison *Daily News*, May 21, 1874.
5 Fort Worth *Democrat*, May 17, 24, 1873; Hunter, *The Trail Drivers of Texas*, 310–11, 704.

Even deputy United States marshals had to go in squads for self-protection. "A company of forty men, known as Gallagher's band, bid defiance of law and are fearless of the United States cavalry. This band infests the cattle trail, and its members have friends everywhere that keep them posted as to the movements of the marshals and the military. Stealing horses is an everyday occurrence, and murder and robbery seem to equal that sin."[6]

II

On the Kansas prairies, Wichita and Ellsworth again were the chief contenders for the Texas cattle trade. Each town was improving its facilities and getting ready to send fast talkers to meet the drovers and try to win their favor. In Wichita the city council again hired James Bryden, on the same terms as in 1872. They also engaged, for a longer period, Abel H. (Shanghai) Pierce, who had worked for the Santa Fe a year earlier. Pierce received $200 a month for ten months for using his influence to induce Texas cowmen to market at Wichita.

Wichita, which boasted of three thousand inhabitants, was putting up many new buildings. It was proud of the new $19,000 First National Bank at First and Main—a two-story brick structure with a basement. Its second floor was occupied by Masonic lodge rooms and had a carpet that cost five hundred dollars. On the opposite corner was a two-story grocery that did a brisk business.

On the south side of Douglas Avenue, near Main, William Greiffenstein was putting up a pair of two-story brick business houses. Elsewhere, James R. Mead was completing a $10,000 home, said to be the finest in southern Kansas. It was a brick house of two stories and basement and had a mansard roof covered with slate. Also under construction by a stock company was the Metropolitan Hotel, at Main and Second. This was a three-story building designed to have seventy-six rooms. Completion was promised by September. Meanwhile, the Baptists had met to form a church.

Spring rains had put the pastures about Wichita in fine condition, and citizens were confident of getting a large share of the cattle trade. On May 2, agents of the Santa Fe heard that twenty thousand

[6] *Western Independent*, August 21, 28, 1873.

head of Longhorns had arrived at a ranch south of Caldwell. They immediately set out to meet the drovers. They wanted not only to persuade them to sell at Wichita but to conduct the herds there by a route that would avoid trouble with farmers.

Soon the trail drivers began to pour into town. As the hotels were crowded, many cowboys slept in the Blue Front store, which had a big supply of blankets and buffalo robes. Early in June, a visitor found Wichita in "a lively condition. Hundreds of the long-haired Texans are encamped in the vicinity. Three or four brass bands keep the place flooded with music. Soon the Longhorns will begin to move eastward by rail."[7]

In addition to cattle, Wichita was shipping large quantities of buffalo hides. Wagon trains brought the hides in from the southwest, over the Medicine Lodge road. Sometimes a cattle outfit would pass a train of fifteen to twenty wagons, each drawn by six or eight mules. The hides, which made light freight, were piled high and were held in place with poles and ropes. Other freighters and settlers brought in buffalo and cattle bones, for which dealers paid fifty cents a load. Vast piles of the bones lined the railroad, awaiting shipment to carbon factories.

Not only in shipping but in entertainment, Wichita did a flourishing business. "Everything goes in Wichita," read signs on the roads at the edge of town. "Leave your revolvers at police headquarters and get a check. Carrying concealed weapons strictly forbidden."

In the wild Delano district at the west end of the Douglas Avenue bridge, John (Red) Beard had built a dance hall beside that of Rowdy Joe. Beard was a big, red-headed fellow, slovenly in dress and walk. He hailed from Illinois and was said to have come from a good family. Whenever he went into town, he carried a double-barreled shotgun, which he placed between his knees when he sat down in a saloon.

On June 2, Red Beard's dance hall was the scene of the first of Wichita's serious gun battles of the season. From their camp south

[7] Proceedings of the Wichita City Council (MS, Office of the City Clerk), February 14, July 16, November 5, 1873; *Kansas Daily Commonwealth*, May 4, 1873; Wichita *Eagle*, May 15, June 12, 1873.

of town, soldiers of the Sixth Cavalry had come in to celebrate. When a soldier and a cowboy wanted to dance with the same girl, their quarrel led to a free-for-all between the Texans and the cavalrymen. The girls and other neutrals stampeded for cover. One man crawled under a bass violin, from which his arms and legs stuck out like the legs of a turtle. As the bullets flew, one soldier and one of Red's girls were killed, while two other persons were wounded.

Gun fights and stabbings continued through the cattle season. At least six victims died violently, and others acquired lasting scars. The biggest gun battle came near the close of the shipping season— on the night of October 27. Red Beard and some of his friends were holding a drunken brawl in his dance hall. After a while they went into Rowdy Joe's place, breaking into the midst of a dance. Red fired a shot that wounded Annie Franklin, one of Joe's girls. Then guns began popping on both sides. Bill Anderson, who had been jailed earlier in the year on a charge of killing a man in a blacksmith shop with his pistol, keeled over, blinded by a bullet just back of his eyes. Red Beard caught buckshot in one arm and one hip. He died a few days later. The police held Joe on $2,000 bail but in December a trial jury acquitted him.

III

Ellsworth was equally alert in going after the Texas cattle business. In the spring the Kansas Pacific Railroad had a new route surveyed from the Indian Territory, leading west of Wichita and direct to Ellsworth. For this task, William M. Cox, general livestock agent for the railroad, left Ellsworth April 6, in company with four well-known cattlemen. The work of marking the new trail, which shortened the distance by twenty miles, was completed about May 1. While Cox returned to Ellsworth, three of the stockmen stayed in the Indian Territory to meet the early drovers.

The new short cut left the original trail at Sewell's ranch, about halfway between the Salt Fork of the Arkansas River and Pond Creek. Turning to the left, it bore a little west of north along Pond Creek to the headwaters of that stream. It crossed Bluff Creek at a point that came to be known as Cox's Crossing. It reached Ellsworth by way of Kingman and Ellinwood, crossing the Arkansas at the latter place.

By traversing the three forks of the Ninnescah River, Antelope Creek, Rattlesnake Creek, and lesser streams, this route offered the drovers an abundance of water for their herds. There were three supply stores: one at Sewell's ranch east of the Pond Creek crossing, one kept by C. H. Stone at Cox's Crossing, and that of E. C. Manning a mile and one-half east of Kingman, where the trail crossed the Ninnescah.[8] Although usually considered a part of the Chisholm Trail, the short cut to Ellsworth sometimes was called Cox's Trail or the Ellsworth Trail.

Ellsworth, eager to be "the livest town in Kansas this year," was making ready for a big influx from Texas. New buildings were rising on every side. Besides the Drover's Cottage, which Mrs. James W. Gore had bought from Moses B. George for $10,000 and renamed the Cottage House, the town had several other hotels. The most imposing was Arthur Larkin's $27,000 brick Grand Central, at Main and Lincoln. Larkin advertised it as "the finest house in Kansas—headquarters for stock dealers." There the Ellsworth Dancing Club had held its balls in the preceding winter. In the spring, Larkin replaced the board sidewalk in front of the hotel with one of magnesian limestone, twelve feet wide.

Even the lesser hotels were being spruced up for the cowmen. J. C. Veatch had enlarged and improved his City Hotel and restaurant. On Main, east of Douglas, John Kelly and his brother had remodeled, enlarged, and refurnished the American House. It offered to serve with "luxury and ease all those fatigued with the toils and labors of the day, especially the Texas drovers upon their arrival after a long and weary journey."

New stores were ready for the drovers; and D. W. Powers and Company, of Leavenworth, had opened a bank for "merchants, stock dealers, and the Texas cattle trade." Besides three hotel bars, the town had thirteen licensed saloons and dram shops. Each paid for a $500 yearly license, a $25 federal license, and a $10 general business license. Saloons, gambling houses, and dance halls stayed open all night. A theater was opened early in June.

Ellsworth tolerated ladies of easy virtue—for a fee. "The city realizes $300 per month from prostitution fines alone," a Topeka

[8] Ellsworth *Reporter*, May 8, 1873; *Guide Map of the Great Texas Cattle Trail* (pamphlet), 1875 edition.

newspaper reported July 1. "The authorities consider that as long as mankind is depraved and Texas cattle herders exist, there will be a demand and necessity for prostitutes. They consider that as long as prostitutes are bound to dwell in Ellsworth, it is better for the respectable portion of society to hold prostitutes under restraint of the law."

Ahead of the cattle herds that spring came not only sporting women but a full array of gamblers and thugs. Ben Thompson, who had stayed home in Texas for nearly a year after retiring from the Bull's Head in Abilene, came to Ellsworth to get in on the pickings. Soon he was joined by his younger brother, Billy, who had come up with a trail outfit. The brothers set up gambling tables in Joe Brennan's saloon, known as the "gamblers' roost." Another gambler was John Sterling, who seemed to win every bet. Also in town were two handsome, wild fellows, Cad Pierce and Neil Cain. They had come up with Texas herds and stayed on as gamblers.

To cope with troublemakers, the town dads promoted to the post of marshal John W. (Brocky Jack) Norton, who had served an apprenticeship in Abilene. They gave him four policemen. The four were John S. Brauham, known for his quick trigger finger; John DeLong, from the Topeka police force; Ed O. Hogue, of French ancestry; and John (Happy Jack) Morco, a surly, illiterate fellow who had just arrived from California. The police judge, Vincent B. Osborne, held court in a room above Larkin's Drug Store, where he tried more than sixty cases during the cattle season. The county sheriff was bearded Chauncey B. Whitney, a veteran of the Civil War and an Indian fighter. One of the policemen, Ed Hogue, doubled as deputy sheriff. A jail was completed in June, 1873, next to the courthouse on the north side of the railroad, two blocks east of Douglas. The local newspaper called it the most comfortable place in town but warned readers that not too many should crowd into it at once.[9]

The drovers did not keep Ellsworth waiting. Even before William Cox arrived back from his survey trip, twenty-eight Texas

[9] Ellsworth *Reporter*, March 6, May 1, July 3, August 28, 1873; *Kansas Daily Commonwealth*, June 4, July 1, 1873; Floyd Benjamin Streeter, "Ellsworth as a Texas Cattle Market," *Kansas Historical Quarterly*, Vol. IV, No. 4 (November, 1935), 388–98; Jelinek, *Ellsworth, Kansas, 1867–1947* (pamphlet), 9–13.

herds were reported to be on the way. Soon Ellsworth people could make out hazy clouds of dust in the south, then the Longhorns themselves. "You see a steer's head and horns silhouetted against the sky line," recalled John Clay, "then another and another until you realize it's a herd."[10]

Early summer found the prairies about Ellsworth filled with herds from the Texas ranges. Among the early arrivals were herds brought or sent by such leading Texas cowmen as Colonel John J. Myers, Major Seth Mabry, Captain Eugene Millett, Willis McCutcheon, Jesse L. Driskill, John R. Blocker, and Mark and Richard Withers. On May 29, the *Reporter* estimated that 100,000 head were on hand. The number rose to 125,000 on June 5 and to 143,000 a week later. From his big ranch on San Miguel Creek in Frio County, William Perryman and his Mexican trail hands arrived in June with five thousand head.

Excursionists from Kansas City who visited the western cattle markets about July 1 estimated that Ellsworth had 135,000 head, compared with only 56,000 head at Wichita. Before July ended, some estimates of the Texas cattle about Ellsworth rose to 177,000 head. "The great droves cover the hills and knolls," said one observer, "and the valleys are dark with them for miles around." One of the biggest sales in Ellsworth during the season was that of L. B. Harris of San Antonio, who received $210,000 for his seven thousand steers.[11]

Trail drivers who liked excitement could find it in Ellsworth as readily as in Wichita. "As we go to press," reported a weekly newspaper in a rival town, "hell is still in session in Ellsworth."

This wild life reached its peak on the afternoon of August 15. At Joe Brennan's saloon, Ben Thompson had put John Sterling in a monte game in which the stakes were unusually high. Sterling said that if he won he would split his winnings with Ben. Continuing to drink as he played, Sterling won more than a thousand dollars, which he pocketed, and walked off.

Later in the afternoon, Ben saw Sterling in Nick Lentz's saloon and asked for his share of the winnings. This so angered Sterling that

[10] Clay, *My Life on the Range*, 107.
[11] Ellsworth *Reporter*, May 1, 29, June 26, 1873.

he struck Ben in the face. A policeman, Happy Jack Morco, separated the men. But a few minutes later Morco and Sterling appeared together at the front door of Brennan's saloon, both heavily armed. Morco didn't have much use for the Thompsons. On June 30, he had arrested Billy for assaulting him with a pistol. The next day Billy had paid a ten-dollar fine and fifteen-dollar costs.

On this August afternoon one of the men in Brennan's doorway shouted into the saloon at Ben, telling him to come out and fight. Ben ran out through the back door and up to Jack New's saloon, where he picked up his pistol and repeating Winchester. Meanwhile, Billy rushed in and grabbed Ben's double-barreled shotgun.

In front of the saloon, Billy, who had been drinking and was handling the shotgun carelessly, fired one barrel by accident. The charge hit the sidewalk, just missing the feet of two Texas cowmen, Major Seth Mabry and his partner, Captain Eugene Millett. Seeing that Morco and Sterling were coming after them, the Thompson brothers headed for the railroad, where they could fight a gun battle without danger to innocent bystanders.

From the railroad track, near the west end of the station, Ben shouted defiance to his foes and dared them to come out and fight. By that time, Sheriff Whitney, who was in front of Veatch's restaurant, had become aware of the fracas. In his shirt sleeves and unarmed, he walked over to the Thompsons.

"Boys," he advised, "let's not have any fuss or any difficulty."

"We don't want any trouble, but we'll defend ourselves if they want to fight," replied Ben. He accused Happy Jack of picking on Texans. But the sheriff, offering his protection, persuaded them to come back with him toward Brennan's saloon. As they were entering the door, W. A. Langford, a Texas cowman, shouted to Ben, who was behind:

"Look out, Ben! Here they come with guns!"

Turning, Ben saw Happy Jack running down the street toward him, with a six-shooter in his hand. Ben aimed his rifle at the policeman, but Jack dodged into Jerome Beebe's store. Ben's bullet missed him and hit the door casing.

Then Billy and Sheriff Whitney, who had gone into the saloon, heard the shot and rushed out. From the store, Happy Jack ventured out again, with his pistol ready for action. Billy, who still had Ben's shotgun, loaded with buckshot, aimed it at Jack. But, perhaps as a result of his drinking, he stumbled as he pulled the trigger. The charge intended for Jack struck Sheriff Whitney.

As the sheriff reeled and sent for his wife, Ben shouted to his brother: "Billy, you've shot our best friend!"

While bystanders carried the wounded sheriff to his home, two blocks away, Ben urged Billy to flee. A Texan brought his horse and handed him a roll of bills. Ben gave him more money and a pistol. But Billy refused to be hurried. He rode about, shooting the pistol, then went to the Nauchville section to see his girl friend, Molly Brennan, before heading toward Texas. Three days later, Sheriff Whitney died of his wounds.[12]

Whitney's death did not end the violence in Ellsworth. Soon afterward a new policeman, Ed Crawford, got into an argument with Cad Pierce, the Texas cowman who had turned gambler. The quarrel ended with Crawford's killing of Pierce. The next day Happy Jack ran Pierce's partner, Neil Cain, out of town. Vigilantes, alarmed over the shootings, ordered a dozen thugs to leave Ellsworth and raided the Grand Central Hotel, making a haul of six-shooters belonging to Texans.

In November, Ed Crawford, who had left town for his own safety after killing Pierce, returned. After patronizing the bars, he went to a brothel in Nauchville. There he engaged in a quarrel with another man and was shot to death.

IV

Although the number of Texas cattle trailed to Ellsworth in 1873 was estimated at 150,000 or more—a third of all those taken into western Kansas—only 30,540 were shipped from there. This was only three-fourths of the number loaded a year earlier, from a smaller drive, and was much below the 65,831 shipped from Wichita. Lesser shipments were made from other towns on the Kansas Pacific. To the south, the Santa Fe was developing new cattle markets in

[12] Walton, *Life and Adventures of Ben Thompson*, 110–31; Floyd Benjamin Streeter, *The Kaw*, 136–48. Three years afterward, Billy Thompson was arrested in Texas and later was tried in Ellsworth. He was acquitted on the ground that his shooting of Sheriff Whitney was an accident.

addition to Wichita. That year it shipped 11,144 head from Great Bend, 1,291 from Hutchinson, and 2,580 from Granada, across the line in Colorado.

About 25,000 Longhorns were wintered on the prairies near Ellsworth, while many herds were trailed on to new ranges in the Northwest. William G. Butler trailed to Nebraska; Dillard R. Fant sent herds to Nebraska and Wyoming; and the Snyder brothers took Longhorns to Wyoming and Idaho. Probably more cattle would have been shipped from Kansas in 1873 except for the financial panic which struck the East in September and spread to the cattle country a month later.

This economic disaster, one of the worst that ever hit the nation, was an aftermath of wars on both sides of the Atlantic and of too rapid expansion in industry and wild speculation in business. In the East, pandemonium broke loose on September 18, when the big banking and securities firm of Jay Cooke and Company closed its doors. Following closely the failure of several other large eastern firms, that of Jay Cooke shook the nation. This company had floated big government loans during the Civil War. Later it had been a leader in financing railroad construction. Heavy advances to railroads led to its downfall.

"This has been the wildest day on the Exchange that I ever have known," wrote Collis P. Huntington, the California railroad builder, who was in New York. "No one can be safe in a panic like this."

The next day many remembered as Black Friday. The Jay Cooke crash closed the Stock Exchange for ten days, sent President Ulysses S. Grant in haste to New York, broke many banks, and pushed a host of companies and individuals into bankruptcy. It threw thousands of men out of work and put skids under prices, including those of cattle.

Those Texas drovers who had sold early in the season had done well, even though a short corn crop had cut down the number of feeder buyers. Those who had held on found the market paralyzed by the panic. A few lucky ones sold to men who had contracts to supply beef to Indian agencies, but this buying made only a small dent in the supply. Again men killed thousands of cattle for their hides and tallow, and they obtained little more money for many of those they sold for other purposes. Shanghai Pierce and James D. Reed, who had both money and nerve, joined hands to buy cattle at panic prices. They acquired seven thousand head, which they wintered in central Kansas.

During the fall and winter, the depression that came after the panic became a chilling blizzard. It reached even the most remote cattle ranges. It was bound to have an effect on the size of the 1874 Texas drive.

XIII

GRASSLAND EMPIRE

As drovers started more herds up the Chisholm Trail in the spring of 1874, those with sharp eyes could see the beginning of changes in the broad Texas cow country. Stockmen who read the signs foresaw the close of the era of the open range. The big cowmen, instead of depending wholly on state-owned land for grazing their herds, were buying choice pastures that bordered on good streams and were fencing in as much grass and water as they could.

Building fences on the Texas plains was laborious and expensive. Both wood and stone were scarce in most sections, and the cost of wire put it beyond the reach of all but the most prosperous ranchmen. Yet some went ahead building fences of rails, planks, or smooth wire. The barbed wire that rival Illinoisans were trying to patent wasn't yet on the market.

Shanghai Pierce, who had become one of the leading cowmen, recalled with a wry grin the fences he had built for W. B. Grimes in Matagorda County, on the coastal plains. When Pierce, then a lanky youth of nineteen, had come to Texas late in 1853, his first job was to split rails for a stake-and-rider fence. For this work, Grimes, who had a wide spread on Tres Palacios Creek, paid him fourteen dollars a month and board.

In the spring of 1874, fences were becoming more common. In southern Texas, Captain Richard King, who owned a ranch of about 150,000 acres—with 50,000 cattle, 20,000 sheep, and 10,000 horses—had begun fencing in 1871. Now he had an enclosed pasture of 70,000 acres. A few ranchmen were building sod fences, and many were growing hedges. The most popular plant for hedging was the thorny Osage orange, or *bois d'arc*. Closely planted, it would become "horse high, bull strong, and pig tight."

Fencing made it easier for foresighted cowmen to improve their herds. The grading up of the Texas Longhorns, which Joe McCoy had noted two years earlier, was becoming more marked. Captain King, who had turned to ranching after running a steamboat on the Rio Grande, had just imported many fine Kentucky cattle to breed with his native stock. Others, too, were bringing in blooded bulls of modern breeds, most often the Durham or Shorthorn. "The people are becoming tired of raising Longhorns," reported the Weatherford *Times*. "Shorthorns are coming in every few days. Yesterday we saw a herd of fifteen or twenty Shorthorn bulls, from one to three years old. Some of them had been sold, to go to Keechi Valley. Colonel Tom Lewis was bargaining for some of them when we saw them. That is the right way to improve the native stock."[1]

Several stockmen from the Dallas area imported pedigreed Kentucky bulls. In Johnson County, Tilghman Fowler, of Cleburne, paid a Kansas City dealer $586 for three thoroughbred Shorthorns from Kentucky—two heifers of fifteen months and a bull of thirteen months.[2] That price sounded big to some grizzled Texans who, not many years earlier, had sold yearlings at one to three dollars a head. But most of them realized the need to improve the beef herds and thus do away with having to sell Texas cattle at a discount from the regular price. Texas fever took some of the imported stock, but enough survived to breed out part of the roughness and toughness of the Longhorns.

As the 1874 trail season opened, the market still was suffering from conditions brought on by the panic of the preceding fall. With many herds still on the Kansas ranges, buyers were inactive. In Kansas City the cattle market was reported in February as lifeless. In

[1] Quoted in the Denison *Daily News*, April 17, 1874.
[2] Dallas *Herald*, May 20, 1874.

Chicago cows and heifers had been selling during the winter at $1.50 to $2.25 per hundred pounds. With the average weight about seven hundred pounds, these cattle brought only about $13.50 per head. To ship a cow from Baxter Springs to Chicago cost $6.50 for freight, plus an average of $2.00 for feed, commissions, and losses from death or injury. With $8.50 deducted from the $13.50 received in Chicago, the drover had only $5 to cover the original cost of the animal and the cost of trailing to Kansas. That wasn't enough to enable him to come out even. Fat beeves brought higher prices but also cost more in Texas.

Conditions in the Southwest, too, pointed to a drive smaller than that of 1873, in which drovers walked half a million Longhorns north to Kansas. Cowmen who went out after wild stock and mavericks had cleaned out most of the ranges and were finding it harder to gather trail herds. Those who had their own branded herds already had sold most of their surplus stock. Many wanted to keep and graze their better male calves until they became mature steers and would bring higher prices.

On the favorable side for the drovers was a mild winter that had left most of the cattle in better condition for the market than had been the case a year earlier. The sagging demand for beef did not deter all the Texas stockmen. Some wanted to convert their cattle into cash at any price. Others hoped for a firmer market later in the season. Still others, like Jim Daugherty, could make a profit by selling on contract to Indian agencies.[3]

San Antonio and Fort Worth were astir to outfit and provision the drovers. On the south side of Fort Worth's public square, Joseph H. Brown did a flourishing business. The season was late; but by April 15, about forty-eight thousand head had passed through or near Fort Worth. About half of the outfits were beef herds. Most of the other herds—the mixed ones—were made up of cattle of inferior grade. Fort Worth dealers looked for a drive about half the size of that of 1873.

Meanwhile, Texas, with two railroads edging into the cow country, continued to ship some cattle directly to the Kansas City, St. Louis, and Chicago markets. At Dallas, drovers could load on the Texas and Pacific for St. Louis or on the Houston and Texas Central,

[3] Daugherty, notebook, MS.

which had connections with the Missouri, Kansas and Texas at Denison. More of the cowmen shipped directly from Denison for Kansas City or St. Louis.

A bit disappointed that their new rail line had failed to wean most of the drovers from the old cow paths, some Denison people were trying a new tack to draw business their way. With the help of Colonel William H. Day, they built a packing plant to slaughter cattle and ship the meat in the new refrigerator cars, which cost $1,110 each. The meat sold in New York at six cents a pound. The new firm, the American and Texas Refrigerator Car Company— later the Texas and Atlantic—hired Joseph G. McCoy of Abilene fame to promote its business.

Denison boosters had high hopes for this project. On February 5, 1874, a visitor reported, "Already three trains of ten cars each, containing the dressed carcasses of more than four hundred cattle have reached the Washington market. There competent judges pronounce the beef as sweet and perfect as if just killed." A month later, on March 4, the *Daily News* declared that the success of the company was no longer in question. The latest shipment, it added, had found a ready and profitable market in New York. "This company paid more for fat cattle at the yards in this city than the drovers could have realized by shipping to St. Louis or Chicago. The advantage of Denison as a cattle market is apparent."

Early in May, McCoy and Colonel Day ranged as far west as Gainesville to buy cattle for the packing plant. They contracted for a thousand head of fat beeves. The capacity of this local plant, though, was too small to make much dent in the trail driving.[4]

In Kansas, Wichita and Ellsworth were girding for a new battle for the Texas herds. Shanghai Pierce, who had worked for the Wichita market in 1873, enlisted under the Ellsworth banner for the 1874 season.

Wichita, closer to Texas, was determined to capture a lion's share of the trade. After enlarging its stockyards, of which John Cline was in charge, it sent to buyers and dealers a circular advertising its cattle market and signed by the mayor and councilmen. The first two Texas herds arrived in the opening week of May, and a large one of James D. Reed, of Goliad, followed soon. Cattle ship-

[4] Denison *Daily News*, March 4, 5, 7, April 29, May 10, 1874.

ments started late that month, with prices better than they had been in the fall after the panic struck. To avoid having the herds crowd through their business streets, Wichita people had the trail changed to cross the Arkansas River three miles below town.

Ellsworth received its first trail herds on May 6. There were seven herds that day, of which the largest—1,200 head—was that of William G. Butler. Six more herds reached town the next day. The thirteen herds totaled about 8,880 head, or 677 to the herd.

In the lead of the herds arriving at Ellsworth on May 6 was one of a thousand head owned by Willis McCutcheon and George W. West of Lavaca County. Sol West, a younger brother of one of the partners, had brought this herd up the trail. The outfit had left on February 27 and had run into trouble in the Indian Territory. Along Rush Creek, Indians had burned much of the grass. Farther north, on Hell Roaring Creek, this outfit and that of Al Fields, of Victoria, just behind on the trail, were hit by an April blizzard. All their horses froze to death, and their cattle scattered. Later George West figured the profit of the drive at $1.50. When he handed young Sol 75 cents as his share, he asked his brother whether he intended to use his new capital to buy a herd of his own or to start a bank.[5]

Other drovers, too, had poor luck on the trail that spring. Two brothers who left Matagorda County with eleven hundred steers had so many stampedes that they arrived at Wichita with only eight hundred head. Bill Perryman, who took a thousand fat beeves from the thickets below Pearsall, left the Shiner pasture March 5. The outfit put up with storms and stampedes all the way through Texas and had to swim the herd across the Red River. A man from one of the two other outfits that crossed the same day fell into the water and was drowned.

In the Indian Territory, the men in the Perryman outfit had time to rope and shoot a few buffaloes. They ran into little trouble there; but Ed Chambers, in charge of a herd for Tucker and Duncan, was killed at Pond Creek. Reports that the Indians had gone on the warpath along the Chisholm Trail during the summer led the Perryman outfit to return home by way of Coffeyville and the old Shawnee Trail. The outfit of D. C. Choate, which had taken a Choate and

<hr />

[5] Wichita *Eagle*, January 16, May 8, 15, 22, June 4, 1874; W. D. Hornaday in San Antonio *Express*, August 7, 1910.

Bennett herd from the Druce Rachel ranch on Nueces Bay, San Patricio County, followed the same detour back to Texas. After grazing this herd along the Ninnescah during the summer, Choate had sold in the new market at Great Bend. R. R. Savage of Corpus Christi also had pointed a beef herd to Great Bend, selling to Bruce Parsons there.[6]

With the 1874 drive cut to less than half that of the preceding year, prices did not sink as low as a bigger trail movement might have pushed them. They were noticeably lower, though, than those of earlier years. The Rev. George W. Slaughter and his son, C. C. (Lum) Slaughter, obtained only $60,000 for their herd of two thousand head. That compared with $66,000 received in 1872 and 1873 for herds of the same size.

Low Kansas prices led Ben Juvenall to trail on to Julesburg, Colorado. Juvenall had a mixed herd of about three thousand head that belonged to his brother, J. C. Juvenall. The outfit had gathered these Longhorns at the Jackson ranch on Bull Hide Creek, near the line of Bell and McLennan counties. The men marked each animal for the trail with an apple brand on the left loin. The herd set out on April 1. Three days later, after the cattle had crossed the Brazos at Fort Graham, a blizzard caused some of them to freeze to death. Farther on, they swam the Red River safely; but beyond Wild Goose Creek, they headed into another storm that froze several of the cattle and horses. In Kansas the men had to keep a close watch to prevent buffaloes from stampeding the horses.

At least one outfit on the trail that spring had a woman along. When D. M. (Doc) Barton of Mason County started north with five hundred Longhorns, his wife insisted on going with the herd and taking their young baby. While the baby rode in the chuck wagon, under the eye of the cook, Mrs. Barton mounted a cow pony and worked as a trail hand. When the chuck wagon stuck in the mud one day, several Indians helped pull it out. Mrs. Barton rewarded them with a jar of cookies.[7]

Perhaps the most nearly accurate estimate of the size of the 1874

[6] S. M. Lesesne in Galveston *News*, April 2, 1911; Hunter, *The Trail Drivers of Texas*, 119, 417–19.
[7] Hunter, *The Trail Drivers of Texas*, 756; Taylor, *The Chisholm Trail and Other Routes*, 164–65; Poage, "Drive to Cheyenne in 1874," MS; J. B. Cranfill in Dallas *Morning News*, July 20, 1941.

drive would be one based on a record of the Texas herds that entered Kansas at the dusty town of Caldwell. There C. H. Stone, a pioneer merchant, kept a list in which he noted each herd and its number of cattle. Up to about the last of July, his tally showed a total of 162,127 head.[8] As the trailing season was nearly over and as not a great many herds missed Caldwell, the total drive probably did not much exceed 175,000 head. That was little more than a third of the half million head for 1873.

In the division of the Texas cattle business in Kansas, even the trumpeting of Shanghai Pierce was of little help to Ellsworth. Wichita, much closer to the source, captured the biggest shipping business. This was a victory, too, for the Santa Fe over the Kansas Pacific. The more northern road shipped only 18,500 head, or 12,000 fewer than in 1873. The Santa Fe shipped 75,929 head, including 49,730 from Wichita, 16,513 from Great Bend, and 4,127 from Hutchinson. The other cattle were consumed on the frontier, used to fill Indian or Army contracts, trailed on to the Northwest, or wintered on the Kansas prairies.

II

Sprawled in the dust and mud on the bank of the Arkansas River, Wichita had become the chief of the Kansas cow towns. Beyond the few brick and stone buildings on the main streets, new false-front wooden stores and saloons were rising. Farther out were the livery stables, corrals, and homes—most of them hastily built. Hitching racks and posts lined the rutted streets. Some of the downtown buildings had new board sidewalks in front; elsewhere people used dirt paths. Among the merchants was Jake Karatofsky, who had moved down from Ellsworth in the fall of 1872. He had a big stock of clothing and dry goods and the widest show windows in town.

Texas cowmen who came up the Chisholm Trail called Wichita the most rip-roaring town in the whole West. In the saloons, gambling rooms, and honky-tonk dance halls, many tried to help the place live up to its reputation. One of the busiest spots was the two-story Keno Hall, at the northwest corner of Douglas and Main. There W. W. (Whitey) Rupp presided over faro, monte, poker,

[8] Wichita *Beacon*, August 4, 1874.

roulette, and other games. Those who passed by could hear the shout of "Keno!" at all hours of the day and night. In afternoons, during the cattle season, a brass band played in the balcony. Rupp had a long bar, and next door was Pryor's Saloon. On Main Street were two other popular bars, the Southern and the Empire.

Across the street to the east from Keno Hall was the New York Store. There the cowboy who hadn't blown all his pay could outfit himself with new duds and guns. A block west of Keno Hall were two hotels—the Douglas Avenue, at the southwest corner of Douglas and Water Street, and the Texas House, diagonally across. The Texas House had as a dishwasher and bootblack an ambitious young fellow named Edward L. Doheny.

East of the Texas House was Horse Thief Corner, where horses were sold at auction. It acquired its name from the belief that many of the mounts sold there were stolen ones.

The town's police court, where Judge Ed B. Jewett held out, was in the basement of the courthouse at First and Main. Outside hung a big triangle of bar steel, on which a policeman sounded an alarm whenever a gun battle or some other outbreak called for action. Prisoners marked time elsewhere in the courthouse basement or in a near-by shack.

Wichita's variety theater put on nightly shows with scantily dressed cuties. Other entertainment included several street shows. Back of the Steel and Smith real estate office on Main Street, Professor S. Gessley, the armless wonder, drew a daily crowd. Near-by attractions included a child wonder and a freak pig. A man with a hand organ put out popular tunes all day to draw a crowd. On a high plank platform across the street, a brass band blared from morning until late at night to bring suckers into the gambling booths. In town to extract dollars from the Texas cowmen were at least three hundred sporting women and about two hundred men—gamblers, con men, and other parasites. Among the gamblers was Ben Thompson, who had followed the cattle business from Ellsworth.

Also on hand was William Martin, a Texas desperado better known as Hurricane Bill. Southeast of Abilene in 1870, Hurricane Bill and his outlaw band had stolen sixty head of cattle from a trail herd; but the drovers, with the aid of a posse from Marion, had recovered them. For several weeks in 1874, Hurricane Bill and his toughs imposed a reign of terror on Wichita. They galloped through the streets, yelling, shooting, and putting residents in fear of their lives.

Forces trying to keep order in Wichita were headed in 1874 by Mayor James G. Hope, who was serving his second year. Hope was a partner in the firm of Hope and Richards, wholesale dealers in wines, liquors, and tobacco, on North Main Street. On April 15, the city council had named William Smith to be city marshal. He succeeded William Meagher. Smith had Daniel Parks as assistant, with James Cairns and William Dibb as policemen. In May, as the Texans began to liven the town, the police force added two patrolmen, John Behrens and J. F. Hooker. The work of these men enabled Judge Jewett to collect more than $5,600 in fines during the cattle season. P. H. Massey was county sheriff.

Defiance of the law by a band of Texans put Wichita in an uproar in the last week of May. On the night of May 25, a Texan became involved in a quarrel with a Negro hod carrier, Charley Saunders. Officers arrested both men. Outraged at this treatment, the Texan sought revenge. With the backing of armed friends, he walked up to Saunders on the afternoon of the twenty-seventh, while the Negro was at work on the Miller Building on Main Street. The Texan shot his unarmed victim twice—in the ear and in the breast.

Marshal Smith happened to be near by; but, looking into the muzzles of a dozen six-shooters, he could do nothing. While the marshal was held thus, the killer mounted a horse and fled down Main Street, out Douglas, and across the toll bridge. Scores of citizens grabbed weapons and gave chase, but they were unable to overtake the speeding horseman. Saunders died two days later.

This brazen killing and a shooting affray on the west bank of the river, in which a sporting woman and two soldiers were wounded, aroused many of the citizens. The *Eagle* warned local officials to enforce the ordinance against carrying firearms. It called on the mayor to strengthen the police force. Several Texas drovers denounced the cowardly shooting and offered to help local officers prevent similar crimes. While the city added two men—Samuel Botts and Samuel Burris—to the police force, a hundred citizens bound themselves by oath in an armed vigilance committee.

As Hurricane Bill and some of his fellow Texans kept on shooting up the town, still another policeman—Wyatt Earp—was hired on June 17. Trouble came to a head again on the late afternoon of July 6. One of the new policemen, Sam Botts, had disarmed a trouble-making cowboy and was about to take him to jail. Before he could get him away, a dozen or more Texans drew their six-shooters on him. Then the police alarm sounded; and more than forty vigilantes popped out of stores and houses, armed with Henry rifles and shotguns. Among them were Judge William P. Campbell of the District Court and S. M. Tucker, a lawyer.

The citizens caught up with the Texans at Horse Thief Corner as some of the latter were entering the Texas House. Several in both groups drew their guns, ready for battle. Bill Smith, the marshal, fearing wholesale bloodshed, asked the vigilantes to disperse.

The men refused. "This is the third time I've been out on this kind of call," said Tucker, "and I've never made an arrest. I'm not afraid of trouble—I'm used to it. Point out the man you want arrested, and I'll arrest him—kill or get killed."

"All right," replied Smith, "arrest Hurricane Bill."

In tense silence, the men in both parties kept their eyes fixed on Tucker. Quickly cocking one trigger of his shotgun, he called on Hurricane Bill to surrender. The outlaw started to raise his guns to defend himself. But as he looked into the barrels of Tucker's weapon, he changed his mind. Dropping his six-shooters, he allowed the citizens to march him and the other Texans to the police station. There Judge Jewett fined them $600.

After that incident, although there were many cases of disorderly conduct and sporadic shootings, Wichita had no more concerted and open defiance of the law.[9]

111

Warm March days in 1875 saw Texas cowmen out on the range, gathering and road-branding new herds for the Chisholm Trail. Reports indicated a drive almost as large as that of 1874. In Austin, on April 2, Colonel William H. Day wrote that about 30,000 head

9 Wichita *Eagle*, May 28, June 4, July 9, 1874; Streeter, *Prairie Trails and Cow Towns*, 160–73; Streeter, *The Kaw*, 160–66; Stuart N. Lake, *Wyatt Earp, Frontier Marshal*, 95–134.

had crossed the Colorado River at that point. "They were looking pretty well," he said, "considering the shortness of the grass." By the last of the month, about 110,000 head were said to have crossed the Colorado at Austin, most of them pointed toward Kansas.[10]

As the early herds drew near, Fort Worth was confident of good business as an outfitting and supply center. "This city is on the nearest and best route," assured the *Democrat*. "The country in the vicinity of the Silver Creek crossing has been settling up rapidly during the last year. Fencing will be a serious obstacle to herdsmen in many places. This route also allows the owners and herdsmen a better opportunity of securing supplies than is afforded by any other route."

The reference of the *Democrat* to fencing was not mere speculation. Henry B. Sanborn and his partner, Judson P. Warner, arrived in Texas as agents for the newfangled barbed wire. From Gainesville, Sanborn set out in a buggy and sold eleven reels of wire in northern Texas. Later he obtained at Rockport an order for a carload. Meanwhile, Warner sold a carload at Austin.[11]

In Fort Worth, though, people weren't yet worrying over fencing. There saloonkeepers and merchants were ready for the trail herds. Especially so was Joseph H. Brown, who had done most of the supply business in 1874. On the south side of the public square he leased extra space and had his store piled high with goods that the trail outfits likely would want. Along with other supplies, he had brought in bacon, flour, and molasses by the wagon load. For the cowboys' lariats, he had hundreds of coils of rope.

The first herd to reach Fort Worth was that of John Redus, who ran the V2 brand in Medina County. His 1,020 beeves were grazing a few miles south of town by April 9. They were reported to be in fair condition for this early in the season and to have stood the trip well. Redus had become a big dealer in Longhorns. Down the trail he had been buying the herds of other cowmen. He planned to sell them in Fort Worth or farther north. This first herd he sold in Fort Worth about a week later to a Missourian, George Miller. The buyer planned to trail the cattle to Baxter Springs.

[10] Dallas *Herald*, April 10, May 1, 1875.
[11] Cox, *Historical and Biographical Record of the Cattle Industry*, 500; Amarillo *News-Globe*, June 17, 1928.

Early in April, both the Santa Fe and the Kansas Pacific had rival agents in Fort Worth to induce Texas drovers to ship over their railroads in Kansas. By the middle of the month, two beef herds and four mixed herds had arrived. Many others were on their way up the trail from the south.[12]

As more bellowing Longhorns reached the ranges outside Fort Worth in late April and through May, trading reached a high pitch. Before the month ended, 135,112 head were reported to have gone through or past the town. At the Transcontinental Hotel, where many of the drovers shed some of the dust and sweat of the trail and talked with buyers, some of the herds changed owners. John Redus sold his second herd, one of 1,500 mixed cattle, to Belcher and Company of Grayson County for $21,000. Jesse L. Driskill of Austin sold a herd of 2,000 beeves to an Iowa buyer for $44,000.

Also at the Transcontinental was E. M. Butler, speaking up for the Missouri, Kansas and Texas Railroad. He was urging the cowmen to ship at Denison instead of making the long drive to Kansas. Some followed his advice, while others loaded at other Texas rail towns. Dallas, which had two railroads—the Houston and Texas Central and the Texas and Pacific—was not overlooking the cattle trade. Sixty cars of Longhorns went north over the Texas Central on May 26, reported the *Herald*. By that time, the Texas and Pacific, beginning to recover from the panic of 1873, had laid its rails on to Eagle Ford, six miles west of Dallas, on the way to Fort Worth. The Eagle Ford railhead was a loading point for some cattle that season. On June 1, seventeen carloads were waiting there to be coupled into a train; and shippers had ordered five more cars.[13]

Texas cowmen who took or sent herds up the Chisholm Trail in 1875 included such veteran drovers as Dillard R. Fant, J. J. Ellis, James Hickey, William G. Butler, W. B. Grimes, and several members of the Slaughter family. The biggest trailing enterprise of the year was that of four Texas cowmen, all Confederate veterans, who joined as partners. Their herds made up two-thirds of the whole Texas drive.

This quartet was formed by the merger of two partnerships that

12 Fort Worth *Democrat*, March 13, April 10, 17, 24, 1875.
13 *Ibid.*, May 1, 8, 15, 22, 29, 1875; Dallas *Herald*, weekly edition, May 22, 29, June 5, 1875.

had been active on the trail for several years. Captain Eugene B. Millett of Seguin, who had trailed Longhorns to Illinois in 1866, had joined Major Seth Mabry in supplying contract beef on the hoof to Indian agencies in Dakota Territory. Likewise, John O. Dewees, who had a big spread in Atascosa, Karnes, and Wilson counties, had thrown in with Colonel James F. Ellison of Caldwell County in trailing herds north for sale to ranchmen and Indian agencies.

Before the start of the 1875 drive, Mabry and Millett added to their own stock by buying up other Texas herds. Before long they had fifty-two thousand head, mostly three-year-olds and up. They had paid an average of eight dollars for the cows and twelve dollars for the steers. To dispose of part of their holdings, they obtained contracts to supply the Sioux reservations.

To strengthen their market position and to gain help in handling this vast operation, Mabry and Millett brought Dewees and Ellison into the partnership. The latter pair owned or controlled about fifty thousand head of cattle. From a camp near San Antonio, the partners checked in the herds and pointed them north. Ellison's son, known as Little Jim, had charge of one of the trail herds, while Mack Stewart was boss of another. Young Jim found the drive unusually hard but put the cattle through. About the Wichita Mountains, the men saw buffaloes and antelope.

With herds strung along the trail from southern Texas to the Platte, the four partners sold cattle in Kansas, Nebraska, Colorado, Wyoming, and Dakota. At least one of their herds was taken to Dodge City, which the Santa Fe had reached in September, 1872.[14] At first ignored as a possible cattle market, Dodge had shipped a mere 318 head in 1874. It loaded 5,826 cattle in 1875.

Another who trailed to Dodge that year was J. W. Driskill, a nephew of Jesse L. Driskill. With about 1,450 head belonging to himself and his brother, Driskill had to see his herd go without water for four days in the Indian Territory. He was about to give up hope for his thirsty brutes when his outfit struck water just before sundown. Despite this close brush with disaster, Driskill and his four drivers delivered the herd with the loss of only one cow.

[14] Hunter, *The Trail Drivers of Texas*, 476–78, 539, 940–42; Floyd Benjamin Streeter, "Famous Cattle Drives," *Cattleman*, Vol. XXXIV, No. 8 (January, 1948), 130–32.

Fortunately for the cowmen, Indian raids along the trail were becoming less serious. The slaughter of the buffalo herds, on which the roving plains Indians had depended for food and clothing, was forcing them to come to terms with the whites. In the summer of 1875, the last small band of half-starved Comanches straggled in to Fort Sill, near the Wichita Mountains. With buffaloes scarce, their horses gone, and their tepees burned, they were ready to surrender. They still might be a nuisance as beggars and petty thieves, but the trail outfits would have little cause to fear them.

In the Kansas cow towns, trail-weary Texans celebrated as wildly as ever. One who saw the bubbling night life of Wichita in the cattle season described it thus:

As the evening approaches, the business of the day draws to a close and the business of another class begins. In one place we find a Negro mounted on a high elevation, picking on his guitar and singing planta- tion melodies to attract a crowd to an auction room. Saloons are lighted up, the billiard tables are uncovered. Back rooms, though not secreted, are filled with others who seek a more solid amusement at cards, poker, monte, and faro. In another place we hear a man in a hall on the second floor calling out loudly the numbers in the game of keno. Going around, we find a large hall containing from one hundred to two hundred and fifty players. Large amounts of money, though in small sums, are lost.

At about nine o'clock in the evening, the band from the beer gar- dens strikes up. Going around, we find a crowd of men and women dancing to the music as it screeches out on the still night air. There is still another class of houses, numbering perhaps twenty or thirty, filled with females. But while these nightly revels are going on, the churches are lighted up and ministers are preaching within the sound of the keno man's voice.[15]

Among the herds trailed to Wichita in 1875 were four—totaling 14,000 head—sent by Hughes, Nunn, Hood, and Birchfield of Uval- de. Wichita was the top Kansas shipping point again that year. It ac- counted for 22,569 of the 54,553 head sent over the Santa Fe. Settle- ment of the interior Kansas country by farmers had made Ellsworth about done for as a cattle market, although it and other towns in the Kansas Pacific did some shipping. The Leavenworth, Lawrence

15 Wichita *Eagle,* June 24, 1875.

and Galveston loaded 19,537 head and the Missouri River, Fort Scott and Gulf 12,730 head.[16] The government estimate for the year's drive was 151,000 head, marking a slight decline from the figure for 1874.

IV

In Texas, some people were irked a bit at seeing so many herds still trailed to Kansas after railroads were available to haul them to market. But that was a day in which the officials of some railroads were too busy extending their lines and selling shares of stock to go out after freight business. Too, some of them lacked proper cars and loading facilities for handling a big livestock business.

In Fort Worth, Captain B. B. Paddock, the peppery Ohio-born Confederate veteran who edited the *Democrat*, took to task the new Texas and Pacific Railroad. Perhaps impatient that this line hadn't yet reached Fort Worth, he prodded its officials to go more actively after their road's share of the cattle business. Noting that four Kansas railroads and the Missouri, Kansas and Texas had alert agents in Fort Worth contending for the cattle trade, he deplored what he viewed as inaction by the Texas and Pacific. He wrote:

Exceeding strange is the fact that one road that, above all others, would most naturally claim and take the major portion of this trade, has no representative in the field to compete for even a share. The Texas and Pacific is without a representative in this part of the state.

Why is this? Have they not an interest in this immense traffic? Is it nothing to them, or do they expect that the cattle will naturally come to them without an effort? We would feel pride in seeing the Texas and Pacific secure this trade. It is essentially a Texas road. But good wishes will not give it the cattle trade. It must make an effort for itself. It must secure rates equal to those of any other line and show the shippers all the advantages it possesses.

A do-nothing policy will not secure the cattle trade for any line. Let the Texas and Pacific expend the same energy in the interest of this trade that the Kansas Pacific does; and, instead of witnessing nineteen-twentieths of the trade passing on through to Kansas for shipment, the greater proportion of the cattle would be shipped over that line to north-

[16] Fort Worth *Democrat*, April 8, 1876; Hunter, *The Trail Drivers of Texas*, 707–708, 763.

ern and eastern markets. Texas, as well as her most important railway, would be greatly benefited.

Although Fort Worth hadn't yet heard the snort of the Iron Horse, the *Democrat* already was predicting that the place would become a large meat-packing center. Pointing out that Fort Worth had ample herding grounds and an abundance of water and soon would have a rail line, it asserted that the town would be "an admirable point for packing beef."

Texas ranges still were teeming with cattle, and most of the herds increased by about a third each year. Stock cattle sold at $5.50 to $8.00 a head, while fat beeves brought $20 to $30. In the stock-raising sections of the state, butchers retailed beef of good quality at two and one-half to three cents a pound. In the larger towns, it brought five to seven cents.

Two weeks after he had twitted Texas and Pacific officials for tardiness in going out after the cattle business, Paddock took up the subject again. This time he tried to give a detailed answer to the frequently asked question of why most Texas cattle still were walked five or six hundred miles to Kansas when there were railroads to haul them.

The Texas and Pacific and the Missouri, Kansas and Texas roads, he wrote, "are not making anything like the effort to secure this important trade that the Kansas roads are making, and they are not offering rates equal to those of the Kansas roads. In this way, the Texas roads are losing traffic that belongs to them. They seem to be perfectly willing that the Kansas roads should reap this vast benefit that could be theirs for the asking and making the effort to secure."

The editor cited figures to show why Texas cowmen found it cheaper to trail their herds all the way to Kansas instead of shipping them by rail from Denison, Eagle Ford, or Dallas:

Two thousand head of cattle, or one hundred carloads, cost by the Missouri, Kansas and Texas to St. Louis $10,000 and by the Texas and Pacific from Eagle Ford or Dallas $11,500, being a difference of $1,500 in favor of the Missouri, Kansas and Texas road.

To drive two thousand head to Ellsworth, Kansas, costs $1,000. Thence by rail to St. Louis $7,500, total $8,500, making a difference in favor of the Kansas routes of $1,500 over the Missouri, Kansas and Texas and $3,000 over the Texas and Pacific.

These differences are altogether too great. So long as they exist, we may certainly look for the trade to go where it has always gone—to Kansas. The difference even between the Texas and Pacific and the Missouri, Kansas and Texas rates amounts to 75 cents per head. Between the M. K. and T. and the Kansas route 75 cents per head, and between the Texas and Pacific and Kansas routes $1.50 per head.

If our Texas roads do not want this traffic, they are pursuing the policy not to get it. If they want it, they must compete for it, and they must show the stock shippers that the expense of shipping by their routes is at least somewhere within the bounds of reason compared with the expense of the Kansas routes.

No officer of the Texas and Pacific road has ever visited the country west of Dallas with the view of working up or bringing into notice the facilities of the road. The officers of both the Texas and Pacific and the Missouri, Kansas and Texas roads seem to have entirely forgotten or neglected an important shipping west of Dallas.[17]

Paddock's advice did not attain immediate results, but the cattle business kept on bringing prosperity to the Texas ranges. Cowmen began to look even farther for markets. With Europe clamoring for more beef, an enterprising Galveston man arranged for the shipment of twenty choice beeves from that city to Liverpool by the S. S. *San Antonio*. He hoped to make this the start of a lucrative export business. Meanwhile, the cattle country was spreading. As fencing continued to close some of the once open range, many cowmen trailed their herds to new pastures in the northwestern part of the state. This movement within the state was said to have embraced not less than 200,000 head in 1875.

More of the cowmen were improving their stock with bulls from other sections. In September, Fort Worth residents noticed a bunch of thirty-five Durham or Shorthorn bulls being trailed through their town. Twenty of them were for C. C. (Lum) Slaughter, who was grading up his western herds. The Shorthorn, predicted the *Democrat*, "will soon be as familiar on the Texas prairies as the Longhorn

[17] Fort Worth *Democrat*, April 24, May 8, 1875. After they reached deeper into the Texas cow country, the Texas and Pacific and the Missouri, Kansas and Texas became heavy carriers of cattle and were active in soliciting this business.

is now." It would take many imported bulls many years, though, to erase the traits of the iron-muscled Longhorn.[18]

[18] *Ibid.*, July 31, September 25, October 16, November 6, 1875. Slaughter, who had begun buying Shorthorn bulls from Kentucky in 1871, bought the grand champion bull at the Columbian Exposition at Chicago in 1893. While retaining his cattle interests, he became a banker in Dallas, where he died in 1919.

XIV

NEW TRACKS IN THE WEST

For many Texans, the year 1876 was one of change and revived spirits. It seemed to mark the close of one era and the opening of another. Thousands of young men who had come of age since 1860 were looking forward to voting for President for the first time. The choice of most of them would be the free-soil Democrat who was governor of New York—Samuel J. Tilden. Well-to-do families on the frontier were buying fancy duds for a trip to Philadelphia. They wanted to visit the big Centennial Exposition, marking the one-hundredth anniversary of the signing of the Declaration of Independence. There they could see such recent inventions as the high-wheel bicycle and Alexander Graham Bell's telephone.

In the West, the prairies and plains still were attracting new settlers. Colorado, filling up with cowmen as well as miners, was clamoring for admission as the Centennial State. In the Northwest, Indian troubles still clouded the horizon. From Montana came news of the defeat and death of the dashing George A. Custer and many of his men in a battle on the Little Big Horn on June 25.

In the Texas cow country, change was in the air. Many cattle raisers were trailing their herds to new ranges in unsettled country to the west. Some were giving a trial to the much talked-about barbed wire. An energetic young Illinoisan, John W. Gates, who had just turned twenty-one, landed in Texas as a salesman for the new wire. Henry B. Sanborn and Judson P. Warner, who had arrived a year earlier as agents for the wire, had settled in Houston, where they continued to make some sales. But they had done little to show ranchmen how to use the wire or to convince cowboys that it wouldn't throw them out of jobs. The time was ripe for a more aggressive sales push.[1]

Meanwhile, the outlook was for a much larger trail drive than that of 1875. Captain M. B. Loyd, who had gone down the trail to San Antonio in the early spring for the Kansas Pacific Railroad, was enthusiastic over the prospect. The winter had been unusually open, and new grass began carpeting the prairies early. San Antonio and Fort Worth were laying in stocks for a big trail business.

The cowman who stopped in San Antonio could find entertainment as long as his money lasted. The old town still had much of its Spanish cast, although new frame buildings—of materials from Sam Maverick's lumberyard on the north side of Alamo Plaza—were going up beside the older ones of stone and adobe. The staid Menger Hotel still held most of the quality trade, but there was plenty of patronage for the Central, Schmitt's, and half a dozen other small hostelries.

In the plazas the visitor occasionally might see the Alamo Rifles or the new Milam Rifles on dress parade. Almost any day he could listen to hand organs, watch rooster fights, or lend his ear to some old-timer, such as Big Foot Wallace, the celebrated Indian fighter, who had come in for supplies. He could bathe at Gulhon's barbershop on Main Street and play billiards at the Crystal or Jack Harris'. He could attend a Mexican bull fight on Sunday afternoon and, on occasion, take in a horse race on the prairie turf at the edge of town. By day or night, he could lose his best pony at monte or other games at the Silver King, the Banner, or any one of a score of other gambling joints.

When thirsty, he need walk only a few steps to the nearest bar. There he could order anything from the local Degan's beer to te-

[1] Cox, *Historical and Biographical Record of the Cattle Industry*, 500; Amarillo *News-Globe*, June 17, 1928.

quila from below the border. Prominent among the saloons was Lockwood's—with its big clock, card room, and newspaper reading room—on the west side of Alamo Plaza. Walker's Exchange, on Main Street, also had a reading room. The Old Stand, on the north side of Main Plaza, was known for the quality of its free lunch. Well patronized also were George Horner's Bar Room, the Bull's Head, and a host of others, ranging down to J. Vigie's Mexican nickel bar-room on Military Plaza. Two women crusaders had started picketing the saloons that spring, but they soon became discouraged.

If the free lunch in the saloon didn't satisfy his hunger, the cow-hand could burn his insides with chili and enchiladas at one of the Mexican stands. Or he could fill up on German food at Adolph Scholz's Palm Garden on Alamo Street, carve steaks at William Ernst's on Commerce Street, or dine on venison at the Menger. One who liked fresh oysters could have a whole dozen—stewed, fried, or raw—for fifty cents at either Ernst's or Eugene Dietrich's Plaza House.

At the Vaudeville House on Soledad Street the visitor could find plenty of laughs. If he craved theatrical entertainment of a higher class, he occasionally could enjoy the performance of a traveling company at Casino Hall. On any night, he could find excitement at a dance hall or succumb to the lure of girls in thin kimonos who called or beckoned from doorways, windows, and balconies. San Antonio policemen, who had acquired their first uniforms that spring, tried to curb violence but seldom bothered the sporting women or the gamblers.

The Alamo city, despite its Spanish buildings and Mexican lingo, was in many respects a typical Texas cow town. The streets and plazas echoed the jangle of spurs and the popping of buckskin whips. Thousands of cowhides lay in high piles, awaiting shipment. Towns-people sometimes squawked because a cowboy, instead of tying his mount outside a store, fastened one end of a rope to the pony's bridle and carried the other inside with him. The rope, held taut across the sidewalk, hampered traffic and often caused tempers to flare.

Although hogs still roamed at large, the city council had just banned loose cattle from the streets. The Longhorn herds still grazed at the edge of town, and some of them had trampled the graves and headstones in the burial ground on the hill. After hearing many

NEW TRACKS IN THE WEST

complaints, the councilmen were considering having a fence built around the cemetery.

Fort Worth, although smaller, did its part in saving the trail men from boredom. It had ample saloons, several dance halls, and a host of sporting women eager to trade their charms for cash. Joseph H. Brown, an old hand at such merchandising, had laid in a big supply of flour, sugar, molasses, coffee, hams, sauerkraut, pickles, prunes, raisins, hams, smoked fish, cigars, rope, and other items.[2]

Fort Worth had just chosen as marshal a tall, nervy fellow, T. I. Courtright. People called him Long Hair Jim because he often let his hair grow to his shoulders, as did some of the Indian scouts of his day. He carried two pistols in his belt and was quick on the draw. The new marshal had help from two policemen for day work and two others for night patrol. On Saturday nights in the trailing season, the bluecoats sometimes crowded twenty-five to thirty miscreants into the two cells and dungeon of the log jail at Second and Commerce streets. Although rough on killers and horse thieves, Long Hair Jim was tolerant of gamblers. He not only allowed his policemen to loaf in the casinos and variety theaters when they might have been patrolling but he often tried his own hand at the gaming tables.

While serving the trail outfits, Fort Worth people were looking to the east and to the west. From Eagle Ford, the Texas and Pacific was laying its rails westward toward Fort Worth, which hoped to see its first Iron Horse in midsummer. But news from the west was a cause for concern. Some drovers were blazing a new cattle route that would miss Fort Worth.

Leaving the Chisholm Trail at Belton, these cowmen went up the Leon River to the northwest. Then they pointed north by way of Fort Griffin, a frontier outpost that had become the headquarters of most of the Texas buffalo hunters. They crossed the Red River at a ford beside which Jonathan Doan, from Ohio, had built a picket house with a roof of mud and grass and a buffalo hide flapping in the doorway. From there they headed on through the Indian country to the new market at Dodge City, Kansas, on the Santa Fe.

[2] San Antonio *Herald*, September 28, 1874, February 24, 1875, January 14, March 6, 27, April 8, 14, 21, 1876; Fort Worth *Democrat*, March 4, 18, 25, 1876. The Sam Maverick who operated a lumberyard in San Antonio was a son and namesake of the lawyer whose name had been given to unbranded range cattle.

Dodge City was in a position to profit from an action of the Kansas Legislature that moved the cattle quarantine line farther west. This change put Wichita in the forbidden area and made Dodge the most convenient market in the part of the state left open to Texas drovers. Cowmen still could take their herds up the Chisholm Trail for most of the way, turning northwest toward Dodge from Elm Spring or some other point in the Indian Territory. But many, especially in the western ranges, could save miles and time by following the new and more direct trail by way of Fort Griffin and Doan's Crossing.

The hardy frontiersmen of Fort Griffin welcomed this new business. "Cattle from the south are coming in rapidly," wrote a correspondent on April 22. "The cattle drive to the north *via* this point, Cantonment, and Dodge City is an assured fact. It is estimated that 125,000 head will be driven upon this trail this season."

For the moment, Fort Worth was too busy with its own trail herds to give much heed to this rival trail in the west. The first herd of the season, one of 1,850 beeves belonging to Miller and Carson, had arrived on the morning of April 7. Before the month ended, there were several scores of herds, including five mixed ones of Major Seth Mabry, totaling 12,000 head. The drive was running well ahead of that of 1875. "The trail is swarming with cattle," reported the *Democrat*.[3]

Probably the biggest movement of Longhorns in 1876 was that of Captain Richard King. From his vast spread in southern Texas, King sent north 30,000 head, divided into twelve herds. With each herd he sent a boss, a cook, and fifteen trail hands. He paid the boss $100 a month, the cook $30, and the punchers $25 each.

The first herd of the King cattle, one of 2,300 head in charge of R. Walker, reached Ellis, Kansas, on the Kansas Pacific west of Hays, early in June. Two days later came the second herd, of which A. Allen was boss. Then Walker went on with his herd to the Red Cloud agency. By the middle of the month, the Smoky Hill River ranges held several thousand King cattle. Other thousands were on the trail to Ogallala, Nebraska.[4]

[3] Fort Worth *Democrat*, April 8, 22, 29, 1876.
[4] San Antonio *Herald*, March 6, 1876; Wichita *Eagle*, March 23, 1876, quoting the San Antonio *Express;* Fort Worth *Democrat*, August 30, 1876; Streeter, "Famous Cattle Drives," *Cattleman*, Vol. XXXIV, No. 8 (January, 1948), 130–33.

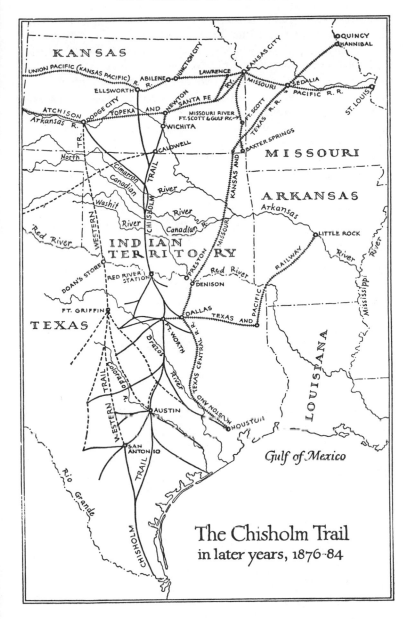

KANSAS

UNION PACIFIC (KANSAS PACIFIC)
ABILENE
ELLSWORTH
DODGE CITY
ATCHISON
Arkansas R.
TOPEKA AND
NEWTON
SANTA FE
WICHITA
CALDWELL
JUNCTION CITY
LAWRENCE
KANSAS CITY
MISSOURI
SEDALIA
PACIFIC R. R.
MISSOURI RIVER
FT. SCOTT & GULF RY.
FT. SCOTT
TEXAS R. R.
BAXTER SPRINGS
QUINCY
HANNIBAL
ST. LOUIS

MISSOURI

North
Cimarron
Canadian
River
Washit
River
CHISHOLM TRAIL
Canadian
Red River
River
Canadian R.
PRESTON
Arkansas
ARKANSAS
LITTLE ROCK
River

INDIAN TERRITORY

DOAN'S STORE
RED RIVER STATION
Red River
DENISON
MISSOURI
KANSAS AND
RAILWAY
PACIFIC
Mississippi River

FT. GRIFFIN
DALLAS
FT. WORTH
TEXAS AND

TEXAS

WESTERN TRAIL
Brazos River
TEXAS CENTRAL R.
LOUISIANA

Colorado R.
AUSTIN
GNV. NELSON
HOUSTON

WESTERN TRAIL
SAN ANTONIO

Rio Grande
CHISHOLM TRAIL

Gulf of Mexico

The Chisholm Trail
in later years, 1876-84

Although the perils of the trail were diminishing, a few outfits ran into trouble that season. Young Branch Isbell, in charge of a herd belonging to R. R. Savage, of Corpus Christi, lost thirty head in a stampede near Monument Rocks one stormy night. After a search, he found the missing cattle in a pen near Beaver Creek. He was able to recover only twenty. The other ten he had to leave with a band of heavily armed ruffians who demanded them as pay for looking after the lost cattle. Later Isbell and his men cut off the trail to the northwest. After grazing the Longhorns on Kansas pastures, they sold them at Dodge City in July.[5]

For some of the other drovers, life on the trail wasn't entirely smooth. From Matagorda County, on the Gulf Coast, a veteran cowman, W. B. Grimes, gathered two mixed herds, one of 2,300 and the other of 2,600 head. Many of the Longhorns were half-wild timber cattle that had to be handled cautiously. Grimes had them all road-branded with the letter G and sent Asa H. Dawdy as trail boss to take them north. In a thunderstorm that came up about midnight after the men had bedded down the herds near Gonzales, the cattle stampeded. In the rush, several steers suffered broken legs or broken horns.

After crossing the Colorado at Montopolis, three miles below Austin, the men pointed the herds north. They reached Fort Worth late in May. On the eastern edge of that town, barking dogs stampeded one of the herds, but soon it was under control again. North of Fort Worth, the outfits found several of the water holes fenced in with the new barbed wire. The trail hands, without hesitation or qualm, cut the wire and let their thirsty cattle drink. But the loose wire tangled with the horns and tails of some of the Longhorns, causing them to stampede. At this stage, several of the farmers whose fences had been cut appeared and set their dogs on the cattle. The punchers, outraged at this action, promptly shot the dogs.

Finding the Red River a raging torrent, the Grimes outfits and a score of others had to wait for the flood waters to subside. On the second day of waiting, an inspector stationed at the crossing told the trail bosses that he would check the herds the next day. He said they would have to pay him an inspection fee of ten cents a head. The next morning, the men of one outfit invited the inspector to

<hr/>

[5] Hunter, *The Trail Drivers of Texas*, 577–78.

have breakfast with them. But, instead of feeding him, they tied his hands and feet and tossed him into a near-by plum thicket, where he was at the mercy of flies and mosquitoes. The punchers turned loose his fine Kentucky mare, whose return home would lead to the release of the inspector two days later. Then all the outfits crossed the river safely. They had saved a big phony inspection charge, besides keeping several hundred strays that they could sell in Kansas.

The Grimes outfits had no Indian trouble except for the nuisance of roving beggars. But at the Salt Fork one of them ran into grief of another kind. The chuck wagon, driven in advance of the herd, crossed this stream just ahead of a sudden rise. By the time the Longhorns arrived, the river was so flooded that the lead steers refused to try to swim it. The trail hands, separated from their food and cook, killed a fat beef and ate their fill of unsalted meat roasted over a camp fire.

The men were satisfied with this fare for the moment; but after the river had remained in flood for six days, they began to clamor for a more varied diet. They sent a scouting party across Wild Horse Creek, which also was out of its banks. The riders found an army camp and obtained a supply of flour, bacon, sugar, salt, and coffee, which they placed in a tub. One of the scouting party, Charles A. Siringo, guided the tub across the swollen creek. Two days later the outfit crossed the Salt Fork and caught up with the cook. Despite the new quarantine, the men took the Grimes Longhorns to the prairies near Wichita. There they grazed them, with frequent excursions into town for entertainment, until they sold them in the following spring.[6]

The 1876 drive turned out to be more than double that of 1875. Late in July, the Fort Worth *Democrat* reported that 313,248 head had gone up the trails. Of these, 204,438 had taken the Chisholm Trail through Fort Worth. The others had used the new Western Trail by way of Fort Griffin. In addition, the newspaper estimated that about 60,000 head were being grazed near Fort Worth, waiting for shipment over the new railroad. The government estimate for the 1876 drive was 321,928 head, which compared with 151,000 for 1875.[7]

[6] Fort Worth *Democrat*, May 27, 1876; Charles A. Siringo, *A Lone Star Cowboy*, 40–46.
[7] Fort Worth *Democrat*, July 29, 1876. Large shipments went off not only from

A large proportion of the Texas cattle walked north in 1876 were trailed on to the Northwest to stock new ranches. The Santa Fe shipped 21,590 head from Kansas and Colorado points. This included 14,643 head from Wichita, 9,540 from Dodge City, and 1,380 from Great Bend.

On the Texas ranches, more stockmen were beginning to grade up their Longhorns. On June 10, the Fort Worth *Democrat* noted that Messrs. Boaz and Godwin, in from their ranch, "report the grass good and the cattle fat. The Shorthorn stock they took out this spring are in good condition. The idea that Durhams will not do well in Texas has about exploded."

After the completion of the 1876 drive and the arrival of the new railroad, celebrated with a big barbecue, Fort Worth could give overdue attention to civic improvements and reform. The *Democrat* called attention to the condition of the streets, on which cattle occasionally went on a rampage. "There are so many loose stones in the streets," it said, "that the progress of vehicles is greatly impeded." Only Main and Houston streets had paving worthy of the name, and there were few sidewalks. "No city in northern Texas can boast such a limited supply of good sidewalks," wrote the editor. He advocated building a sidewalk down Houston or Main to the depot.

The dance halls also came in for notice. Within a week, two "soiled doves," one of them from the Waco Tap dance hall, had killed themselves by taking poison. Later two dance girls at the Theatre Comique pitched into one another. Each pulled and scratched the other and tore her clothes. The mayor closed all three dance halls on Main Street and fined the owners ten dollars each. But soon they were open again and indulging in their nightly orgies.[8]

II

Howling blizzard gales opened the year 1877 on the ranges of northwestern Texas, freezing many cattle and horses. Thousands of

Fort Worth but from Denison. In its issue of April 9, the Denison *Daily Cressett* said: "It is expected that the cattle season will be in full blast by the middle of May. The M. K. and T. stockyards are now the largest in the state and can accommodate five thousand head."

[8] Fort Worth *Democrat*, November 24, 25, 29, December 13, 20, 21, 1876.

carcasses were strewn over the prairies. But milder weather soon brought recovery for the survivors. By January 27 it was balmy enough for a horse race on the track outside Fort Worth.

Out on the unsettled plains, an estimated fifteen hundred hunters were killing the buffaloes for their hides. From headquarters in Fort Griffin, they worked in small groups, peeling and drying the hides as the animals were killed. Fort Griffin had about four acres covered with piles of hides. Wagon trains took them to Fort Worth to be shipped east by rail. One morning a Fort Worth reporter noted a train of ten wagons. "In front were twelve yoke of oxen driven by one man and dragging after them four large new wagons, heavily laden. Two other teams, with seven yoke each, drawing three wagons, followed. There probably were from 2,500 to 3,000 hides in the train." Another observer was impressed with one lot of 60,000 hides piled high on a platform near the railroad. During the season, Fort Griffin sent in about 200,000 hides, which brought the hunters about one dollar each.

Progressive stockmen continued to bring in better breeding cattle to grade up their herds. The Millett brothers, announced the Fort Worth *Democrat*, "have a fine bunch of blooded cattle at the stable of Wims and Johnson. There are twenty-five or thirty in all. A few are for sale, but most of them are for their ranches in Baylor County. Two or three of the animals occupy stalls and are blanketed like horses. One of them, Stonewall Jackson, is a descendant of some of the families of $20,000 renown and is a bovine beauty."

Some of those who were buying land and improving their stock were building fences of the new barbed wire. But many were skeptical. Some said the wire wouldn't hold the Longhorns. Others feared the barbs might injure their cattle or horses. In San Antonio, the enterprising wire salesman John W. Gates decided to show them. He had a circular fence built in Military Plaza and invited cowmen for miles around. He obtained sixty Longhorn steers and engaged seasoned cowhands to give an exhibition of cutting and bulldogging. Then he had forty of the steers driven into the fence. Stampeded by two men with flaming torches, they lunged against the wire. One post pulled loose; but, to the surprise of most of the spectators, the fence held. Barbed wire had proved its strength, and sales began to zoom.

Cowmen were beginning to join forces for their common good. In February, about forty of them gathered under an oak at the frontier village of Graham. They formed the Stock Raisers Association of Northwest Texas. Their purpose in this was to divide their section into districts for cow hunts and to protect their herds against rustlers.

In Fort Worth, while stockmen gathered at the bar of the Cattle Exchange, the editor of the *Democrat* renewed his attack on filthy streets. "Some people dam up water," he wrote, "and others dump gravel and refuse. Ladies are seen with gaiters, stockings, and skirts bedraggled with mud from the puddles." Yet, no matter how messy its streets, Fort Worth was growing. It was building the three-story El Paso Hotel of gray limestone and was starting work on a new $65,000 courthouse.

In March, a Fort Worth slaughter house shipped its first carload of fifty refrigerated beeves to St. Louis. Undeterred by the failure of the Denison firm formed several years earlier to ship beef by iced cars, the Fort Worth enterprise hoped to profit from the better ventilation offered by the new cars. Those of the Tiffany Refrigerating Company of Chicago were said to keep meat fresh and untainted for great distances. The use of these cars, confidently predicted the *Democrat*, would end the trailing of cattle from Texas to Kansas.

Yet such an outcome was still in the future. In April and May, outfits taking Longhorn herds up the Chisholm Trail crowded Fort Worth as usual. Despite the diversion of some herds to the new Western Trail, Fort Worth was kept busy. Among the drovers still following the older route were Ellison and Dewees, the Milletts, Sol West, and Colonel Dillard R. Fant. The cowhands found plenty of refreshment at Tivoli Hall, the Trinity Saloon, and other bars. The dance halls were in full blast in spite of an ordinance intended to ban them. Joe Lowe was tried on a charge of operating a dance hall on Main Street but was acquitted for lack of evidence that he was the owner. The mayor's court fined frequent offenders for drunkenness, assault and battery, and the use of profane and abusive language.

Not all the cattle herds went on foot beyond Fort Worth. The Texas and Pacific shipped 51,923 head from there during the year.

More than two-thirds of these Longhorns went to St. Louis and nearly all the others to Chicago.[9]

Among the herds that Ellison and Dewees sent up the Chisholm Trail in 1877 was one in charge of Colonel James F. Ellison's brother, Nat P. Ellison. He had a mixed herd of about 2,600 head. With him were eight cowboys, a wrangler, and a Negro cook who had two yoke of oxen hitched to his wagon.

This herd, thin after a dry, cold winter, left the pastures near Lockhart early in April. The cattle stampeded one night on Maze Prairie, near Onion Creek, but were recovered before long. They had to swim the Colorado River but came into fine grazing along the Trinity River near Fort Worth. The outfit found the Red River too swollen to cross and had to wait. There, at midnight, the guards discovered a panther standing on his hind legs eating a beef that the cook had hung from a tree near the wagon. The consequent shooting stampeded the cattle. It took the men several days to find them and to put them across the river.

In the Indian Territory the cattle benefited from good grass and began to regain some of their lost weight. They had to swim both the Washita and the North Canadian but did so without much trouble. The camp had a few Indian visitors, headed by Chief Spotted Tail. The boss sent them off with four or five lame yearlings from the drag. At one place on the trail, the men were saddened at seeing a mound of freshly dug earth topped by a pair of cowboy boots. Above the Salt Fork, the outfit turned the herd off to the northwest and reached Dodge City a week later.

Rainy weather plagued Jerry M. Nance, as it did Nat Ellison and others. Nance left Hays County on April 15 with 2,100 Longhorns, forty ponies, and a wagon drawn by two yoke of oxen. The herd crossed the Colorado below Austin and swam the Brazos above Waco. At Fort Worth the outfit bought from York and Draper enough supplies for the drive to Kansas. The men had to swim the cattle and horses across both the Washita and the North Canadian. They pulled the supplies across by raft. At the Salt Fork, on June 8, a norther brought rain and such cold that eight ponies in near-by

[9] *Ibid.*, January 2, 6, 14, 17, 28, 31, February 3, 13, 16, 17, March 25, April 17, May 3, 22, 25, June 12, 13, 17, 22, July 1, August 10, December 2, 1877, January 3, 1878; Lloyd Wendt and Herman Kogan, *Bet a Million! The Story of John W. Gates*, 42–49.

outfits died from exposure. The Nance cattle stampeded, but the men recovered all of them. Pointing northwest to Dodge City, Nance took the herd on to Ogallala and Cheyenne.

The westward surge of farm settlement, which gave Dodge City its advantage over Wichita, showed no sign of slackening. Kansas farmers still were hostile toward the drovers. T. J. Garner, who went with a Hood and Hughes herd from Uvalde to Caldwell, had a taste of their venom. After the herd was sold, he and Hank Leedy trailed 640 of the steers to feeding pens at the head of the Elk River, near Eureka. They were about a mile from the pens when ten French ranchmen popped out of a gulch and said they were going to hang Hank Leedy for bringing in the steers three days to early. But when Garner, from the protection of a four-foot boulder, pointed his Winchester in their direction, they quickly changed their minds.

The low esteem in which many Kansans held Texas cowboys was deepened by news from Big Springs, Nebraska, on the night of September 18. There six masked men in cowboy outfits held up and robbed the eastbound Union Pacific express. They took $60,000 in gold and $458 in paper money from the express car, then robbed the passengers in the coaches. Two of the bandits were Joel Collins and Sam Bass, Texas cowboys who had taken a Longhorn herd up the trail in 1876. They had gone on to the Deadwood mining camp in the Black Hills, where they squandered their cattle money in gambling and, with new companions, held up several stagecoaches.

By this time, the new Chisholm Trail cutoff to Dodge City was becoming a beaten path, used by more herds than the older trails to Wichita and Ellsworth. While shipments of cattle from Wichita dwindled to 4,102 head in 1877, those from Dodge City—fed by both the Chisholm and Western trails—rose to 22,940 head. Dodge City not only could be reached with less trouble from the nesters and their fences but was a more convenient stopover point for those who planned to trail on to Ogallala or Cheyenne.

Dodge City was beginning to perk up under the impetus of its new cattle trade. The village, which had had a railroad since September, 1872, had used it for little except shipping buffalo hides. Now it had a full array of saloons, gambling rooms, dance halls, and bagnios. It was trying to live up to its new reputation as the wickedest town on the plains.

Thus far, law enforcement in Dodge hadn't quite caught up with crime and vice. In 1876, Larry Deger had been marshal, with Wyatt Earp, a former Wichita policeman, as chief deputy. In 1877 the law was represented mainly by two trigger-fingered brothers. William Barclay Masterson, better known as Bat, was sheriff. Edward J. Masterson was deputy marshal. Bat was an even more foppish dresser than Wild Bill Hickok had been, but he was becoming known as one of the most deadly gunmen on the frontier.[10]

Although Dodge City was on the up in 1877, the total cattle drive for that year suffered from the hard winter in Texas. The government estimate was 201,159 head. That was slightly less than two-thirds of the figure for 1876.

III

Fort Worth merchants, eager for the bellowing and the dust of new trail herds, greeted the first arrivals of the 1878 season on April 7. There were two herds that day—one of 3,000 mixed cattle and one of 2,700 fine beeves belonging to J. P. Morris. Both herds were headed for the Platte River country to be distributed to the Indian agents. In Fort Worth at that time, yearlings were bringing $6.50 to $7.00. Two-year-olds were worth $11 to $12.50, and four-year-olds $22 to $25. Cows sold at $12 to $16. Stockmen said that the spring grass never had been better.

Soon Fort Worth was crowded with hilarious trail hands who made the rounds of the bars and dance halls. Late on the night of April 9 a dozen or more of them mounted their horses outside the Red Light, drew their six-shooters, and fired twenty to thirty shots into the air. Putting spurs to their mounts, they galloped to the railroad station. There they reloaded and fired another volley. Later, peace officers arrested three of the merrymakers at the Waco Tap and lodged them in the calaboose.

Elsewhere that spring, some Texans were putting six-shooters to other use. Sam Bass, back from Nebraska with his share of the Union Pacific loot, formed a new band and held up four passenger trains. Texas Rangers and local posses were chasing this elusive

[10] Hunter, *The Trail Drivers of Texas*, 105–108, 228–35, 648–49, 687–90; Robert M. Wright, *Dodge City, the Cowboy Capital;* Stanley Vestal, *Queen of Cowtowns: Dodge City.*

brigand through the hills and hollows without catching up with him.

At Fort Griffin, where buffalo hunting showed signs of playing out, merchants were picking up new business in supplying cow outfits on the Western Trail. Irked at the success of Fort Griffin in diverting much of this trade, the *Democrat* in Fort Worth berated the merchants there for letting this business slip out of their hands. "This through drive is worth thousands of dollars to any city," it said. "That our merchants should have lost sight of the importance of having a representative to offset the influence of Fort Griffin's enterprise at Belton is singular indeed."

A few weeks later the editor of the *Democrat* was hammering at this subject again. He credited the energy and enterprise of Fort Griffin citizens with drawing 150,000 of the trail cattle for the season, leaving only 100,000 for Fort Worth. "Had our businessmen been equally active in securing this immense drive, the season drive would not have fallen short of 200,000. Experience is a dear teacher. We hope that their eyes will be opened to their best interests next year."

Of the 82,450 head of trail cattle that had passed Fort Worth by May 23, 38,550 were headed for Wyoming Territory, 27,550 for Kansas, 7,900 for Colorado, and 8,450 for the Texas Panhandle. Twenty thousand more were expected during the remainder of the season. Among the biggest drovers of the year were the Snyder brothers, who sent about 25,000 head to Wyoming.

The European demand for beef was still strong. Sailing from New York early in the summer, the *France* gave over part of what usually was passenger space to make room for five hundred Texas steers. In the same week, twelve hundred head were shipped from Boston to Liverpool, despite a freight charge of $25 to $30 a head.[11]

Among the few Texas cowmen who trailed to Wichita in 1878 was Joe Shiner. With Louis Enderle as foreman, he took a herd north from the San Antonio River. Except for a stampede on a creek near Kerrville, in the hill country, the outfit pushed through without much trouble.

T. J. Garner ran into rain and fog when he pointed one of the Snyder herds up the Chisholm Trail to Dodge City and on to Ogal-

[11] Fort Worth *Democrat*, April 9, 10, 13, 18, May 8, 23, July 9, 1878; Wayne Gard, *Sam Bass.*

lala and Julesburg. Often the restless cattle would drift in a fog and
stampede. Then they would run for the rest of the night. For three
weeks, Garner didn't get to unroll his bedding or to sleep more
than an hour or so each night.

From the lush coastal ranges of Refugio County, Thomas Welder and Doug Williams trailed two herds to Dodge City for J. J.
Welder. On the prairies near Gonzales they were caught in a severe
freeze. In the Indian Territory they found at the entrance to each
reservation a sign demanding "one wohaw" as payment for grazing.
The bosses complied, preferring to lose a steer rather than to have
the Indians stampede their herds. Welder, riding ahead after crossing
the North Canadian, was approached by seven Indians who demanded that he swap horses with them. But, drawing his pistol and
spurring his horse, he eluded them until his outfit came into view.
Except for a few hard hailstorms, the herds reached Dodge City
without any further mishap.

Torrential rains made trouble for Virgil Johnson, who took a
mixed herd of two thousand head up the Chisholm Trail for Woodward and Oge of Frio County. While this and a dozen other herds
were waiting to cross the flooded Red River, a thunderstorm struck
with great force. A bolt of lightning killed nine cattle in the Johnson
herd and caused the others to stampede. A few days later, the outfit
swam the cattle across, ferrying the chuck wagon. Four steers bogged
in a bar of quicksand, but some of the men swam out and pulled
them loose. Near the Wichita Mountains the cattle had to go without
water for two days, but they had plenty of lush grass. The cook
was able to vary his menu when two of the trail hands roped and
butchered a young buffalo bull, and again when one of them killed
a big turkey gobbler.

Although the year's drive of 265,649 head was considerably
larger than that of 1877, cattle shipments from Dodge City dropped
to 16,237 head. For most of the drovers that year, Dodge City was
not the end of the trail but a mere stopping point on the way farther
north. Some of those who did dispose of their herds at Dodge sold
not to shippers but to cowmen who trailed on north or west.[12]

Yet Dodge, no matter what its figure for cattle shipments, was
livelier than ever in 1878. At the Comique, Eddie Foy and his troupe

[12] Hunter, *The Trail Drives of Texas*, 262–66, 293–95, 472, 649.

played to a full house. Hundreds of Texas cowboys crowded the three south-side dance halls and packed the saloons. Shootings and other offenses made plenty of work for the peace officers. Charles E. Bassett was marshal at $100 a month. On the payroll at $75 a month each were Wyatt Earp, assistant marshal, and John Brown and James Masterson, policemen.

I V

Looking ahead to the 1879 cattle season, Fort Worth leaders acted on the advice of the *Democrat*. They engaged Dave Blair as a spokesman and sent him down the trail to talk with the drovers. Late in February, and again early in March, he sent back assurance that those cowmen he had seen would use the Chisholm Trail through Fort Worth. A severe winter had caused the loss of some cattle and had left others in poor condition, but the drive was expected to be only slightly smaller than that of 1878.

By the middle of April the boisterous laughs and whoops of the trail hands were again enlivening Fort Worth. The town was profiting from its enterprise in soliciting business. Instead of seeing most of the herds pointed through Fort Griffin, as in 1878, it had the larger number on the Chisholm Trail. But Fort Griffin could not be downed. Its Western Trail offered better grazing along the way and greater freedom from nesters and their fences.

In April, after extravagant boasts by Dave Blair, the Fort Griffin *Echo* began to taunt Fort Worth. It reported that one of its citizens, Frank E. Conrad, was ready to bet $500 or $1,000 that more cattle would be trailed by Fort Griffin than by Fort Worth in the 1879 season. The Fort Worth *Democrat* issued a bristling answer. Two unnamed Fort Worth cowmen, it assured, would wager up to $2,500 that at least three-fourths of the 1879 drive would go up the older trail. The editors battled back and forth, each accusing the rival town of bluffing. The *Echo* stated that, on May 22, Conrad sent a check for $500 to a Dallas bank, for a bet on the *Democrat's* terms; but there were no Fort Worth takers.

If this wager had gone through, Fort Worth would have lost. It handled more than half the Texas trail cattle that year but fewer than three-fourths. By June 24, 101,010 head had gone by the Western Trail and 135,847 by the Chisholm Trail—236,857 in all. The season total was estimated at 250,927 head.[13]

Among the larger trail herds of the 1879 season was a mixed one of 3,500 head that the veteran Mark A. Withers, of Lockhart, took up the Chisholm route. The herd left on April 2 and stampeded on the first night out. Pieced together again, it crossed the Colorado River at Webberville. At Taylor, about twenty days from the home range, the travelers ran into a blizzard that killed several horses and cattle. The herd drifted in the sleet and cold, wind-driven rain. The weary men had to go without supper, sleep, and breakfast to keep the Longhorns in hand. When, the next noon, they went to the camp for dinner, they were disgusted to find the cook under blankets in the wagon. He said he couldn't build a fire in the rain. After Withers had sent the cook packing, the men built a fire and soon had a warm meal. A new cook took over the next day.

At Turkey Creek, in the Indian Territory, about thirty-three miles above the North Canadian, Withers had his outfit leave the Chisholm Trail and point the herd northwest. After traveling one hundred miles over a route marked with a buffalo head about every half-mile, the herd reached the Western Trail at Longhorn Roundup on the Cimarron or Red Fork. At Dodge City, Withers sold his yearling steers to the Day brothers. Then he went on to the Smoky Hill River, where he sold his cows to John R. Blocker. The trail hands, with money burning their pockets, struck out for Ogallala.[14]

By this time, Ogallala was challenging, but not quite usurping, the position of Dodge City as the Gomorrah of the plains. Dodge still had more saloons, bolder women, and more sensational shooting affrays. On the night of Saturday, April 5, its crowded Long Branch Saloon had been the scene of a gun battle over a woman. The duelists were Frank Loving, a young gambler, and Levi Richardson, a well-known freighter. After eleven shots, from pistols so close that they almost touched, Richardson received a mortal wound, while Loving escaped with a scratch.

[13] Fort Worth *Democrat*, February 26, March 7, April 17, May 10, June 25, 1879; Fort Griffin *Echo*, April 19, 26, May 17, 31, August 9, 1879.
[14] Hunter, *The Trail Drivers of Texas*, 219–21, 236–38, 253–54.

XV

SONGS OF THE PUNCHERS

His long hair didn't mean that the Texas cowhand who guided bawling Longhorns up the Chisholm Trail had any highbrow streak in him. If anyone had called him a musician, he would have been amused if not insulted. Likely he took more pride in his cussing than in his singing.

Usually his untrained voice wasn't anything to brag about. Often it sounded like the bray of a burro with a cold. Jack Thorp, who collected many of the cowboy ballads, said he never knew a cowboy with a good voice. "If he had one to start with, he always lost it bawling at cattle, sleeping in the open, or telling the judge he didn't steal that horse."

Yet the rough men on the trail gave the nation some of its most popular songs. Those who sang on horseback had a strong sense of rhythm—a rhythm that often was set by a pony's gait. Usually the singers were free from self-consciousness and had an instinct for the appropriate. They chose loud, vigorous songs to prod laggards in the drag and crooned soft ones to keep the cattle quiet after they were bedded down for the night.

When the trail hand gargled his throat, as some called it, he usually had a practical purpose. In threatening weather, when the cattle began to drift and showed signs of stampeding, a hymn or a ballad might quiet them. "The confidence a steer's got in the dark," observed Charlie Russell, "is mighty frail." Songs were the best antidote to rumbling in the sky or the howl of a lobo wolf on a distant hill.

When the cattle stampeded and had to be gathered again, songs helped to wear off their excitement. Methodist hymns were popular for this purpose, wrote one observer in 1873, "although good old-fashioned Negro minstrel songs have been found equally effective in soothing the breast of the wild Texas steer." In one such instance, Charlie Siringo reported that after the men had sung a few lullabies to the steers, they all lay down and started snoring.[1]

Like Big-Mouth Henry, the Negro cowboy whose voice seemed to charm the Longhorns, the cowpuncher who could sing better than the average had an advantage. In his long days in the saddle, songs helped to speed the hours and to keep him from growing lonesome. In the evening around the campfire, they gave a bit of diversion before the tired men hit their bedrolls. The hands on night guard used songs not only to keep the cattle quiet but to keep themselves awake.

Some trail bosses didn't like to hire a fellow who couldn't sing, said J. M. Grigsby of Fort Worth. "We boys would consider it a dull day's drive if we didn't add at least one verse. On bad, dark nights the cowboy who could keep up the most racket was the pet of the bunch. We called him the bellwether, and he always brought up his side of the herd."

Even after the Longhorns were penned in some Kansas cow town and were ready to be loaded, singing might be needed. Joe McCoy said that many times he sat on the fence of a shipping yard and sang to an enclosed herd while a train roared past. The cattle would remain quiet as long as they could hear his voice, he said. But if they failed to hear it above the din of the train, they would rush against the enclosure and sometimes break out.[2]

[1] Kansas City *Journal of Commerce*, June 19, 1873; Charles A. Siringo, *A Texas Cowboy*, 1950 ed., 59.
[2] McCoy, *Historic Sketches of the Cattle Trade of the West and Southwest*, 101.

Occasionally some trail hand would bring along a musical instrument. One Texas cowman made a habit of putting a few mouth organs in his chuck wagon. A fiddler was likely to be popular. Lake Porter, who made several trips up the trail in the early seventies, used to take along his fiddle. Although he said that the only tunes he could play to perfection were "Seesaw" and "Sawsee," he did well enough on others to suit his fellow punchers. Among those they remembered were "Dinah Had a Wooden Leg," The "Arkansas Traveler," and "The Walls of Jericho."[3]

In the early days of trail driving, the songs of the cowboys generally were those they had learned back home and ones that were popular over the country. Wash Adams, a Negro cook, used to sing an old plantation melody, "Oh Mary, My Mary." Many sang hymns and sentimental ballads. Among the favorites were "Lorena," "Green Grow the Lilacs," "When You and I Were Young, Maggie," and "Darling, I Am Growing Old." Such tunes seemed to fit in with the creaking of saddle leather and to soothe the restive steers.

Soon disappointed gold miners began to drift back from California, bringing ballads of the Forty-Niners and of the settlers who had gone out in covered wagons. Among those the cowpokes liked were "The Days of Forty-Nine" and "Sweet Betsy From Pike." Before long they were making up songs about their own experiences— of the girls they left behind, of the joys and tribulations of life on the trail, and of bad men whose careers had ended in clouds of six-shooter smoke. Some of the words they sang to hymn tunes would have shocked a preacher and scorched a printed page.

II

Horses, which played an essential and intimate part in the daily life of the trail hand, were the heroes of many of his songs. One of the ballads, "The White Steed of the Prairies," recalled legends of the herds of wild horses and the famous pacing white mustang. It told of the futility of trying to rope this proud monarch that sped over the plains like a creature of light and that had no fence to his range save the mountains and sky.

[3] Hunter, *The Trail Drivers of Texas*, 837–38; Cora Melton Cross, "Up the Trail With Nine Million Longhorns," *Texas Monthly*, Vol. V, No. 2 (February, 1930), 135.

Closer to the cowboy's own everyday life were songs dealing with the riding of wild or outlaw horses. These included "The Horse Wrangler," "The Wild Bronc Peeler," and "The Zebra Dun." The trail hand's affection for his own faithful mount was made evident in several early ballads. One of the strongest in appeal was "Old Paint," whose variant versions became known as "I Ride Old Paint" and "Good-by, Old Paint." In the western cow country, this popular song came to replace "Home Sweet Home" as music for the final waltz at a cowboy breakdown.

> *My foot's in the stirrup; my pony won't stan'.*
> *Good-by, old Paint, I'm a-leavin' Cheyenne.*
> *I'm a-leavin' Cheyenne; I'm off for Montan'.*
> *Good-by, old Paint, I'm a-leavin' Cheyenne.*

Often the cowboy song was a parody or an adaptation of an earlier song, or at least it used an old tune. The popular "Whoopee Ti Yi Yo, Git Along, Little Dogies" appears to have been derived, by stages, from an English ballad. "Red River Valley" was localized from "The Bright Sherman Valley," which in turn was an adaptation of an upstate New York song, "The Bright Mohawk Valley."

Several of the trail songs had their origin in dramatic incidents in the cow country or elsewhere. "Rattlesnake," was a stuttering, semi-comic version of the colonial ballad "Springfield Mountain," which told of the death of a young man from a snake bite in Massachusetts in 1761. "The Cowboy's Stroll" and its variant, "Jack o' Diamonds," apparently were adapted, by stages, from an Irish ballad, "The Forsaken Girl."[4]

Other songs related the adventures of cowboys, peace officers, or brigands. In the later years of trail driving, one of the most popular of such ballads was "Sam Bass." Before he turned to robbing stagecoaches and trains for easy money, Bass had gone up the trail with a herd in 1876. Betrayed by one of his associates, Jim Murphy, Bass was fatally wounded in a gun battle with Texas Rangers and other officers at Round Rock, Texas, in 1878. The song, the original version of which was attributed to John Denton, of Gainesville, showed deep scorn for the traitor:

[4] Ruth Speer Angell, "Background of Some Texas Cowboy Songs" (Master's thesis, Columbia University, 1937), 50–66.

Jim had borrowed Sam's good gold and didn't want to pay.
The only shot that Jim could see was to give poor Sam away.
He sold out Sam and Barnes and left their friends to mourn—
Oh, what a scorching Jim will get when Gabriel blows his horn!

The ballad did much to make Bass a folk hero of the Robin Hood type among the cowboys, and its simple tune was useful to trail hands on night duty. Charlie Siringo found that this song, more than others, had a quieting effect on a herd of Longhorns during a thunderstorm.[5]

Less than four years after the death of Sam Bass, that of Jesse James, the Missouri bandit leader, gave rise to a similar ballad that became popular among the cowboys. It minced no words in condemning the man who, after accepting Jesse's hospitality, killed him in hope of a reward. Of "that dirty little coward," the song noted that "he ate of Jesse's bread and he slept in Jesse's bed" then "came along like a thief in the night and laid poor Jesse in his grave."

Not all the heroes of cowboy songs were outlaws. The top hand, the bronc peeler, the Pecos puncher, the Texas Ranger, and even the bullwhacker came in for attention. One popular song, "Mustang Gray," dealt with a frontiersman, Mayberry B. Gray, who came from South Carolina in 1835, at the age of twenty-one. He took part in the battle of San Jacinto and later joined in skirmishes against the Indians and in raids on Mexican ranches. In the war with Mexico in 1846–47, he commanded a company. He acquired his nickname during a buffalo hunt. After losing his horse, he had to live on buffalo meat for several days. Finally he made a *riata* of buffalo hide, caught a mustang when it came to drink, and rode the wild horse back to the camp of his friends, who had given him up as lost. The song told of his imprisonment in Mexico and his release by a smitten *señorita*.

Another song, "The Texas Ranger," recounted the exploits of a youth who joined the frontier defense force and quickly had his fill of Indian fighting. He advised other youths in search of adventure to stay at home.

One of the most impressive songs heard on the cattle trail was "The Buffalo Skinners." With Homeric frankness and simplicity, it told the story of cowboys who were hired at Jacksboro to go out

[5] Charles A. Siringo, *Riata and Spurs*, 101; Gard, *Sam Bass*.

on the plains beyond the Pease River and skin buffaloes. Indians picked off some of the skinners, and the others complained of hard life and sorry chuck. When, at the close of the season, the boss refused to pay them, that was the last straw. They "left old Crego's bones to bleach on the range of the buffalo."

This song had a variant, "The Hills of Mexico," that substituted Fort Griffin for Jacksboro and cattle herding in New Mexico for buffalo skinning along the Pease. But the outcome was the same. Both songs appear to be western adaptations of an early Maine loggers' song called "Come All Ye Jolly Lumbermen" or "Canada I–O." Another offshoot of this New England ballad was a popular lumber-camp song, "Michigan I–O."

Not all the trail songs had words and phrases that would blister the hide off a Texas alligator. Some indulged in homesick or romantic sentiment, and a few touched on religion. One of the favorites was "The Cowboy's Dream," known also as "The Great Roundup" or "The Dim, Narrow Trail." This hymn of the cow country pointed beyond the stars in the prairie sky and into the future:

> There's goin' to be a great big roundup,
> When the cowboys like dogies will stand,
> Cut out by the Rider from heaven,
> Who'll be there and know every brand.

The appeal of this song was such that at least one Texas revivalist used it at frontier camp meetings to draw cowboys to the mourners' bench.

Many of the cowboy songs were doleful. They dealt with sudden death that might catch up with the trail hand far from his family. One ballad, called "The Cowboy's Lament" or "The Dying Cowboy," recounted the sad story of a puncher who was shot in a gambling brawl. Usually the locale was the border town of Laredo, though in some versions it was Tom Sherman's barroom or elsewhere. The dying narrator admitted that he'd done wrong, warned his fellows to avoid his fate, and asked for a military funeral. The song seems to have stemmed from an early Irish ballad, "The Unfortunate Rake" or "The Unfortunate Lad," or perhaps more directly from a feminine version, "The Bad Girl's Lament."[6]

6 J. Frank Dobie, "Mustang Gray: Fact, Tradition, and Song," *Publications of*

Equally sad was the popular trail song "Oh, Bury Me Not on the Lone Prairie." "More than once," said Mark Withers, "I caught myself singing the cattle to sleep with that favorite of the range." A sentimental dirge, it reflected the cowboy's lonely life and his dread of lying in a neglected grave, far from his loved ones. It is a plains version of an early salt-water ballad, "The Ocean Burial," sometimes called "Burial at Sea" or "Oh, Bury Me Not in the Deep, Deep Sea."

Some of the songs recalled trials and hardships of the long drive. One, called "The Trail to Mexico" or "The Trail of '83," told of a cowboy who, after going off with a herd, learned that his sweetheart, instead of waiting for him as she had promised, had married another. He turned back to the cattle range

> Where the girls are few and the boys are true
> And false-hearted love I never knew.
> I'm goin' back to Mexico,
> Where the Longhorn steers and cactus grow.

III

For day riding, the song most popular of all was the one about the Chisholm Trail itself. In couplet form, it was easy to add to, and it gathered hundreds of stanzas, many of them unmailable. "The Old Chisholm Trail" was no crooning song but a vigorous ballad for a man on a trotting horse. Its tune seemed to be an adaptation of Stephen Foster's "Old Uncle Ned." The opening usually ran:

> Come along, boys, and listen to my tale;
> I'll tell you of my troubles on the old Chisholm Trail.
>
> Come a ti yi yippy, yippy yay, yippy yay,
> Come a ti yi yippy, yippy yay.

The troubles that the singer recalled were many. They included bucking horses, downpours of rain, and midnight stampedes. This

---

the *Texas Folklore Society*, Vol. X (1930), 109–25; Angell, "Background of Some Texas Cowboy Songs" (Master's thesis, Columbia University, 1937), 76–87. The name Tom Sherman in one version of "The Cowboy's Lament" may have been a folk variant of that of Tom Sheran, who bought the Bull's Head Saloon in Abilene, Kansas, in July, 1871.

was a great trail song, said Bill Walker. "It could put life into a footsore cow herd and a saddle-sore puncher. It has been known to throw several kinds of panic into a bunch of Mexican cow thieves and into Indians on the warpath."[7]

In the later years of the Chisholm Trail, as barbed wire and political quarantines restricted the drives and as the open range in Texas was being parceled out into fenced ranches, stanzas added to the song told of an intention to turn from cowboy life to farming:

> Good-by, old trail boss, I wish you no harm;
> I'm quittin' this business to go on the farm.
>
> I'll sell my old saddle and buy me a plow;
> And never, no, never will I rope another cow.

The puncher viewed a more settled life also in another song that became popular in the declining years of the Chisholm Trail. "A Home on the Range," which had its origin in northern Kansas in 1873, spread quickly up and down the cow trails. The words of the song stemmed from a poem, "Western Home," which Dr. Brewster Higley, a frontier physician and homesteader, wrote in his one-room dugout on the bank of West Beaver Creek, northwest of Smith Center.

After showing this poem to some of his friends, Dr. Higley was encouraged to have it published. It appeared in the Kirwin *Chief* on March 21, 1874. Soon afterward Daniel E. Kelley set the words to music. Kelley was an enterprising young farmer and contractor who lived in the village of Harlan, south of Smith Center. A former Army bugler, he had an interest in music. With his wife and her two brothers, he had formed a small orchestra that was in wide demand for dances and celebrations. The tune he provided for Dr. Higley's words reminded some of an old church song, "Home for the Soul."

Although the Kelley music was not published at the time, the song caught on rapidly and soon was familiar over most of the West. It became known under various titles, including "My Home in the West," "Home Where the Buffalo Roam," "Colorado Home," and "An Arizona Home." Often the words were changed and localized, and fresh stanzas were added. Rocky Mountain versions had allu-

---

[7] D. F. Baber, *The Longest Rope*, 92. Other stanzas are quoted on pages v, 124, 134, 162, and 264.

sions to prospecting and mining. Some luckless cowboy must have added this stanza:

> *Oh, give me a jail where I can get bail,*
> *If under the shining sun.*
> *I'll wake with the dawn, I'll chase the wild fawn,*
> *I'll ride with my saddle and gun.*

Some singers unfamiliar with Kansas were a bit stumped by the reference in the song to "the graceful white swan." But early Kansas did have wild swans, and Dr. Higley probably had seen them. The swans were attested not only by pioneer settlers but by French explorers, who named one of the Kansas rivers Marais des Cygnes, "Marsh of the Swans."

"A Home on the Range" swept through the square dances and the country singing schools. In one form or another, it came from the lips of thousands of trail hands and others who lived on the frontier. In time, more than any other cowboy ballad, it was adopted as a song that belonged to all Americans.[8]

On the Chisholm Trail there were almost as many songs as there were riders. The Mexicans brought lilting tunes from below the Rio Grande, some of them echoing airs from Spain. The Texas cowhands made up songs of their own or changed the words of those they had heard and added new stanzas. The many songs later set down in print or on phonograph records were only a small segment of the cowboy repertory and often missed the more interesting versions or stanzas. Yet enough of the ballads survived to put the nation in debt to the trail driver as one of the most prolific contributors to its treasury of folk music.[9]

[8] John A. Lomax, "Half-Million-Dollar Song," *Southwest Review*, Vol. XXXI, No. 1 (Fall, 1945), 1–8; Kirke Mechem, "Home on the Range," *Kansas Historical Quarterly*, Vol. XVII, No. 4 (November, 1949), 313–39. Rediscovered by John A. Lomax in 1908 and published by him two years later, "A Home on the Range" was issued in sheet-music form in 1925. It quickly became popular and in 1934 was one of the top song hits. In 1947, by legislative action, it became the state song of Kansas.
[9] N. Howard (Jack) Thorp, *Songs of the Cowboys;* John A. Lomax and Alan Lomax, *Cowboy Songs.* Much credit is due to the late John A. Lomax for snatching many of the cowboy songs from obscurity and publishing them and to Carl Sandburg for broadening their popularity by including them in his recitals of folk music.

XVI

BARBED-WIRE BARRIERS

Hard-pressed by the rival route farther west, hemmed in by quarantine laws and barbed-wire fences, the Chisholm Trail seemed doomed. Yet it received a temporary reprieve in June, 1880. In that month the Santa Fe extended rail service to Caldwell, near the southern edge of Kansas. Caldwell was so close to the border of the Indian Territory that it was not affected by the embargo which kept drovers from trailing their herds on north.

Business leaders in this frontier town were quick to see their advantage. They issued a circular and sent copies to the Indian Territory and Red River Station, inviting Texas drovers to sell at Caldwell. At this new market, optimism ran high. "Dodge City has lost the cattle trade," confidently boasted the Caldwell *Post*.[1]

Caldwell, which had been astride the Chisholm Trail since the original village took root in 1871, was prepared not only to ship cattle but to give the trail hands the kind of entertainment they liked. By the time it loaded its first cattle on June 16, the town had several small hotels and livery stables and seven saloons, each with its gambling room. One of the saloons, the Red Light, also ran a dance hall

[1] Caldwell *Post*, February 26, May 20, 1880.

and an upstairs bagnio housing ten to twelve sporting girls. Horse-race fans could find exciting matches every few days in the bottoms between Bluff and Fall creeks.

For years Caldwell had heard the whoops of Texas cowboys. It had had many shootings and was known as a tough town. One visitor, after a call at the Red Light Saloon on a Saturday night, said the scene reminded him of early times in Cheyenne, when murder ran riot and the pistol was the only argument. The streets were lined with drunken rowdies. The Red Light girls, most of them from Wichita but a few recruited locally, openly solicited business in the streets. George Wood, who had come from Wichita, ran the Red Light Saloon. His wife, Mag Wood, was in charge of the girls upstairs.[2]

Only three days after its first shipment of cattle, Caldwell had another shooting. George W. Flatt, who had been dismissed from the post of marshal for drunkenness, had refused to obey the ordinance against gun-toting. This action and his continued rowdiness gained him the enmity of the policemen, but they didn't dare try to disarm him. On Saturday morning, June 19, soon after midnight, Flatt was walking along Main Street with a friend when about a dozen pistol shots barked in quick succession. The former marshal fell with wounds from which he died after a few minutes.

Caldwell was becoming hardened to such conduct. Another shooting occurred on the evening of October 8, during a dance at the Red Light. Frank Hunt, a local policeman, was sitting in one of the windows when an assassin slipped up in the shadows. The gunman fired at close range, causing Hunt's death several hours later.[3]

The start of the shipping season found several Kansas City and Chicago cattle buyers in Caldwell. On hand, too, was Joseph G. McCoy, whose active figure and booming voice had become familiar in Abilene, Wichita, and Kansas City. He was gathering livestock statistics for the United States Census Bureau.

Texas herds began arriving at Caldwell as soon as the railroad was ready to handle them. Among the early drovers to reach the

[2] *Ibid.*, May 20, June 17, 1880; Freeman, *Midnight and Noonday*, 284–303.
[3] Caldwell *Post*, June 24, October 14, 1880; Freeman, *Midnight and Noonday*, 290–96.

new market were C. C. (Lum) Slaughter, with 1,000 fat beeves, and John Dawson, of Fort Worth, with 1,900 stock cattle. W. H. Murchison arrived with 3,400 head for John W. Gamel. Murchison had blazed a new trail from the head of Persimmon Creek to Pond Creek, which he said was fifteen miles shorter than the old route.[4]

The 1880 drive from Texas, despite unusual rainstorms, crowded the beaten paths more than had that of 1879. It added up to 394,784 head, compared with 257,927 a year earlier. The Western Trail carried most of the herds; a report on July 2 showed that 244,784 head had passed Fort Griffin.

The new market at Caldwell, though, took some business from Dodge City and outdid it in cattle shipping for the season. While Dodge City shipped 17,957 head, a slight drop from 1879, Caldwell loaded 25,531 head. Dodge City, which drew from both trails, received many more cattle than Caldwell -187,000 head by the end of August—but most of the herds were trailed on to Nebraska or beyond.

Because of a severe winter, the 1881 drive started late. As in earlier years, the western competition didn't keep the Chisholm Trail from feeling the hoofbeats of many Longhorn herds. William B. Slaughter took two herds of steers from Palo Pinto County to Caldwell, which had improved its stockyards. More went by Red River Station and Dodge City to Ogallala. Tom Taylor walked one of Colonel Jim Ellison's herds by that route. Colonel Ike T. Pryor sent fifteen herds of about three thousand head each by the same path, some of them going on to Wyoming or Dakota Territory. T. M. O'Connor sold seven hundred horses to Dillard R. Fant at Goliad and delivered them at Ogallala.[5]

Although the 1881 drive of about 250,000 head was smaller than that of 1880, both Caldwell and Dodge City shipped more cattle. Caldwell loaded 31,644 head and Dodge City 33,564 head. This meant that a smaller proportion of the herds were pointed on to new ranges in the Northwest.

[4] Caldwell *Post*, June 3, July 1, 1880. McCoy had been living in Kansas City, where he was a commission dealer in livestock. In 1881 he moved to Wichita, where, at various times, he sold groceries, flour and feed, and real estate. He died in Kansas City in 1915 and was buried in Wichita.

[5] Hunter, *The Trail Drivers of Texas*, 104, 178–79, 817, 872–73.

Both these Kansas cow towns had some excitement during the shipping season. In Caldwell, on the evening of August 18, a patron of the Red Light quarreled with one of the girls. When George Wood, the owner of the place, took the girl's part, the visitor pulled a Colt improved forty-five and shot the unarmed Wood twice, killing him almost instantly.[6]

Dodge City, even before the first Texas herds arrived, had a lively street battle. James Masterson, besides acting as marshal, had been running a saloon and dance hall in partnership with A. J. Peacock. Jim quarreled with their bartender, Al Updegraph, and wanted to dismiss him; but Peacock objected. Then Jim or one of his friends sent for Jim's trigger-fingered brother Bat, who was in New Mexico.

A few moments after he had alighted from the midday train, Bat Masterson saw Peacock and Updegraph in the street. All three reached for their guns and hastened to find cover. Bat dropped behind the railroad embankment, while the others dodged behind the calaboose. A friend of Bat came to his assistance; and before the guns were empty, Updegraph had a bullet pass clear through his body. Although this wound did not prove fatal, Mayor A. B. Webster arrested Bat, who paid a fine of eight dollars. "It costs eight dollars," commented the Medicine Lodge *Index*, "to shoot a man through the lung in Dodge City."[7]

Higher cattle prices in 1882 spurred speculation not only in stock but in the Texas grasslands. Cowmen who foresaw the end of the open range and its free grass wanted to grab all the land they could and fence it with barbed wire. Some borrowed large sums at 18 to 24 per cent interest. Too, outside capital was coming in from the East and from Britain.

In size the 1882 Texas drive matched that of the preceding year, but it was made up more largely of young steers. Many stockmen were holding back their cows and heifers for use in breeding on new ranges in the west. A mild winter had left the trail cattle in unusually good condition. Among the larger drovers this spring were Reed and Byler with thirty thousand head and Jesse L. Hittson with a like

---

[6] Caldwell *Post*, August 25, 1881; Freeman, *Midnight and Noonday*, 297.
[7] *Ford County Globe*, April 19, May 10, 1881.

number. Shanghai Pierce passed San Antonio in late April with three thousand head.[8]

Among the prominent Texas cowmen in Caldwell when that town began shipping in the last week of May were James D. Reed, J. W. Simpson, and L. M. Kokernot. From the Texas Panhandle, J. W. Carter had broken a new trail to Caldwell. Leaving the Western Trail near the crossing of the Washita River, he pointed his herd northeast and reached the Chisholm Trail at Pond Creek. More of the 1882 cattle, compared with those of 1881, were shipped from southern Kansas instead of being trailed farther north. Dodge City loaded 69,271 head and Caldwell 64,007 head.

This was Caldwell's peak year as a point for shipping cattle—and a boisterous one when the Texans were in town. On June 22 a pair of trail hands carried their rowdiness to more than the usual lengths. After extensive patronage of the Red Light bar, they went upstairs to visit some of the girls. Their profane and obscene shouting and their frequent firing of six-shooters so annoyed near-by residents that the marshal, George S. Brown, was sent to arrest them. As he neared the head of the stairs, the Texans fired three shots, and the marshal reeled and fell dead on the landing. The killers rushed across the street to take their horses from the livery stable and escaped to the Indian Territory. The slain marshal was succeeded by B. P. (Bat) Carr. He had as assistant, John Henry Brown, who recently had come from Texas.[9]

II

The spring of 1883 found many Texas ranges overstocked with young cattle. Although a late winter blizzard had killed some stock in the western counties, the coastal prairies benefited from a big 1882 calf crop. Despite plentiful grass in the early spring, much of the state began to suffer from drouth. Even the moving out of 267,-000 head in the season's drive to Kansas left too many cattle for streams that were drying up and grass that was becoming scorched. In some pastures, racing fires destroyed what grass had survived the blistering sun.

[8] Caldwell *Post*, May 11, 1882, citing the *Texas Live Stock Journal* of April 29. Shanghai Pierce later was active in introducing Brahman or Zebu cattle to Texas. He was a millionaire at the time of his death in 1900.

[9] Freeman, *Midnight and Noonday*, 299–311.

As the tough Longhorns grew thin from scant fare and began to bawl for water, many of the smaller cowmen blamed the new fences for their plight. Some of the fencers had enclosed not only their own ranches but much public land that should have been open to all stockmen. Many had blocked roads. Those whose herds were cut off from grass and water took matters into their own hands. In the dark of the moon they went out on fence-cutting forays. Soon some of them were snipping lawful fences along with the others. This fence-cutting war became so extensive and so serious that Governor John Ireland called a special session of the Texas Legislature to deal with the fence problem.[10]

The 1883 drive saw Dodge City regain its dominance as a market for Texas cattle. While the number shipped from Caldwell dropped to 28,379 head, the figure for Dodge City rose to 74,237 head.

Fencing on the trail was becoming a more thorny problem for the drovers. In March the Cherokee Strip Live Stock Association gave notice that fences had closed the branch of the Chisholm Trail from Red Fork Ranch, in the Indian Territory, to Dodge City. It added that "the Chisholm Trail is entirely unobstructed from the Red River to Caldwell," but many cowmen switched to the Western Trail.[11]

In Dodge City a reform element was trying to make the town less rowdy. A new ordinance forbade gambling and banned the use of musical instruments in saloons. One of the operators most affected was Luke Short. A former Texas cowboy, Short had become a gambler and had bought an interest in Dodge's biggest and most popular saloon and gambling house, the Long Branch. On the demand of the marshal, he started to obey the law. He dismissed the young woman who had been playing the piano at the Long Branch.

But a few days later this same young lady turned up at a rival place, the Alamo, owned by Mayor Webster. There she played the piano as lustily as ever and drew customers from the silent Long Branch.

Luke Short was incensed. He sent telegrams summoning Wyatt Earp, Bat Masterson, and other friends whose reputations as pis-

10 Wayne Gard, *Frontier Justice*, 104–19.
11 *Texas Live Stock Journal*, March 24, 1883.

toleers were well known. After this "peace commission" had been in Dodge a few days, the difficulty was straightened out. Again gambling and saloon music were in full blast at the Long Branch and other places of entertainment.[12]

In the spring of 1884, many Texas drovers realized that trailing cattle to Kansas and beyond had about played out. Fences were hemming in the trails and threatening to cut them off, and quarantine laws were becoming more restrictive. Yet some cowmen were willing to risk one more big surge. They pointed about 300,000 Longhorns north during the year. Both Caldwell and Dodge City showed an upturn in shipments, Caldwell shipping 57,112 head and Dodge City 79,525.

These shipments included local cattle and some raised in the near-by Indian Territory. A severe Kansas winter had taken a heavy toll of the cattle being grazed in the Blue Stem Hills and the pastures to the west and had left the survivors in poor condition. Prairie fires had destroyed much of the grass. Too, the spread of farms and fenced ranches across southern Kansas was limiting the open pasture lands.

Caldwell, on the eve of its shipping season, was still having trouble keeping a marshal. It had dismissed Bat Carr in 1882 and promoted John Henry Brown to the post. Ben F. Wheeler, from Texas, became his assistant. Brown, who had ridden with Billy the Kid and later had served as constable in the Texas frontier town of Tascosa, was popular in Caldwell. He had married a local girl and had kept order so well that grateful citizens presented him with a gold-mounted Winchester.

Late in April, 1884, Brown rode out of Caldwell with his deputy and two other men. They said they were going after horse thieves. But on the morning of May 1 they turned up at Medicine Lodge, sixty miles to the west. There they tried to rob a bank and killed two of its officers. By midnight or soon afterward, all four of the bandits had died by vigilante action. Caldwell councilmen adopted a resolution heartily approving of the execution.[13]

Dodge City, too, was having troubles that season. The demand for Texas cattle and cow ponies was falling off, and local business

[12] *Ford County Globe*, June 5, 1883.
[13] Freeman, *Midnight and Noonday*, 153–59.

was dull. Drovers were complaining of trail troubles. Cowmen grazing herds in the northern part of the Indian Territory had stretched barbed wire across the trails, and drovers had to wait while soldiers removed it. Those who wanted to take their herds beyond Dodge City were restricted to a narrow trail marked by furrows.

The old hands still were finding ways to push through. Some of the Texas cattle arriving at Dodge in 1884 bore such familiar brands as those of John Blocker, Dillard R. Fant, Seth Mabry, Shanghai Pierce, John N. Simpson, and Dudley H. Snyder. But the herds were thinning.

To bolster Dodge's slipping prestige, A. B. Webster, former mayor, planned to have the town celebrate the Fourth of July with two days of bullfighting. He and other businessmen raised ten thousand dollars, recruited a dozen ferocious-looking Longhorn bulls from near-by pastures, and imported five matadors from Mexico.

Several hundred cowboys turned out, and Kansans from many towns poured in by train. The crowd filled all four thousand seats of the grandstand at the fair grounds between the town and the river. The cowboy band blared, and spectators cheered as the Mexicans—in blue tunics, red jackets, and white stockings—taunted the bulls. Some of the Longhorns put up a good fight, and one of them was killed. But soon the effects of the celebration wore off. Dodge, as a booming and boisterous cow town, was still on the skids.[14]

One more gun battle enlivened the town that summer. For several months, a feud had been brewing between Thomas Nixon, a former buffalo hunter who had become assistant marshal, and Dave Mather. A deputy sheriff and a former marshal, Mather was known as Mysterious Dave. He and a partner had operated a dance hall in the opera house, but official action had closed it. Mather suspected that Nixon had been back of the closing, and the two had had one encounter.

On the evening of July 21, as Nixon was walking toward the opera house, Mather stepped out and called, "Oh, Tom!" As Nixon turned toward the speaker, Mather fired at close range. After Nixon fell to the sidewalk, Mather put three more bullets into his body.

[14] Dodge City *Democrat*, July 5, 1884; *Ford County Globe*, July 8, 1884; *Kansas Cowboy*, July 12, 1884; Kirke Mechem, "The Bull Fight at Dodge City," *Kansas Historical Quarterly*, Vol. II, No. 3 (August, 1933), 294–308.

When his friends reached the scene, Nixon was dead. Mather was arrested and tried, but the jury acquitted him on the ground of self-defense.[15]

Officials of the Santa Fe took a hand in applying a damper to the roaring at Dodge. Through train passengers complained of the din, especially at night. Too, the rail men could see that the Texas cattle business was drying up. They wanted to build their freight traffic on a more lasting basis. When they promised Dodge a round-house, a hospital, and other facilities—on their terms—the town dads decided to close the dance halls.[16]

III

After the season of 1884, the Chisholm Trail was virtually closed. Cattle shipments from Caldwell in 1885 were less than a third of the 1884 figure and came mainly from local, heldover, and Indian Territory herds. Loadings continued to diminish rapidly through the remaining eighties. Barbed wire was blocking the drovers. Too, railroads were piercing deeper into the Texas ranges and were offering better facilities and more favorable rates for stock shipment.

Dodge City, left with only one main trail, had its last big year as a cow town in 1885. After that, use of the Western Trail, too, tapered off rapidly. By 1890 the trailing of cattle over long distances had almost ended, although cowmen pointed a few herds north through Colorado to Wyoming or the Dakotas in the nineties. As late as 1901, William B. Slaughter walked a herd from Clifton, Arizona, to Liberal, Kansas. Trailing continued from ranches to rail points, which, in some instances, might be fifty or even a hundred miles. But in these shorter treks the cowhand found scant adventure.

Some Texas cowmen refused to give up their long drives without a fight. Through 1883, 1884, and 1885, they called on Congress to open a national trail. They wanted a route that would be on federal land and thus free from the fences of nesters. Their proposal, although opposed by Kansas farmers, drew support from livestock interests at Dodge City.[17]

[15]*Kansas Cowboy*, July 26, 1884; Stanley Vestal, *Queen of Cowtowns: Dodge City*, 247–65.

[16] *Kansas Cowboy*, July 19, 1884.

[17] *Ford County Globe*, January 16, 1883, March 25, 1884; *Kansas Cowboy*, July 5, 1884.

In St. Louis in November, 1884, a national convention of stock-men gave attention to this proposal. It adopted a resolution offered by one of the Texas delegates, Judge J. A. Carroll, of Denton, asking Congress to lay out and maintain a trail from the Red River to Canada. As a result, a committee of nine stockmen went to Wash-ington the next month. This group planned to ask Congress to set aside a strip of land through the public domain in Kansas, Nebraska, and Dakota, following roughly the Western Trail.

Because of a hostile attitude in Kansas, the sponsors altered this plan to route the trail along the eastern edge of Colorado. Early in 1885, Texans introduced in both houses of Congress bills to establish such a trail. The Texas Legislature adopted a resolution supporting this proposal, while the Texas Live Stock Association and similar groups gave added backing. But the shortness of the time and the press of other legislation caused the bills to die in committees.

This inaction led Colonel John N. Simpson, president of the Texas Live Stock Association, to call a meeting to open in Dallas on May 15. This group asked for a trail similar to the one sought in Congress. Some Texas drovers followed this route in 1885, with-out official sanction, and more did so in 1886. In the latter year, the new town of Trail City, on the Arkansas River at the eastern edge of Colorado, became a lively cow town and acquired some business from Dodge City. By July 29, about 135,000 cattle had gone up this trail. The total drive for the year, for all trails, was esti-mated at 350,000 head.

Despite the pressure from Texas, Congress still failed to set aside public land for a national trail. In 1887, with the northern ranges overstocked, cattle prices down, and a part of southeastern Colorado opened for settlement, large-scale trailing declined abruptly. Home-steaders and their fences quickly closed the Colorado route. This action blasted the dream of Texas cowmen for a durable trail to the north.[18]

IV

As barbed-wire fences cut off the Chisholm Trail, wind and rain began to beat out the prints of millions of Longhorn hoofs. Soon a carpet of new grass spread over the battered path. At some of

[18] Floyd Benjamin Streeter, "The National Cattle Trail," *Cattleman*, Vol. XXXVIII, No. 1 (June, 1951), 26–27, 59–74.

the river crossings, men would point out traces of the trail for many years, but on most of the prairies it was erased so quickly that its exact route became a subject for frequent argument.

On the nation's economy, the trail had made a more lasting impression. It had spurred the settlement of the northern ranges, including those of Colorado, Wyoming, Montana, and the Dakotas. A Wyoming editor noted that the season of 1871, the peak year of the Chisholm Trail, was "a memorable one in the stock business on the plains. Its success was doubted by many newcomers, but the year has closed with their unlimited confidence in the complete practicality and profits of stock growing and winter grazing. The number of cattle is double, if not four times larger than in 1869."[19]

To Wyoming the trail brought not only cattle to stock the plains and the mountain valleys but ponies for use in tending the northern herds. In many instances, Texas cowhands who had come up with their herds stayed on in Wyoming. Mastery of their art enabled them to command high wages. Often they were needed to teach green northern cowpokes the finer points in the use of the lariat and the branding iron. Some of the transplanted Texans set up homesteads and began acquiring herds of their own.

This migration, along with travel up and down the trail, helped to lessen in the West the sectional animosity that the abolition movement and the Civil War had engendered. The trail cattle trade, observed Joseph G. McCoy in 1874, was a means "of bringing about an era of better feeling between Northern and Texas men by bringing them in contact with each other in commercial transactions. The feelings today existing in the breasts of all men from both sections are far better than they were six years ago."[20]

Cattle taken up the Chisholm Trail filled a need for more beef and brought the price down for the housewife. Although some of the early Texas beef was tough and had to be sold at a discount, the feeding of Longhorn steers in the Midwest soon overcame this handicap. As early as 1869, two years after the opening of the trail, the directors of the Union Stockyard and Transit Company of Chicago noted this change. In their third annual report, they observed that consumers "demand this Texas stock as it lessens to them the price

[19] Cheyenne *Leader*, April 11, 1872.
[20] McCoy, *Historic Sketches of the Cattle Trade of the West and Southwest*, 56.

of beef." Before the trail was closed, the grading up of Texas cattle by the use of bulls of British breeds had further improved the quality of the beef. On thousands of American dining tables, beef had replaced pork as the chief meat item. The trail drives were a big factor in this change.

Even Europe felt the impact of the Chisholm Trail. In the 1870's, Texas beef began to reach Europe in large quantities. It went on the hoof, in tubs, in tin cans, and in the form of frozen sides. While consumers welcomed it, European cattle raisers became aroused against this competition from across the Atlantic. In several countries they induced their governments to bar imported beef by means of either high tariffs or quarantines based on imagined diseases.[21]

In the American Midwest, the Chisholm Trail spurred the growth of Chicago and Kansas City as centers for beef packing. Although Cincinnati remained the chief meat-packing city until after the Civil War, Chicago had done some slaughtering as early as 1820, shipping meat over the lakes to Detroit, Buffalo, and Rochester. By 1850 the city had three small stockyards. Drovers often grazed their herds in pastures just west of the Chicago River before driving them into the city. The Union Stockyards, owned principally by the nine railroads entering Chicago, began business on Christmas Day, 1865. Beef packing took a big spurt as Texas Longhorns began coming in by the trainload.

In frontier Kansas City, businessmen were not content to see the Texas beeves shipped through their town to Chicago. On the levee two blocks east of Grand Avenue, J. L. Mitchener had built a small packing plant in 1859, in the period of the Shawnee Trail; but the Civil War had ended its operation. In 1868, as Longhorns from the Chisholm Trail came in from Abilene by rail, a new packing plant was built near Ninth and Mulberry streets. In the following year Kansas City handled three million dollars in cattle money.

Kansas City, with seven railroads, had four packing plants in operation in 1871. One of them was leased in that year to the Milwaukee meat-packing firm of Plankinton and Armour and became its branch. In the same season, Kansas City built stockyards in the

[21] Joseph Nimmo, "The Range and Ranch Cattle Traffic of the United States," in *Report on the Internal Commerce of the United States*, Part III, Bureau of Statistics, Washington, 1886.

West Bottoms and erected at Twelfth Street and State Line a one-and-one-half-story frame Livestock Exchange.

This packing business grew rapidly and attracted cowmen from distant ranges. To entertain them, Kansas Citians built lavish gambling houses. The Marble Hall and the House of Lords—each in a brick building furnished with a mahogany bar, crystal chandeliers, and thick carpets—knew the faces of most of the Texas cattle kings.

The trail gave incentive also to railroad building and to the development of refrigerator cars and meat canning. Railroads in Kansas and adjoining states hastened construction to tap the cattle routes. Meanwhile, lines building into the Southwest pushed on to reach the Texas ranges and thus make unnecessary the long drive to the north.

The first refrigerator car, which appeared in 1867, the year the Chisholm Trail was blazed, was a mere icebox on wheels. From direct contact with the ice, the meat became discolored and often spoiled after removal. Soon improved cars kept the meat and ice in separate compartments. George H. Hammond began shipping refrigerated meat from the Chicago area to Boston in the summer of 1869. Twelve years later, Gustavus F. Swift was doing such shipping on a larger scale. Soon use of the refrigerator car and the canning of meat led to the spread of meat packing to such cities as Omaha, Wichita, and Fort Worth, which were nearer the sources of beef.

For much of Texas, the Chisholm Trail offered a way of escape from the poverty in which the Civil War had left the state. It brought quick cash for a product that the ranges had in abundance. Selling the surplus cattle, along with the annual yield, relieved the pastures from overgrazing and enabled the cowmen to pay off their debts. Many sold enough trail cattle to buy land for new ranches, to build fences, and to bring in improved breeding stock.

Even for the puncher who viewed the drive less as a business venture than as a lark, the Chisholm Trail had lasting rewards. Every trail hand carried memories of far horizons, winding rivers, faithful mounts, and thundering stampedes. He had survived dangers that made the hazards of a more settled life seem tame. He had stories of buffaloes and Indians that grandchildren would ask for again and again. He might sing

With my knees in the saddle and my seat in the sky,
I'll quit punchin' cattle in the sweet by and by;

but he would treasure to his last moment the vision of a Longhorn herd strung out on the green prairie or bedded down for the night under the gleaming stars.

BIBLIOGRAPHY

MANUSCRIPTS

Baker, J. H., Diary, 1858–1918, Transcripts in University of Texas Library.

Barry, James Buckner, Reminiscences, University of Texas Library.

Caldwell, Frank, Letter, Austin, Texas, to the author, December 22, 1949.

Daugherty, James M., Papers, 1870–92, University of Texas Library.

Day, William H., Letters. In possession of his grandson, James T. Padgitt, Coleman, Texas.

Doan, C. F., Letters, Vernon, Texas, to J. Frank Dobie, Austin, Texas, 1924–25.

Goodnight, Charles, Letter, Goodnight, Texas, to Howard W. Peak, Fort Worth, Texas, October 28, 1923

Gross, Charles F., Letters, Chicago, to J. B. Edwards, Abilene, Kansas, 1922–28. In J. B. Edwards Papers, Kansas State Historical Society, Topeka.

Hanna, James R., Letter, Blue Bluffs, McLennan County, Texas, to Abner Hanna, Parish, Des Moines County, Iowa, August 18, 1856, Fort Worth Woman's Club.

Indian-Pioneer Papers, University of Oklahoma Library.

Lemmon, G. E., Reminiscences, 1943, J. Frank Dobie, Austin, Texas.

Loving, Oliver, Letters, 1862, Texas State Library, Austin.

McCoy, Florence L., Information furnished at Wichita, Kansas, to Mrs. Hortense B. C. Gibson, October 24, 1938, Kansas State Historical Society, Topeka.

McCoy, Joseph G., Letter, Wichita, Kansas, to J. B. Edwards, Abilene, Kansas, June 14, 1911. In J. B. Edwards Papers, Kansas State Historical Society, Topeka.

Matthews, Warren L., and Others, Letters on the route of the Chisholm Trail from the Indian Territory to the Arkansas River, 1936, Kansas State Historical Society, Topeka.

Matthews, Warren L., Map of the Chisholm Trail from the Indian Territory to the Arkansas River, Kansas State Historical Society, Topeka.

Maverick, Samuel A., Papers, University of Texas Library.

Mead, James R., "Reminiscences of Frontier Life," 1898, Kansas State Historical Society, Topeka.

Nicholson, John C., "The Chisholm Trail," 1941, Kansas State Historical Society, Topeka.

Norton, Edith, "The Story of Coffeyville, Kansas," Carnegie Public Library, Coffeyville.

Oatts, Tom C., Diary, 1871. In possession of his daughter-in-law, Mrs. W. K. Oatts, Austin, Texas.

Pierce, Abel H. (Shanghai), Papers, University of Texas Library.

Poage, William R., "Drive to Cheyenne in 1874," Transcript in University of Texas Library.

Pryor, Ike T., "The Cattle Industry of the United States and the Part Played by the Old Trail Drivers," 1924, E. E. Dale, Norman, Oklahoma.

Rivington, Tom, Letters, Omaha, Nebraska, to J. B. Edwards, Abilene, Kansas, October 20, 26, 1926. In J. B. Edwards Papers, Kansas State Historical Society, Topeka.

Shepherd, John, Letter, Elk City, Oklahoma, to George Saunders, July 8, 1932.

Snyder, Dudley H. and John W., Papers, University of Texas Library.

Starr, James H., Papers, University of Texas Library.

Stevens, Robert S., Letters, 1871, Files of Missouri-Kansas-Texas Lines.

Taylor, T. U., Papers, University of Texas Library.

Withers, Mark A., Reminiscences, J. Frank Dobie, Austin, Texas.

UNPUBLISHED THESES

Angell, Ruth Speer. "Background of Some Texas Cowboy Songs." Columbia University, 1937.

Choitz, John F. "Ellsworth, Kansas: The History of a Frontier Town." Fort Hays Kansas State College, 1941.
Donnell, Guy Renfro. "The History of Montague County, Texas." University of Texas, 1940.
Haley, John Evetts. "A Survey of Texas Cattle Drives to the North, 1866–1895." University of Texas, 1926.
Howard, Dwight Martin. "Southeastern Kansas Cow Towns." University of Kansas, 1946.
McArthur, Daniel Evander. "The Cattle Industry of Texas, 1685–1918." University of Texas, 1918.
Marr, John Columbus. "The History of Matagorda County, Texas." University of Texas, 1928.
Moore, Bonnie Cathryn. "The Northern Drives of Texas Cattle After 1866." University of Oklahoma, 1934.
O'Banion, Maurine M. "The History of Caldwell County." University of Texas, 1931.
Rossell, John. "The Chisholm Trail." University of Wichita, 1931.
Thompson, George G. "Bat Masterson: The Dodge City Years." Fort Hays Kansas State College, 1939.

PUBLIC RECORDS

Abilene, Kansas, Minute Book of the Board of Trustees and the City Council, 1870–71. Office of the City Clerk.
Abilene, Kansas, Ordinance Book, 1871. Office of the City Clerk.
Dickinson County, Kansas, Deed Records. Office of the Recorder of Deeds, Abilene.
Ellsworth, Kansas, Proceedings of the City Council, 1871–73. Office of the City Clerk.
Ellsworth, Kansas, Docket of the Police Judge, 1872–73. Office of the City Clerk.
Ellsworth County, Kansas, Records of the District Court, 1873–77. Office of the District Clerk, Ellsworth.
Kansas Governors' Correspondence, Letters, depositions, reports, and other papers in criminal cases against Silas Fearl and J. N. Howard, charged with stealing cattle from the Indian Territory and driving them into Kansas, 1865–67. Kansas State Historical Society, Topeka.
Kansas Governors' Correspondence, Letters of William H. Lamb and others to Governor Samuel H. Crawford, 1867. Kansas State Historical Society, Topeka.
Palo Pinto County, Texas, Records of Cattle Sales, 1867–69. Office of the County Clerk, Palo Pinto.

Republic of Texas, MS map, Sketch Showing the Route of the Military Road From Red River to Austin, Colonel William G. Cooke, Commanding, William H. Hunt, Engineer, 1840. Drawn by L. L. Upshur, 1841. Texas Land Office, Austin. Duplicate in University of Texas Library.

Supreme Court of Kansas, *McCoy* vs. *Kansas Pacific Railway Company*, July Term, 1871.

Wichita, Kansas, Proceedings of the Town Trustees and the City Council, 1870–75. Office of the City Clerk.

PUBLIC DOCUMENTS

Colorado: *General Laws and Private Acts of the Territory of Colorado,* 1866–67.

Cooke, Colonel William G. Report on the survey of a military road from Austin to the Red River, November 14, 1840. In *Journals of the House of Representatives of the Republic of Texas,* 5 Cong., 1 sess., 1840–41.

Eighth Census of the United States: Agriculture.

Illinois: *Public Laws of Illinois,* 1867, 1869.

Kansas: *General Laws of the Territory of Kansas,* 1859; *General Laws of the State of Kansas,* 1861, 1862; *Laws of Kansas,* 1865, 1866, 1867, 1872, 1876, 1877, 1879.

Kentucky Laws, Adjourned session, 1867.

Missouri: *Revised Statutes of the State of Missouri,* 1855; *Laws of Missouri,* 1860–61, 1867.

Mohler, John R. *Texas or Tick Fever and Its Prevention.* United States Department of Agriculture, Farmers' Bulletin No. 258.

Nebraska Laws, 1867.

Nimmo, Joseph. "The Range and Ranch Cattle Traffic of the United States," in *Report on the Internal Commerce of the United States,* Part III, Bureau of Statistics, Washington, 1886. Printed also as 48 Cong., 2 sess., *House Exec. Doc. 267,* Serial No. 2304.

Reports of the Commissioner of Agriculture, 1866, 1870.

Supreme Court of Kansas, Brief of the Defendant in Error, *Kansas Pacific Railway Company* vs. *McCoy,* July Term, 1871.

Tenth Census of the United States: III—Agriculture.

Texas: *Laws of the State of Texas,* 1860, 1866, 1870, 1871.

NEWSPAPERS

Abilene (Kansas) *Chronicle,* 1870–72.
Abilene (Kansas) *Daily Reflector,* April 24, 1925; June 12, July 3, 1938.

Abilene (Kansas) *Weekly Reflector*, April 30, 1925.
Amarillo *News-Globe*, June 17, 1928; August 14, 1938.
Austin *Republican*, 1869–70.
Austin *State Journal*, 1870.
Austin *Statesman*, April 26, 1874; August 27, 1875.
Caldwell *Post*, 1879–83.
Cheyenne *Leader*, April 11, 1872.
Chicago *Daily Democratic Press*, October 11, 1854.
Cincinnati *Enquirer*, October 17, 1872.
Clarksville *Standard*, November 4, 1871.
Colorado Tribune, Matagorda, Texas, July 21, 1854.
Corpus Christi *Star*, February 10, 1849.
Dallas *Herald*, 1859–76.
Dallas *Morning News*, 1885–1953.
Denison (Texas) *Daily Cressett*, April 9, July 29, 1876.
Denison (Texas) *Daily News,* 1873–74.
Dodge City *Democrat*, July 5, 1884.
Dodge City *Times*, 1876–82.
Ellsworth *Reporter*, 1871–74.
Ford County Globe, Dodge City, April 19, May 10, 1881; January 16,
     June 5, 1883; March 25, July 8, 1884.
Fort Griffin *Echo*, 1879.
Fort Worth *Democrat*, 1873–79.
Gainesville *Weekly Register*, October 14, 1926.
Galveston *News*, 1865–76; November 4, 1900; May 12, 1907; April 2,
     1911.
Hannibal *Messenger*, July 10, 1858.
Houston *Chronicle*, April 19, 1936.
Houston *Telegraph*, March 8, 1849.
Illinois State Journal, Springfield, 1859–60.
Independent Press, Sedalia, Missouri, November 15, 1866.
Junction City *Weekly Union*, 1867–70.
Kansas Cowboy, Dodge City, July 5, 12, 19, 26, 1884.
Kansas Daily Commonwealth, Topeka, 1870–73.
Kansas Daily Tribune, Topeka, August 8, 1869.
Kansas State Record, Topeka, August 5, 1871.
Kansas City *Journal of Commerce*, June 19, 1873.
Kansas City *Star*, November 15, 1925; May 20, 1936; April 2, 1946; June
     4, 1950.
Kansas City *Times*, August 23, 1907.
Leavenworth *Daily Conservative*, August 11, 1866.

Missouri Republican, St. Louis, July 20, 1857; March 27, 1868.
Missouri Statesman, Columbia, June 24, 1859.
New York *Times*, August 19, 1858; December 7, 1930.
New York *Tribune*, July 4, 1854; November 1 and 6, 1867.
Oklahoman, Oklahoma City, July 13, 1930.
Quincy *Whig*, July 3, 1854.
Republican Daily Journal, Lawrence, Kansas, April 6, 1869.
Rockford *Register*, February 14, 1863.
St. Louis *Intelligencer*, October 30, 1854.
Saline County Journal, Salina, Kansas, July 20, 1871.
San Antonio *Express*, March 10, 1905; June 15, September 6, 1908; August 7, 1910; July 3, 1930.
San Antonio *Herald*, August 28, 1866; May 17, June 28, 1867; 1874–76.
Semi-Weekly Farm News, Dallas, May 19, June 26, 1931; February 28, March 6, 13, 20, 26, 1936.
Southwest Plainsman, Amarillo, November 21, 1925; June 26, 1926.
Texas Live Stock Journal, Fort Worth, 1882–84.
Texas National Register, Washington, Texas, August 28, 1845.
Texas State Gazette, Austin, July 6, August 6, 1850; July 29, August 5, 1854; April 21, 1855.
Topeka *State Journal*, March 8, 1913.
Waco *Tribune-Herald*, October 30, 1949.
Watonga (Oklahoma) *Republican*, 1952.
Western Independent, Fort Smith, Arkansas, August 21, 28, 1873.
Western Journal of Commerce, Kansas City, Missouri, January 9, June 20, 1859.
Wichita *Beacon*, August 4, 1874.
Wichita *Eagle*, 1872–75; March 23, 1876; March 1, 1890; June 1, 1913.
Wichita *Vidette*, 1870–71.

PERIODICALS

Adams, Ramon F. "Hoss Wranglers," *Western Horseman*, Vol. XVI, No. 1 (January, 1951), 8–9, 32.
———. "Singin' Cowboy," *Southwest Review*, Vol. XXXI, No. 2 (Spring, 1946), 170–73.
———. "Sundown Slim on Singin' to 'Em," *Arizona Highways*, Vol. XXV, No. 1 (January, 1949), 14–17.
Ambulo, John. "The Cattle on a Thousand Hills," *Overland Monthly*, New Series, Vol. IX (March, 1887), 225.
Ashton, John. "The Texas Cattle Trade in 1870," *Cattleman*, Vol. XXXVIII, No. 2 (July, 1951), 21, 74–75.

Baker, A. Z. "Today's Chisholm Trail," *Cattleman*, Vol. XXXIII, No. 12 (May, 1947), 24.

Barnes, Will C. "The Chisholm Trail—For Whom Was It Named?" *Producer*, Vol X, No. 8 (January, 1929), 2–7, No. 9 (February, 1929), 2–8.

Bell, James G. "A Log of the Texas-California Cattle Trail, 1854," ed. by J. Evetts Haley, *Southwestern Historical Quarterly*, Part I, Vol. XXXV, No. 3 (January, 1932), 208–37, Part II, Vol. XXXV, No. 4 (April, 1932), 290–316, Part III, Vol. XXXVI, No. 1 (July, 1932), 47–66.

"Captain Diego Ramón's Diary of His Expedition Into Texas in 1716," ed. by Paul J. Foik, *Preliminary Studies of the Texas Catholic Historical Society*, Vol. II, No. 5 (April, 1933), 1–23.

Cauley, T. J. "Longhorns and Chicago Packers," *Texas Monthly*, Vol. V, No. 1 (January, 1930), 54–62.

Clemen, Rudolf A. "Cattle Trails as a Factor in the Development of Livestock Marketing," *Journal of Farm Economics*, October, 1926, 427–42.

Cook, James H. "The Texas Trail," ed. by E. S. Ricker, *Nebraska History Magazine*, Vol. XVI, No. 4 (October–December, 1935), 228–40.

Cross, Cora Melton. "Up the Trail With Nine Million Longhorns," *Texas Monthly*, Vol. V, No. 2 (February, 1930), 135–53.

Cushman, George L. "Abilene, First of the Kansas Cow Towns," *Kansas Historical Quarterly*, Vol. IX, No. 3 (August, 1940), 240–72.

Dick, Everett. "The Long Drive," *Collections of the Kansas State Historical Society*, Vol. XVII (1926–27), 27–97.

Dobie, J. Frank. "The Chisholm Trail," *Country Gentleman*, Vol. XC, No. 9 (February 28, 1925), 3, 22.

———. "Mustang Gray: Fact, Tradition, and Song," *Publications of the Texas Folklore Society*, Vol. X (1932), 110–15.

———. "Tom Candy Ponting's Drive of Texas Cattle to Illinois," *Cattleman*, Vol. XXXV, No. 8 (January, 1949), 34–45.

———. "Up the Trail to Wyoming," *Western Horseman*, Vol. XVI, No. 3 (March, 1951), 8–9, 43–45.

Duffield, George C. "Driving Cattle From Texas to Iowa, 1866," ed. by W. W. Baldwin, *Annals of Iowa*, Third Series, Vol. XIV, No. 4 (April, 1924), 243–62.

Everett, Malissa C. "A Pioneer Woman," *West Texas Historical Association Year Book*, Vol. III (June, 1927), 59–77.

Foreman, Grant. "The California Overland Mail Route Through Oklahoma," *Chronicles of Oklahoma,* Vol. IX, No. 3 (September, 1931), 300–17.

Gates, Paul Wallace. "Cattle Kings in the Prairies," *Mississippi Valley Historical Review,* Vol. XXXV, No. 3 (December, 1948), 379–412.

Harger, Charles M. "Cattle Trails of the Prairies," *Scribner's Magazine,* Vol. XI, No. 6 (June, 1892), 732–42.

Havins, T. R. "Texas Fever," *Southwestern Historical Quarterly,* Vol. LII, No. 2 (October, 1948), 147–62.

Henry, Theodore C. "Thomas James Smith of Abilene," *Collections of the Kansas State Historical Society,* Vol. IX (1905–1906), 526–32.

Herrington, George Squires. "An Early Cattle Drive From Texas to Illinois," *Southwestern Historical Quarterly,* Vol. LV, No. 2 (October, 1951), 267–69.

Holt, R. D. "From Trail to Rail in Texas Cattle Industry," *Cattleman,* Vol. XVIII, No. 10 (March, 1932), 50–59.

Hutcheson, Virginia Sue. "Cattle Drives in Missouri," *Missouri Historical Review,* Vol. XXXVII, No. 3 (April, 1943), 286–96.

Lomax, John A. "Half-Million-Dollar Song," *Southwest Review,* Vol. XXXI, No. 1 (Fall, 1945), 1–8.

Love, Clara M. "The Cattle Industry of the Southwest," *Southwestern Historical Quarterly,* Part I, Vol. XIX, No. 4 (April, 1916), 370–99, Part II, Vol. XX, No. 1 (July, 1916), 1–18.

McCarthy, Donald F. "The Chisholm Trail," *Frontier Times,* Vol. IV, No. 4 (January, 1927), 29.

McClelland, Clarence P. "Jacob Strawn and John T. Alexander, Central Illinois Stockmen," *Journal of the Illinois State Historical Society,* Vol. XXXIV, No. 2 (June, 1941), 177–208.

McCoy, Joseph G. "Historic and Biographic Sketch," *Kansas Magazine,* Vol. II, No. 6 (December, 1909), 45–55.

McGough, W. C. "Driving Cattle Into Old Mexico in 1864," *West Texas Historical Association Year Book,* Vol. XIII (October, 1937), 112–21.

Mahnken, Norbert R. "Early Nebraska Markets for Texas Cattle," *Nebraska History,* Part I, Vol. XXVI, No. 1 (January–March, 1945), 3–25, Part II, Vol. XXVI, No. 2 (April–June, 1945), 91–103.

———. "Ogallala—Nebraska's Cowboy Capital," *Nebraska History,* Vol. XXVIII, No. 2 (April–June, 1947), 85–109.

Mechem, Kirke. "The Bull Fight at Dodge City," *Kansas Historical Quarterly,* Vol. II No. 3 (August, 1933), 294–308.

———. "Home on the Range," *Kansas Historical Quarterly,* Vol. XVII, No. 4 (November, 1949), 313–39.

Morrison, W. B. "Colbert Ferry on Red River, Chickasaw Nation, Indian Territory: Recollections of John Malcolm, Pioneer Ferryman," *Chronicles of Oklahoma*, Vol. XVI, No. 3 (September, 1938), 302–14.

Nichols, G. W. "Wild Bill," *Harper's New Monthly Magazine*, Vol. XXXIV, No. 201 (February, 1867), 273–85.

Oatts, Tom C. "Chisholm Trail Diary," ed. by Alfred E. Menn, *Texas Preview*, Part I, Vol. IV, No. 3 (March, 1953), 18–19, Part II, Vol. IV, No. 4 (April, 1953), 27, 38.

Padgitt, James T. "Colonel William H. Day: Texas Ranchman," *Southwestern Historical Quarterly*, Vol. LIII, No. 4 (April, 1950), 347–66.

Paxson, Frederic L. "The Cow Country," *American Historical Review*, Vol. XXII (October, 1916), 65-82.

Reynolds, M. J. "The Texas Trail," *Munsey's Magazine*, Vol. XXIX, No. 4 (July, 1903), 576–81.

Richardson, T. C. "Cattle Trails of Texas," *Texas Geographic Magazine*, Vol. I, No. 2 (November, 1937), 16–29.

Ritchie, F. B. "A Trail Driver Who Kept a Diary," *Cattleman*, Vol. XIX, No. 3 (August, 1932), 14–20.

Rossel, John. "The Chisholm Trail," *Kansas Historical Quarterly*, Vol. V, No. 1 (February, 1936), 3–14.

Streeter, Floyd Benjamin. "Ellsworth as a Texas Cattle Market," *Kansas Historical Quarterly*, Vol. IV, No. 4 (November, 1935), 338–98.

———. "Famous Cattle Drives," *Cattleman*, Vol. XXXIV, No. 8 (January, 1948), 130–33.

———. "The National Cattle Trail," *Cattleman*, Vol. XXXVIII, No. 1 (June, 1951), 26–27, 59–74.

Tennant, H. S. "The Two Cattle Trails," *Chronicles of Oklahoma*, Vol. XIV, No. 1, Sec. 1 (March, 1936), 84-122, Texas (Illinois), 1857, 1850, 1859, 1860, 1861, 1870, 1873.

"The Texas Cattle Trade," *Harper's Weekly*, Vol. XVIII, No. 905 (May 2, 1874), 385–87.

Thoburn, Joseph B. "Jesse Chisholm, a Stalwart Figure in History," *Frontier Times*, Vol. XIII, No. 6 (April, 1936), 330–32.

"Wild Cattle Hunting in Texas," *Leisure Hour*, No. 632 (February 6, 1864).

Wilkeson, Frank. "Cattle Raising on the Plains," *Harper's Monthly Magazine*, Vol. LXXII (April, 1886), 285–90.

Wright, Muriel H. "Historic Places on the Old Stage Line From Fort Smith to Red River," *Chronicles of Oklahoma*, Vol. XI, No. 2 (June, 1933), 798–822.

PAMPHLETS

Austin, Mrs. Mary (Hunter). *The Road to Mammon.* New York, Pegasus Publishing Company, 1938.

Black, A. P. (Ott). *The End of the Long Horn Trail.* Selfridge, North Dakota, Selfridge Journal, n.d.

Edwards, J. B. *Early Days in Abilene.* Abilene, Kansas, C. W. Wheeler, 1938.

Foreman, Grant. *Down the Texas Road.* Norman, University of Oklahoma Press, 1936.

———. *Fort Gibson.* Norman, University of Oklahoma Press, 1936.

Guide Map of the Great Texas Cattle Trail from Red River Crossing to the Old Reliable Kansas Pacific Railway, or *Guide Map of the Best and Shortest Cattle Trail to the Kansas Pacific Railway.* Kansas City, Kansas Pacific Railway Company, 1871. Revised editions, 1872, 1873, 1874, 1875.

Jelinek, George. *Ellsworth, Kansas, 1867–1947.* Salina, Kansas, Consolidated, 1947.

Letters from Old Friends and Members of the Wyoming Stock Growers' Association. Cheyenne, S. A. Bristol Company, 1923.

Lyon, Charles J. *Compendious History of Ellsworth County, Kansas.* Ellsworth, Printed at the Reporter Office, 1879.

Maverick, George Madison, and John Henry Brown. *Re Maverick.* San Antonio, Printed by Guessaz and Ferlet, 1905. Reprinted as *Mavericks.* San Antonio, Artes Graficas, 1937.

McClure, Meade L. *Major Andrew Drumm, 1828–1919.* N.p., 1919.

McGee, Tom. *An Incident on the Chisholm Trail.* Oklahoma City, Times-Journal Publishing Company, 1938.

———. *Who Killed Pat Hennessey?* Oklahoma City, Times-Journal Publishing Company, 1941.

Parker, J. M. *An Aged Wanderer.* Ballinger, Texas, the author, n.d.

Sheedy, Dennis. *Autobiography of Dennis Sheedy.* Denver, 1922.

BOOKS

Abbott, E. C. (Teddy Blue), and Helena Huntington Smith. *We Pointed Them North.* New York, Farrar and Rinehart, 1939.

Adams, Ramon F. *Come an' Get It.* Norman, University of Oklahoma Press, 1952.

———. *Cowboy Lingo.* Boston, Houghton Mifflin Company, 1936.

Artrip, Louise and Fullen. *Memoirs of Daniel Fore (Jim) Chisholm and the Chisholm Trail.* Booneville, Arkansas, Artrip Publications, 1949.

Athanase de Mézières and the Louisiana-Texas Frontier, 1768-1780. Trans. and ed. by Herbert Eugene Bolton. Cleveland, Arthur H. Clark Company, 1914. 2 vols.

Baber, D. F. *The Longest Rope.* As told by Bill Walker. Caldwell, Idaho, The Caxton Printers, 1947.

Baughman, Theodore. *The Oklahoma Scout.* Chicago, Homeward Publishing Company, n.d.

Benton, Jesse James. *Cow by the Tail.* Boston, Houghton Mifflin Company, 1943.

Bolton, Herbert Eugene. *The Spanish Borderlands.* New Haven, Yale University Press, 1921.

Brayer, Garnet M. and Herbert O. *American Cattle Trails, 1540-1900.* Bayside, New York, American Pioneer Trails Association, 1952.

Brown, Dee, and Martin F. Schmitt. *Trail Driving Days.* New York, Charles Scribner's Sons, 1952.

Bunton, Mary Taylor. *A Bride on the Old Chisholm Trail in 1886.* San Antonio, Naylor Company, 1939.

Cavanagh, Helen M. *Funk of Funk's Grove.* Bloomington, Illinois, Pantagraph Printing Company, 1952.

Celiz, Fray Francisco. *Diary of the Alarcon Expedition Into Texas, 1718-1719.* Trans. and ed. by Fritz Leo Hoffman. Los Angeles, Quivira Society Publications, 1935.

Clay, John. *My Life on the Range.* Chicago, privately printed, 1924.

Collings, Ellsworth, in collaboration with Alma Miller England. *The 101 Ranch.* Norman, University of Oklahoma Press, 1937.

Collins, Dennis. *The Indians' Last Fight; or the Dull Knife Raid.* Girard, Kansas, Press of the Appeal to Reason, 1915.

Conger, Roger Norman. *Highlights of Waco History.* Waco, Texas, Hill Printing and Stationery Company, 1945.

Connelley, William Elsey. *Wild Bill and His Era.* New York, Press of the Pioneers, 1933.

Cook, James H. *Fifty Years on the Old Frontier.* New Haven, Yale University Press, 1923.

Cox, James. *Historical and Biographical Record of the Cattle Industry and the Cattlemen of Texas and Adjacent Territory.* St. Louis, Woodward and Tiernan Printing Company, 1895.

Cranfill, James Britton. *Dr. J. B. Cranfill's Chronicle.* New York and Chicago, Fleming H. Revell Company, 1916.

Crawford, Samuel J. *Kansas in the Sixties.* Chicago, A. C. McClurg and Company, 1911.

Cross, Joe. *Cattle Clatter.* Kansas City, Walker Publications, 1938.

Cutler, William G. (ed.). *History of the State of Kansas*. Chicago, Standard Publishing Company, 1883. 2 vols.

Dale, Edward Everett. *Cow Country*. Norman, University of Oklahoma Press, 1942.

———. *The Range Cattle Industry*. Norman, University of Oklahoma Press, 1930.

Dewees, W. B. *Letters From an Early Settler of Texas*. Compiled by Cora Cardelle. Louisville, New Albany Tribune Plant, 1852.

Dick, Everett. *The Sod House Frontier, 1854–1890*. New York, D. Appleton Company, 1937.

Dobie, J. Frank. *The Longhorns*. Boston, Little, Brown and Company, 1941.

———. *A Vaquero of the Brush Country*. Dallas, Southwest Press, 1929.

Dodge, Richard Irving. *The Hunting Grounds of the Great West*. London, Chatto and Windus, 1877.

Douglas, C. L. *Cattle Kings of Texas*. Dallas, Cecil Baugh, 1939.

Eisele, Wilbert E. *The Real Wild Bill Hickok*. Denver, William H. Andre, 1931.

Elliot, W. J. *The Spurs*. Spur, Texas, Texas Spur, 1939.

Emmett, Chris. *Shanghai Pierce: A Fair Likeness*. Norman, University of Oklahoma Press, 1953.

Flack, Captain. *A Hunter's Experiences in the Southern States of America*. London, Longmans, Green and Company, 1860.

———. *The Texan Ranger, or Real Life in the Backwoods*. London, Darton and Company, 1866.

———. *The Texan Rifle Hunter, or Field Sports on the Prairie*. London, John Maxwell and Company, 1866.

Foreman, Grant. *A History of Oklahoma*. Norman, University of Oklahoma Press, 1942.

Freeman, G. D. *Midnight and Noonday, or Dark Deeds Unraveled*. Caldwell, Kansas, G. D. Freeman, 1890. 2nd ed., with illustrations, 1892.

Gard, Wayne. *Frontier Justice*. Norman, University of Oklahoma Press, 1949.

———. *Sam Bass*. Boston, Houghton Mifflin Company, 1936.

Gay, Beatrice Grady. *Into the Setting Sun: A History of Coleman County*. N.p., c. 1936.

Gibson, J. W. (Watt). *Recollections of a Pioneer*. St. Joseph, Missouri, Nelson Hanne Printing Company, 1912.

Goodnight, Charles, and Others. *Pioneer Days in the Southwest*. Guthrie, Oklahoma, State Capital Company, 1909.

Green, Rena Maverick (ed.). *Samuel Maverick, Texan: 1803–1870.* San Antonio, privately printed, 1952.

Haley, J. Evetts. *Charles Goodnight, Cowman and Plainsman.* Boston, Houghton Mifflin Company, 1936. New ed., Norman, University of Oklahoma Press, 1949.

———. *George W. Littlefield, Texan.* Norman, University of Oklahoma Press, 1943.

Halsell, H. H. *Cowboys and Cattleland.* Nashville, Parthenon Press, 1937.

Hardin, John Wesley. *The Life of John Wesley Hardin.* Seguin, Texas, Smith and Moore, 1896.

Hastings, Frank S. *A Ranchman's Recollections.* Chicago, Breeder's Gazette, 1921.

Henry, Stuart. *Conquering Our Great American Plains.* New York, E. P. Dutton and Company, 1930.

Hill, J. L. *The End of the Cattle Trail.* Long Beach, California, George W. Moyle Publishing Company, n.d.

Holden, William Curry. *Alkali Trails.* Dallas, Southwest Press, 1930.

Hough, Emerson. *The Story of the Cowboy.* New York, D. Appleton and Company, 1897.

Hunt, Frazier. *The Long Trail From Texas.* Garden City, New York, Doubleday, Doran and Company, 1940.

Hunter, J. Marvin (ed.). *The Trail Drivers of Texas.* Nashville, Cokesbury Press, Vol. I, 1920, Vol. II, 1923. 2nd ed., revised, two volumes in one, 1925.

Jackson, W. H., and S. A. Long. *The Texas Stock Directory.* San Antonio, printed at the Herald Office, 1865. New ed., New Braunfels, Texas, The Book Farm, n.d.

Jones, C. N. *Early Days in Cooke County, 1848–1873.* Gainesville, Texas, 1936.

King, Frank M. *Longhorn Trail Drivers.* Los Angeles, privately published by the author, printed by Haynes Corporation, 1940.

———. *Wranglin' the Past.* Los Angeles, privately published by the author, printed by Haynes Corporation, 1935. Revised ed., Pasadena, Trail's End Publishing Company, 1946.

Knight, Oliver. *Fort Worth, Outpost on the Trinity.* Norman, University of Oklahoma Press, 1953.

Lake, Stuart N. *Wyatt Earp, Frontier Marshal.* Boston and New York, Houghton Mifflin Company, 1931.

Lawrence, A. B. *History of Texas, or the Emigrant's Guide.* New York, Nafis and Cornish, 1844.

Linn, John J. *Reminiscences of Fifty Years in Texas.* New York, D. and J. Sadlier and Company, 1883.

Lomax, John A. and Alan. *Cowboy Songs.* New York, Macmillan Company, 1938.

Long, R. M. (Dick). *Wichita, 1866–1883.* Wichita, Kansas, McCormick-Armstrong Company, 1945.

Lowther, Charles C. *Dodge City, Kansas.* Philadelphia, Dorrance and Company, 1940.

Lucas, Mattie Davis, and Mita Holsapple Hall. *A History of Grayson County.* Sherman, Texas, Scruggs Printing Company, 1936.

McConnell, H. H. *Five Years a Cavalryman.* Jacksboro, Texas, J. N. Rogers and Company, 1889.

McCoy, Joseph G. *Historic Sketches of the Cattle Trade of the West and Southwest.* Kansas. City, Ramsey, Millett and Hudson, 1874. Facsimile reprint, Washington, Rare Book Shop, 1932. Edition with introduction and notes by Ralph P. Bieber, Glendale, California, Arthur H. Clark Company, 1940. New facsimile reprint, Columbus, Ohio, Long's College Book Company, 1951.

McNeal, T. A. *When Kansas Was Young.* New York, Macmillan Company, 1922.

Marshall, James. *Santa Fe, the Railroad that Built an Empire.* New York, Random House, 1945.

Masterson, V. V. *The Katy Railroad and the Last Frontier.* Norman, University of Oklahoma Press, 1952.

Maverick, Mary A. *Memoirs of Mary A. Maverick.* San Antonio, Alamo Printing Company, 1921.

Maverick, Maury. *A Maverick American.* New York, Covici-Friede, 1937.

Nelson, Oliver. *The Cowman's Southwest.* Ed. by Angie Debo. Glendale, California, Arthur H. Clark Company, 1953.

Olmsted, Frederick Law. *A Journey Through Texas.* New York, Mason Brothers, 1857.

Osgood, Ernest Staples. *The Day of the Cattleman.* Minneapolis, University of Minnesota Press, 1929.

Paddock, B. B. (ed.). *History of Texas.* Fort Worth and the Texas Northwest edition. Chicago and New York, Lewis Publishing Company, 1922. 4 vols.

Pelzer, Louis. *The Cattleman's Frontier.* Glendale, California, Arthur H. Clark Company, 1936.

Pichardo, Jose Antonio. *Pichardo's Treatise on the Limits of Louisiana and Texas.* Ed. by Charles Wilson Hackett. Austin, University of Texas Press, 1931–46. 4 vols.

Ponting, Tom Candy. *Life of Tom Candy Ponting.* Decatur, Illinois, 1904. New Ed., Evanston, Illinois, Branding Iron Press, 1952.

Post, Charles Clement. *Ten Years a Cowboy.* Chicago, Rhodes and McClure Publishing Company, 1888.

Potter, Jack. *Cattle Trails of the Old West.* Clayton, New Mexico, Laura R. Krehbiel, 1935.

Powell, Cuthbert. *Twenty Years of Kansas City's Live Stock Trade and Traders.* Kansas City, Pearl Printing Company, 1893.

Prose and Poetry of the Live Stock Industry of the United States. Denver and Kansas City, National Live Stock Historical Association, 1905.

Raine, William MacLeod, and Will C. Barnes. *Cattle.* Garden City, New York, Doubleday, Doran and Company, 1930.

Rainey, George. *The Cherokee Strip.* Guthrie, Oklahoma, Co-Operative Publishing Company, 1933.

Raunick, Selma Metzenthin, and Margaret Schade. *The Kothmanns of Texas, 1845–1931.* Austin, Von Boeckmann-Jones Company, 1931.

Ridings, Sam P. *The Chisholm Trail.* Guthrie, Oklahoma, Co-Operative Publishing Company, 1936.

Roenigk, Adolph. *Pioneer History of Kansas.* Lincoln, Kansas, Adolph Roenigk, 1933.

Siringo, Charles A. *A Lone Star Cowboy, Being Fifty Years Experience in the Saddle as a Cowboy, Detective and New Mexico Ranger, on Every Cow Trail in the Wooly Old West.* Santa Fe, published by the author, 1919.

———. *A Texas Cowboy, or Fifteen Years on the Hurricane Deck of a Spanish Pony.* Chicago, M. Umbdenstock and Company, 1885.

———. *Riata and Spurs.* Boston and New York, Houghton Mifflin Company, 1931.

Smithwick, Noah. *The Evolution of a State; or, Recollections of Old Texas Days.* Compiled by Nanna Smithwick Donaldson. Austin, Texas, Gammel Book Company, 1900.

Sowell, A. J. *Early Settlers and Indian Fighters of Southwest Texas.* Austin, Ben C. Jones and Company, 1900.

Spalding, Charles Carroll. *Annals of the City of Kansas.* Kansas City, Van Horn and Abeel's Printing House, 1858.

Streeter, Floyd Benjamin. *Prairie Trails and Cow Towns.* Boston, Chapman and Grimes, 1936.

———. *The Kaw.* New York, Farrar and Rinehart, 1941.

Taylor, T. U. *The Chisholm Trail and Other Routes.* San Antonio, Naylor Company, 1936.

———. *Jesse Chisholm.* Bandera, Texas, Frontier Times, 1939.

Terrell, C. V. *The Terrells.* Austin, C. V. Terrell, 1948.

Thorp, N. Howard. *Songs of the Cowboys.* Boston and New York, Houghton Mifflin Company, 1921.

Vestal, Stanley. *Queen of Cowtowns: Dodge City.* New York, Harper and Brothers, 1952.

Wallis, Jonnie Lockhart (ed.), in association with Laurance L. Hill. *Sixty Years on the Brazos: The Life and Letters of Dr. John Washington Lockhart, 1834–1900.* Los Angeles, privately printed, Press of Dunn Brothers, 1930.

Walton, W. M. *Life and Adventures of Ben Thompson, the Famous Texan.* Austin, W. M. Walton, 1884.

Waters, L. L. *Steel Trails to Santa Fe.* Lawrence, University of Kansas Press, 1950.

Wellman, Paul I. *The Trampling Herd.* New York, Carrick and Evans, 1939. New ed., Garden City, New York, Doubleday and Company, 1951.

Wendt, Lloyd, and Herman Kogan. *Bet a Million! The Story of John W. Gates.* Indianapolis, Bobbs-Merrill Company, 1948.

Western Texas, the Australia of America. Cincinnati, E. Mendenhall, 1860.

Weston, W. W. (ed.). *Weston's Guide to the Kansas Pacific Railway.* Kansas City, Bulletin Steam Printing and Engraving House, 1872.

Whitman, Walt. *Specimen Days and Collect.* Philadelphia, Rees Welsh and Company, 1882–83.

Williams, R. H. *With the Border Ruffians; Memories of the Far West, 1852–1868.* Ed. by E. W. Williams. New York, E. P. Dutton and Company, 1907.

Wilstach, Frank J. *Wild Bill Hickok.* New York, Doubleday, Page and Company, 1926.

Wright, Robert M. *Dodge City, the Cowboy Capital.* Wichita, Kansas, Wichita Eagle Press, 1913.

Barton, Mrs. D. M.: 211
Barton County, Mo.: 50
Basin Springs, Tex.: 27
Bass, Sam: 236f., 246
Bassett, Charles E.: 240
Bastrop County, Tex.: 33, 90, 127
Bates County, Mo.: 29
Baxter Springs, Kan.: 35, 49, 51ff., 131,
  142, 151, 153, 165, 188ff., 194, 208, 216
Baylor County, Tex.: 233
Bean, Robert: 72
Beard, John (Red): 197f.
Beaumont, Tex.: 25
Beauregard, A. Toutant: 12
Beaver Creek: 79f., 230
Beckers, Matt: 65
Beebe, Jerome: 202
Beecher, Henry Ward: 33n., 192
Beecher's Bible: 33
Beecher-Tilton scandal: 192
Beef Trail: 76
Beeville, Tex.: 76, 142
Behrens, John: 214
Belcher and Company: 217
Bell, Alexander Graham: 224
Bell, George: 39
Bell, James G.: 24
Bell County, Tex.: 127, 211
Belmont, Kan.: 71
Belton, Tex.: 37, 47, 78, 88, 98, 127f.,
  227, 238
Bennett, John: 144
Bennett, William J.: 185
Bent, John J.: 30
Benton, James: 115
Bieber, Ralph P.: vii
Big Bend: 39
Big Bow, Chief: 130
Big Springs, Neb.: 236
Billy the Kid: 257
Black Beaver: 71
Black Dog Trail: 81
Black Hills: 236
Blair, Dave: 240
Blair, Newton: 84
Blanco River: 11
Blocker, John R.: 201, 241, 258
Blue Front Store, Wichita, Kan.: 197
Blue Grove: 79
Blue Stem Hills: 257
Bluff Creek: 81, 198, 252
Boaz and Godwin: 232
Boggy Creek: 89

Boggy Depot, Indian Terr.: 27f., 49, 58, 91
Bolivar, Tex.: 38
Border Tier road: see Missouri River,
  Fort Scott and Gulf Railroad
Borroum, B. A.: 48f.
Borroum, James: 38
Bosque County, Tex.: 156
Bosque Grande, N. M.: 48
Bosque River: 117, 137
Boston, Mass.: 21, 238, 263
Botts, Samuel: 214f.
Brahman cattle: 255n.
Branding: 13f., 45f., 49, 108
Branshaw, Albert: 135
Bratton Hotel, Abilene, Kan.: 64
Brauham, John S.: 200
Brazier City, La.: 142
Brazos River: 7, 10f., 25, 29f., 36f., 39,
  44, 47ff., 78, 88, 97f., 137, 155, 185, 211
Brennan, Joe: 200ff.
Brennan, Molly: 203
"Bright Mohawk Valley, The," song: 245
"Bright Sherman Valley, The," song: 245
Brookville, Kan.: 160, 189
Brown, George S.: 255
Brown, John, abolitionist: 33
Brown, John, policeman: 240
Brown, John Henry: 255, 257
Brown, Joseph H.: 208, 216, 227
Brown's Hall, Junction City, Kan.: 91
Brownsville, Tex.: 11, 60, 76
Brownville, Neb.: 51
Brushy Creek: 141, 155, 185, 188ff.
Bryden, James: 183, 196
Buck, lead steer: 138
Buffalo, N. Y.: 22, 262
Buffalo Gap: 47
"Buffalo Skinners, The," song: 246
Buffalo Springs, Indian Terr.: 81
Buffalo Station, Tex.: 101
Buffaloes: 3, 10, 25, 31, 72, 81, 94, 145,
  150f., 174, 197, 219, 227, 233; on
  cattle trails, 81, 90, 146, 153, 211, 218;
  captured by cowhands, 93, 146, 239
Bull fights: 225, 258
Bull Hide Creek: 211
Bull's Head Saloon, Abilene, Kan.: 163f.,
  168, 176f., 200, 248n.
Bull's Head Saloon, Newton, Kan.: 158

Bull's Head Saloon, San Antonio, Tex.: 226
Bull's Head Stockyards, Chicago, Ill.: 30
"Burial at Sea," song: 248
Burks, W. F.: 156f.
Burks, Mrs. W. F.: 156f.
Burlington, Iowa: 49
Burnet County, Texas: 87
Burris, Samuel: 214
Burwick's Bay: 142
Butler, E. M.: 217
Butler, Pleasant: 146
Butler, William G.: 89, 140, 144, 146, 204, 210, 217
Butterfield Trail: 27
Byler, E. P.: 89, 115, 185
Byler, James: 89, 144, 146

Caddo Indians: 71
Cádiz, Spain: 4
Cain, Neil: 200, 203
Cairns, James: 214
Cairo, Ill.: 47, 59, 61, 87, 96
Cairo *Democrat*: 87f.
Caldwell, Kan.: vii, 117, 153, 190, 197, 212, 236, 251ff., 259
Caldwell County, Tex.: 89, 218
Caldwell *Post*: 251
California: 23ff., 34, 50, 93, 96, 143, 190, 200, 244
California trails: 23f., 143
Camargo, Mexico: 10
Camp cooks: 116, 119f., 122f.
Camp Cooper, Tex.: 47
Camp Ringgold, Tex.: 10
Campbell, Colin: 190
Campbell, Henry: 96
Campbell, James: 24
Campbell, William (Billy): 93f.
Campbell, William P.: 215
Canada: 260
"Canada I-O," song: 247
Canadian River: 26f.; *see also* North Canadian River and South Canadian River
Cantonment, Indian Terr.: 228
Carpetbaggers: 42, 192
Carr, B. P. (Bat): 255, 257
Carroll, J. A.: 260
Carson, Kit: 173, 175
Carson, Thomas: 175
Carter, J. W.: 255

Carvajal, V. J.: 190
Casino Hall, San Antonio, Tex.: 226
Castile: 3, 6f.
Catherwood, S. A.: 148
Cattle Exchange bar, Fort Worth, Tex.: 234
Cattle inspectors: 37, 127f., 141f., 195, 230f.
Cattle prices: 23f., 30f., 40, 43f., 48ff., 55, 87, 89, 93f., 96ff., 100, 103f., 140, 143, 147f., 160f., 208, 211, 218, 221, 237
Cattle rustlers: 127, 138, 155ff., 230
Cattle taxes: 71, 127, 130f., 144f., 153f., 231
Cattle trails: *see* California trails, Chisholm Trail, Loving-Goodnight Trail, Opelousas Trail, Shawnee Trail, and Western Trail
Celiz, Francisco: 6
Centennial Exposition: 224
Central Hotel, San Antonio, Tex.: 225
Chambers, Ed: 210
Champaign County, Ill.: 96
Chapman Creek: 169, 171
Charleston, S. C.: 21
Cherokee Indians: 34, 54, 72, 131, 153f.
Cherokee National Council: 131
Cherokee Strip Live Stock Association: 256
Cherokee Town, Indian Terr.: 102
Cheyenne, Wyo.: 189f., 236, 252
Cheyenne Indians: 128
Chicago, Ill.: vi, 22, 30, 33ff., 49ff., 54, 56ff., 63, 83, 92, 94, 100, 140, 148, 160, 165, 167, 185, 208, 223n., 234f., 252, 261ff.
Chicago River: 262
Chicago, Rock Island and Pacific Railroad: 50
Chickasaw Indians: 27, 153f.
Chickasha, Okla.: vii
Chihuahua, Mexico: 9
Chikaskia River: 61
Childress, H. M.: 48, 82
Chisholm, Jesse: vi, 72–75, 99, 185
Chisholm Trail: v ff.; origin, 3–84; use, 67–241, 251–59; name, 71–76; route, 71–82; closing, 259–64; influence, 260–64
Chisum, John S.: 38, 48, 134
Chisum Trail: *see* Loving–Goodnight Trail
Choate, D. C.: 210f.

Choate, John Henry: 189
Choate, Monroe: 38, 48f., 144
Choate and Bennett: 189, 210f.
Choctaw Indians: 27, 135, 144, 153
Christian County, Ill.: 60, 82
Chuck Wagon: 3, 16f., 119f.
Cimarron River: 73, 80f., 128, 138, 145, 153, 241
Cimarrones: 6, 12
Cincinnati, Ohio: 179n., 262
City Hotel, Ellsworth, Kan.: 199
Civil War: v, 4, 13, 18ff., 23, 30, 37ff., 41ff., 59f., 71, 73, 79, 82, 120, 150, 188, 192, 200, 204, 261ff.
Clark, Jasper: 156
Clark, Joe S.: 143
Clark, L. T.: 97
Clarksville, Tex.: 10
Clay, John: 201
Clay Center, Kan.: 172
Clear Boggy Creek: 27
Clear Creek (Kan.): 103
Clear Creek (Tex.): 79
Clear Fork of the Trinity River: 35
Cleburne, Tex.: 207
Clements, Jim: 153
Clifton, Ariz.: 259
Clifton, Tex.: 117
Cline, John: 209
Clinton, Mo.: 35
Clinton, Tex.: 38
Clinton (Mo.) *Journal*: 35
Cluck, Allie Annie: 155
Cluck, Emmet: 155
Cluck, George W.: 155
Cluck, Mrs. George W.: 155f.
Cluck, Minnie: 155
Coahuila, Mexico: 5, 7
Coe, Phil: 176ff.
Coffee, Holland: 27
Coffeyville, Kan.: 194, 210
Colbert, Benjamin Franklin: 27
Colbert's ferry: 27, 49, 53, 88
Collin County, Tex.: 133
Collins, Dennis: 124
Collins, Joel: 236
Colorado: 36, 47f., 55, 91, 95, 157, 160, 218, 224, 232, 238, 259ff.
Colorado Citizen, Matagorda, Tex.: 193
"Colorado Home," song: 249
Colorado River (Texas): 7, 11, 29, 38, 46, 49, 78, 216, 230, 235, 241
Colt six-shooter: 68, 254
Columbian Exposition: 223n.

Columbus, Christopher: 4
Columbus, Ohio: 21
Columbus, Texas: 38
Comanche Indians: 6, 8, 15, 47, 70, 73, 81, 90, 98, 128f., 145, 155, 219
Comanche Springs, Tex.: 78, 137
Comanche Springs (on Lost Fork of the Red River): 128
Combs, D. S.: 47
"Come All Ye Jolly Lumbermen," song: 247
Comique, Dodge City, Kan.: 239
Concho River: 39, 47f., 117
Concho Trail: 143
Confederate Congress: 37
Congress, United States: 259f.
Conquista, Tex.: 12
Conrad, Frank E.: 240
Cook, James H.: 116, 119, 137f.
Cooke, Jay: 204
Cooke, William G.: 26f.
Cooke County, Tex.: 79, 117
Coronado, Francisco Vásquez de: 4f.
Corpus Christi, Tex.: 17, 96, 157, 211, 230
Cortés, Hernando: 4
Cortinas, Juan L.: 11
Cottage House, Ellsworth, Kan.: 199
Cottonwood Creek: 104
Council Grove, Indian, Terr.: 72
Council Grove, Kan.: 51
Courtright, T. I. (Long Hair Jim): 227
Cow Creek: 52
Cow hunts: 13-15, 44-47
Cow Skin Creek: 81, 147, 185
Cow towns: *see* Abilene, Kan.; Caldwell, Kan.; Dodge City, Kan.; Ellsworth, Kan.; Fort Worth, Tex.; Newton, Kan.; Ogallala, Neb.; and Wichita, Kan.
Cow whips: 21, 44f., 111
Cowboy songs: 242-50
"Cowboy's Dream, The," song: 247
"Cowboy's Lament, The," song: 247
"Cowboy's Stroll, The," song: 245
Cowboys: 9, 13ff., 44-47, 83f., 106ff., 125, 154
Cowden, William: 101
Cox, Fannie: 74
Cox, William M.: 198, 200
Cox's Crossing of Bluff Creek: 198f.
Cox's Trail: 199
Cramer, Joseph: 172
Cranfill, Eaton: 127

Cranfill, James B.: 128
Crawford, Ed.: 203
Crawford, Samuel J.: 66f.
Crédit Mobilier: 192
Creek Indians: 27, 72, 131, 153f.
Cuba: 4, 87
Cude, W. F.: 90, 97, 142
Cuernavaca: 4
Cureton, J. W.: 143
Cureton, Jack: 143
Cureton, John C.: 143
Cureton, W. E.: 143
Custer, George A.: 174, 224
Custer, Mrs. George A.: 174

Daggett, Ephraim M.: 43
Daggett and Hatcher's store, Fort Worth, Tex.: 140
Dakota Territory: 218, 253, 259ff.
Dale, Edward Everett: vii, 130
Dallas, Tex.: vii, 25f., 36, 53, 78, 88, 98, 112, 126, 140, 193, 207f., 217, 221f., 240
Dallas County, Tex.: 107
Dallas Herald: 25, 36, 91, 112, 193, 217
Dalrymple, W. C.: 87
"Darling, I Am Growing Old," song: 244
Daugherty, James M.: 51–55, 141, 208
Davis, Jackson: 186
Davis, Jefferson: 28
Davis County, Kan.: 149
Dawdy, Asa H.: 230
Dawson, John: 253
Day, Addison J.: 98, 128
Day, James Monroe (Doc): 35, 37, 90
Day, Jesse: 33, 36f., 98
Day, William H.: 37, 90, 98, 209, 215
Day brothers: 98, 241
"Days of Forty-Nine, The," song: 244
Deadwood, Dakota, Terr.: 179n., 236
Decatur, Tex.: 70
Declaration of Independence: 114
Decrows Point, Tex.: 12
Deep Fork of the Canadian River: 101
Deer Creek: 80
Deger, Larry: 237
Delano section of Wichita, Kan.: 186, 197f.
Delaware Indians: 71
De León, Alonso: 5f.
DeLong, John: 200
Denison, Tex.: 193f., 209, 217, 221, 231n.
Denison Daily Cressett: 231n.
Denison Daily News: 194, 209

Denton, John: 245
Denton, Tex.: 260
Denton County, Tex.: 38, 51, 78, 97
Denton Creek: 79
Denton Monitor: 46
Denver, Colo.: 36, 48
Detroit, Mich.: 262
Devil's Addition, Abilene, Kan.: 166
Dewees, John O.: 218, 235
DeWitt County, Tex.: 46, 55
Diamond Spring, Kan.: 51
Dibb, William: 214
Dickinson County, Kan.: 68, 180
Dietrich, Eugene: 226
Dignowity Hill, San Antonio, Tex.: 152
"Dim, Narrow Trail, The," song: 247
"Dinah Had a Wooden Leg," song: 244
Do Drop In saloon, Newton, Kan.: 158
Doan, Jonathan: 227
Doan's Crossing of the Red River: 227
Dobbins, John: 52
Dobie, J. Frank: vii, 18
Dodge, Richard Irving: 16f.
Dodge City, Kan.: vii, 218, 227ff., 235ff., 238f., 241, 251, 253ff.
Dodge Trail: see Western Trail
Doheny, Edward L.: 213
Donnell, Henry: 73
Douglas, Stephen A.: 34
Douglas Avenue Hotel, Wichita, Kan.: 185
Driskill, J. W.: 218
Driskill, Jesse L.: 38, 82, 98, 201, 217f.
Drover's Cottage: 65f., 86, 99, 105, 148, 167, 172, 187f., 199
Druce Rachel ranch: 211
Duffield, George C.: 49
Duncan, Okla.: vii
Durham cattle: see Shorthorn cattle
Durkee, John: 33
"Dying Cowboy, The," song: 247

Eagle Ford, Tex.: 217, 221, 227
Eagle Pass, Tex.: 40
Earnest, William: 47
Earp, Wyatt: 215, 237, 240
East Fork of the Trinity River: 133
Eastern Trail: see Chisholm Trail
Ecleto Creek: 190
Edwards, J. B.: 68, 167, 179
Edwards Plateau: 78
Eisenhower, Dwight D.: 66n.
El Paso, Hotel, Fort Worth, Tex.: 234

El Reno, Okla.: vii
Eldorado, Kan.: 75
Elizabeth Creek: 78
Elk River: 236
Elkhorn Saloon, Abilene, Kan.: 163
Ellinwood, Kan.: 198
Ellis, J. J.: 217
Ellis, Kan.: 228
Ellison, James F.: 89, 218, 235, 253
Ellison, James F., Jr. (Little Jim): 218
Ellison, Nat P.: 235f.
Ellsworth, Kan.: vii, 65, 84, 100, 150, 160f., 180, 182, 187–90, 196, 198–204, 209f., 212f., 219ff., 236
Ellsworth Dancing Club: 199
Ellsworth *Reporter*: 201
Ellsworth Trail: 199
Elm Fork of the Trinity River: 117
Elm Spring: 228
Elwood, Kan.: 51
Emmet Creek: 157
Emory, William H.: 71
Empire House, Wichita, Kan.: 182
Enderle, Louis: 238
Enid, Okla.: vii
Ernst, William: 226
Erskine, Michael: 24
Espíritu Santo, Mission of: 6
Eureka, Kan.: 236
Eureka Valley, Indian Terr.: 74
Europe: 8, 222, 262

Fabrique, A. H.: 147
Fall Creek: 81, 153, 252
Fancher, Washburne: 168
Fannin County, Tex.: 31
Fant, Dillard R.: 204, 217, 253, 258
Farmer, W. H.: 53
Farmers' Protective Association: 180
Farragut, David D.: 38
Fencing: 206f., 216, 222, 225, 227, 230, 233, 254, 256ff.
Ferdinand, King of Spain: 4
Ferguson, Dan: vii
Fields, Al: 34, 210
First National Bank, Wichita, Kan.: 196
Flag Springs, Tex.: 143
Flat Top Mountain: 101
Flatt, George W.: 252
Fleetwood Branch: 79
Floresville, Tex.: 44
Forehand and Cockrell: 90
"Forsaken Girl, The," song: 245

Fort Arbuckle, Indian, Terr.: 58, 74, 97, 101
Fort Belknap, Tex.: 47, 71
Fort Cobb, Indian Terr.: 71
Fort Gibson, Indian Terr.: 28, 33, 35, 49, 52, 58, 72, 88, 151
Fort Graham, Tex.: 78, 211
Fort Griffin, Tex.: 227f., 231, 233, 238, 240, 247, 253
Fort Griffin *Echo*: 240
Fort Harker, Kan.: 173
Fort Hays Kansas State College: vii
Fort Holmes, Indian Terr.: 58
Fort Johnson, Tex.: 27
Fort Leavenworth, Kan.: 173
Fort McKavett, Tex.: 39
Fort Preston, Tex.: 27
Fort Richardson, Tex.: 143
Fort Riley, Kan.: 71
Fort Scott, Kan.: 52f.
Fort Sill, Indian Terr.: 144, 219
Fort Smith, Ark.: 61, 72, 195
Fort Stockton, Tex.: 39
Fort Sumner, N. M.: 48
Fort Towson, Indian Terr.: 72
Fort Union, N. M.: 87, 96
Fort Washita, Indian Terr.: 27f.
Fort Wichita, Kan.: *see* Wichita, Kan.
Fort Worth, Tex.: vi, 43, 78, 88ff., 140, 144, 146, 195, 208, 216f., 220ff., 225, 227, 230, 233ff., 237f., 240, 243, 253, 263
Fort Worth *Democrat*: 82, 216, 220ff., 229, 231ff., 238, 240
Fort Yuma, Calif.: 24, 96
Fort Zarah, Kan.: 188
Foster, Stephen: 248
Foster, W. B.: 152
Fowler, Tilghman: 207
Foy, Eddie: 239
France, steamship: 238
Franklin, Annie: 198
Franks, L. A.: 185
Franklin, La.: 23, 198
Fredericksburg, Tex.: 23, 39
Free State Army: 173
Fremont, John C.: 50
Frio County, Tex.: 201, 239
Frio River: 14, 42, 44
Frontier Store, Abilene, Kan.: 64
Funk, Isaac: 21f.

Gainesville, Tex.: 89, 97, 209, 216, 245
Gainsford, James: 175, 177
Galesburg, Ill.: 59

"Lorena," song: 244
Los Angeles, Calif:. 24, 96
Los Ríos, Domingo Terán: 5
Lost Fork of the Red River: 128
Lost Spring, Kan.: 51
Louisiana: 5ff., 23ff., 38f., 43f., 46f.
Love, Bob: 144
Loving, Frank: 241
Loving, Oliver: 34ff., 38, 47f.
Loving–Goodnight Trail: 48, 96
Lowe, Joe: 186, 197f.
Lowe, Kate (Mrs. Joe): 186
Loyal Valley, Tex.: 97
Loyd, M. B.: 225

Mabry, Seth: 87, 164, 201 f., 218, 228, 258
McAdams, William C.: 39, 43
McCaleb, J. L.: 89, 111
McCluskie, Mike: 159
McConnell, Andrew: 171f.
McCoy, James: 59
McCoy, Joseph Geiting: vii, 243, 261;
    early life, 59f.; establishes cattle mar-
    ket at Abilene, Kan., 59–105, 148ff.,
    164ff., 173, 175, 180; work at Newton,
    Kan., 158; at Wichita, Kan., 183ff.,
    191; at Denison, Tex., 209; at Caldwell,
    Kan., 252; death, 253n.
McCoy, William K.: 59, 86
McCoy's Trail: see Chisholm Trail
McCutcheon, William: 33
McCutcheon, Willis: 33, 148, 201, 210
McDonald, James H.: 172, 175
McGehee, George T.: 88
McGhee crossing of the San Marcos
    River: 90
McGough, W. C.: 39f.
McKinney, John: 105
McLaren, J. A.: 148
McLean, Thomas: 64
McLennan County, Tex.: 30, 137, 211
McPherson, Kan.: 55
Maine: 86
Malone, Fred: 142
Malone, Washington: 31f., 113
Manhattan, Kan.: 172
Manning, E. C.: 199
Marais des Cygnes: 250
Marble Hall, Kansas City, Mo.: 263
Marcy, Randolph B.: 28
Marion, Kan.: 127, 213
Marsh and Coffy: 61
Marsh of the Swans: 250
Marshall, Tex.: 43

Martin, William (Hurricane Bill): 127,
    213ff.
Maryland: 21
Mason, Tex.: 96
Mason County, Tex.: 87, 211
Massachusetts: 21, 245
Massanet, Damián: 5
Massengale, W. R.: 146
Massey, P. H.: 214
Masterson, Edward J.: 237
Masterson, James: 240, 254
Masterson, William Barclay (Bat): 237,
    254
Matagorda, Tex.: 120, 143, 193
Matagorda Bay: 12
Matagorda County, Tex.: 206, 210, 230
Matamoros, Mexico: 17
Mather, Dave: 258f
Mathewson, Lizzie (Mrs. William): 74
Mathewson, William: 73f.
Maverick, Sam: 225, 227n.
Maverick, Samuel A.: 12, 227n.
Mavericks: 12
Mayfield, W. H.: 146
Maze Prairie: 235
Mead, James R.: 73ff., 147, 185, 196
Meagher, William: 214
Medford, Okla.: vii
Medicine Lodge, Kan.: 74, 257
Medicine Lodge Index: 254
Medina County, Tex.: 216
Memphis, Tenn.: 38, 165
Menger Hotel, San Antonio, Tex.: 225
Mestenas: 6, 12
Metropolitan Hotel, Wichita, Kan.: 196
Mexican fever: see Texas fever
Mexican War: 13, 39
Mexicans: 8ff., 36, 41f., 117, 201, 225f.;
    deprived of Texas ranches, 10f.; in
    Kansas cow towns, 163, 187
Mexico: 4ff., 39f., 43, 246
Mézières, Anathase de: 7
"Michigan I–O," song: 247
Milam County, Tex.: 190
Milam Rifles, San Antonio, Tex.: 225
Miles, Moses: 172
Military Plaza, San Antonio, Tex.: 226,
    233
Miller, George: 216
Miller, George W.: 153
Miller and Carson: 229
Miller Building, Wichita, Kan.: 214
Millett, Eugene B.: 53, 90, 201f., 218, 233
Milwaukee, Wis.: 262

O'Connor, T. M.: 253
O'Connor, Thomas: 15
Ogallala, Neb.: 228, 236, 238, 241, 253
"Oh, Bury Me Not in the Deep, Deep Sea," song: 248
"Oh, Bury Me Not on the Lone Prairie," song: 248
"Oh Mary, My Mary," song: 244
Ohio: 21, 23, 64, 220, 227
Oje, Louis: 14
Oklahoma: vi f.; see also Indian Territory
Oklahoma, University of: vii
Old Blue, lead steer: 112
"Old Chisholm Trail, The," song: v, 124, 134, 162, 248f., 264
Old Fruit Saloon, Abilene, Kan.: 163, 171
"Old Paint," song: 245
Old Stand saloon, San Antonio, Tex.: 226
Old Trail Drivers Association of Texas: vi
"Old Uncle Ned," song: 248
Oliver Creek: 78
Omaha, Neb.: 263
Onion Creek: 235
Opelousas Trail: 23
Orange, Tex.: 38
Osage Indians: 28, 73, 75, 81, 88, 102, 128, 145, 153
Osage Trace: 28
Osawatomie Creek: 33
Osborne, E. H.: 149
Osborne, Vincent B.: 200
Ottumwa, Iowa: 49
Owens, Peter: 117
Ozark Mountains: 176

Pacific Ocean: 99
Paddock, B. B.: 220ff.
Paine, Randolph: 97
Palacios, Tex.: 87
Palo Duro Canyon: 5
Palo Pinto, Tex.: 101, 105, 148
Palo Pinto County, Tex.: 35, 38f., 43, 89, 100, 143, 253
Panic of 1873: 204f.
Parker County: 35, 120
Parks, Daniel: 214
Parlor Saloon, Newton, Kan.: 158
Parsons, Bruce: 211
Partilleas, Don Felipe: 8, 11
Peacock, A. J.: 254

Pearl Saloon, Abilene, Kan.: 163
Pearsall, Tex.: 210
Pease River: 246
Pecos River: 39, 43, 47f., 143
Pennsylvania: 21
Peril, W. A.: 39, 97
Perry, John T.: 62f.
Perryman, William: 201, 210
Persimmon Creek: 253
Peter, T. J.: 183
Philadelphia, Pa.: 21, 224
Pierce, Abel Head (Shanghai): 25, 131, 184f., 196, 205f., 209, 212, 255, 258
Pierce, Cad: 200, 203
Pierce, William: 134, 158
Pierce City, Mo.: 151
Pinitas, Tex.: 156
Piper, Edward: 23
Plankinton and Armour: 262
Planter's Banner: 23
Platte River: 190, 218, 237
Plaza House, San Antonio, Tex.: 226
Poage, William R.: 109, 122, 126, 129
Polecat Creek: 81
Polly, J. B.: 44
Pond Creek: 73, 81, 146, 188, 190, 195, 198f., 210, 253, 255
Pond Creek, Okla.: vii
Ponting, Tom Candy: 31f., 82, 113
Port Sullivan, Tex.: 39
Porter, Lake: 244
Powers, D. W.: 199
Prairie Creek: 103
Prairie dogs: 64, 81, 98, 125
Prairie Farmer: 54
Presidio, Tex.: 39
Preston, William G.: 27
Preston, Tex.: 26f., 29, 33, 35, 49, 88
Preston Bend, Tex.: see Preston, Tex.
Preston Road: 26
Promontory Point, Utah: 99
Pryor, Ike T.: 129, 253
Pryor's saloon, Wichita, Kan.: 213
Puckett, Dave: 89
Pueblo, Colo.: 36
Pynchon, John: 21
Pynchon, William: 21

Quarter horses: 107
Quincy, Ill.: 33, 35, 51, 54, 63, 148f.

Ramón, Domingo: 6
Randolph, Bud: 27
Randolph Ferry: 34